Start-Up Poland

Start-Up Poland

THE PEOPLE WHO TRANSFORMED AN ECONOMY

Jan Cienski

THE UNIVERSITY OF CHICAGO PRESS

Chicago and London

The University of Chicago Press, Chicago 60637
The University of Chicago Press, Ltd., London

Published 2018
Printed in the United States of America

27 26 25 24 23 22 21 20 19 18   1 2 3 4 5

ISBN-13: 978-0-226-30681-0 (cloth)
ISBN-13: 978-0-226-30695-7 (e-book)
DOI: 10.7208/chicago/9780226306957.001.0001

Library of Congress Cataloging-in-Publication Data
Names: Cienski, Jan, author.
Title: Start-up Poland : the people who transformed an economy / Jan Cienski.
Description: Chicago : The University of Chicago Press, 2017. | Includes bibliographical references and index.
Identifiers: LCCN 2017025013 | ISBN 9780226306810 (cloth : alk. paper) | ISBN 9780226306957 (e-book)
Subjects: LCSH: Entrepreneurship—Poland—History—20th century. | Entrepreneurship—Poland—History—21st century. | Businesspeople—Poland. | Poland—Economic conditions—1990- | Post-communism—Economic aspects—Poland.
Classification: LCC HC340.3 .C55 2017 | DDC 338.092/2438—dc23
LC record available at https://lccn.loc.gov/2017025013

♾ This paper meets the requirements of ANSI/NISO Z39.48-1992 (Permanence of Paper).

For Cecelia . . . obviously

Contents

Preface

Lech Wałęsa is an old man now. His walrus moustache is gray, and his belly strains against his shirt as he sits heavily in a worn armchair and again launches into the story of how he helped lead the Solidarity labor union to victory against the communist regime—setting off a wave of revolutions across Central Europe in 1989 that brought an end to more than four decades of Soviet power in the region.

But there is a little of the old sparkle in his tale of how workers allied with intellectuals to restore Poland's independence more than a quarter-century ago.

That's because Wałęsa is fighting again. He's trying to lead a citizens' movement against the right-wing populist Law and Justice Party government that won power in 2015. He's traveling to towns across Poland, hoping to organize a referendum aimed at curtailing the government's power—a response to Law and Justice's attacks on the country's top constitutional court, its seizure of the public media, and its brawls with the European Union and close allies like the United States.

"There's going to be an ultimatum. Either you agree to democratic solutions, or else we'll help you jump out the window," Wałęsa said, sitting in his office in the European Solidarity Center, a museum in the port city of Gdańsk overlooking the gates of the old Lenin Shipyard, where Wałęsa led the 1980 strike that created Solidarity.

The new government has made Wałęsa a target. Instead of a national hero, winner of the Nobel Peace Prize, and Poland's first postwar noncommunist president, he's seen as a traitor. The progovernment media attack him as a communist stooge, recalling his instances of cooperation with the secret police in the early 1970s, after the bloody suppression of a shipyard strike in 1970.

Wałęsa's greatest success came in 1989, when he led careful negotiations with the still powerful communists that allowed for partly free parliamentary elections. The communists were humiliated in the polls, and by August of that year, Poland had its first noncommunist prime minister since World War II. That allowed for a scrapping of the ludicrous economic policies foisted on Poland by Moscow, and the start of a capitalist revolution.

The decades since then turned Poland from a basket case into one of Europe's fastest-growing countries—a tiger economy on a continent more used to sluggish growth and sky-high unemployment. A key role in that transformation was played by entrepreneurs, people who built businesses that made Poland a power in everything from cosmetics to bus and train construction. Poland became a poster child for capitalism, an example of one of the world's most successful postcommunist transformations.

During the depths of the 2008–9 global financial crisis, the government of the day relished showing colorful maps of the European Union, with every country in red thanks to their deep recessions, and only Poland in green—the sole EU country to emerge from that slump without suffering a contraction.

But the new narrative of the Law and Justice government is very different. Its leader, Jarosław Kaczyński—an old enemy of Wałęsa—sees 1989 not as an astonishing achievement, but rather as a failure, something that left Poland in "ruins" and under the control of foreign bankers, rapacious investors, and deeply dishonest local businessmen who have more in common with gangsters than with entrepreneurs.

Today's Poland "is saddled with the errors of communism," Kaczyński said recently. "The shock of a socialist society, which had been horribly mistreated by the war, encountering liberal permissiveness containing elements of social Darwinism—the idea that whoever is stronger is better, and those who fail are at fault—is very harmful."

Kaczyński and Law and Justice won presidential and parliamentary elections in 2015 by tapping into a broad current of discontent among many Poles who felt they hadn't enjoyed the fruits of the country's economic success. Helped by a generous welfare program promising to pay a child bonus to every family with two or more children and to roll back increases in the retirement age, the party romped to spectacular victories.

By early 2016, several leading businessmen faced criminal charges, and the heads of almost all state-controlled companies had been purged.

Even Wałęsa now recognizes that the earlier rah-rah vision of Poland's success left out a lot of people: especially the old, who had a hard time figuring out how to adapt to the more cutthroat world of capitalism; the badly educated; and those formerly employed by large state-owned companies and farms. Also, many socially conservative Poles proved increasingly uncomfortable with their country's rapid transformation into a mainstream European nation, a place where gays were increasingly comfortable, where the Roman Catholic Church's authority was dwindling, and where people were more interested in making their mortgage payments and getting a promotion at work than in extolling the patriotic heroes of the past.

"Over the last twenty-five years we did as well as we could," Wałęsa said. "But while we were building a new Poland—all those roads and investments—we forgot about the people. We should have helped them more."

While a recalibration of the social costs of Poland's transformation might be in order, there's no escaping the fact that Poland has undergone one of the world's most striking and successful changes. Everything from roads to cars to houses to take-home income is completely different than in 1989—and the largest part of that achievement is due to the work of entrepreneurs.

That's a controversial thesis in today's Poland; but controversial or not, the story is true.

• • •

In 1987, Zbigniew Sosnowski was working as a car mechanic in the unremarkable central Polish town of Przasnysz, fixing the rattling rust buckets produced by Polish auto plants which were so badly built they often needed to be repaired immediately after rolling off the production line.

At about the same time, Andrzej Blikle was studying the mathematics of computer programming at the Polish Academy of Sciences. Leszek Czarnecki was running a small commercial diving company in western Poland. Dariusz Miłek was sweating out wins on the international bicycle racing circuit—promptly taking the crystal trophies and, instead of parking them on a shelf, selling them to bemused French and Italian villagers.

Today all these men are captains of Polish industry, some of the country's wealthiest people and examples of enormously successful entrepreneurs. They are part of a much broader cohort of entrepreneurs who have changed Poland from a gray and stultifying Communist-bloc backwater into a member of the world's wealthy club of nations. Thanks to them, Poland is a place where horses are for pleasure rides, and not for pulling plows or delivering goods on the streets of the capital city; where a luxury good is a Louis Vuitton bag bought at a new silvery shopping mall in central Warsaw, not a roll of toilet paper with the texture of fine-grained sandpaper; and where it makes sense for an ambitious entrepreneur to stay home and build a business instead of fleeing to the West as in decades past.

Today's Poland is a prosperous member of NATO and the European Union, and the only European country not to have suffered a recession in more than two decades. That success is largely the product of the ferment and chaos of the market economy loosed on the country in the late 1980s. Millions of men and women took an enormous risk and opened businesses, starting small, but eventually doing everything from running restaurants and small shops to producing bicycles, buses, newspapers, cosmetics, and computers.

Poland's dramatic resurgence is not just a point of local pride. The story also has implications for debates taking place far outside of Central Europe about rising inequality and the overall fairness of postcrisis capitalism. Of course Poland's transformation suffered from missteps and miscalculations. Rising unemployment and wrenching social change hurt a lot of people. But the country's overall success is a powerful argument in favor of the liberal "shock therapy" economic reforms launched a quarter-century ago, marking the first attempt anywhere in the world to rebuild a capitalist economy after decades of communism. That approach is often viewed today with disapproval, as an example of the discredited "Washington Consensus" of orthodox economic reforms imposed on struggling nations. But in Poland's case they worked. The fact that Leszek Balcerowicz, the architect of Poland's reforms, has now been asked to advise the region's least successful country, Ukraine, is a testament to the attractions of the "Warsaw Consensus."

The problem is that the narrative of success resonated best in Poland's largest cities, where people had decent jobs, rising earnings, and improving prospects. In poorer and more rural areas—especially in the less developed east of Poland, a region that is more religious and more traditional than the rest of the country—that narrative grated and led to growing resentment. In an echo of the rage that made Donald Trump the president of the United States, and gave rise to populists and nationalists across much of Europe, Law and Justice played to that anger in its 2015 victory. It appears set to run the country at least until 2019.

I watched and wrote about large parts of Poland's convoluted transformation: first as a cub reporter looking at the chaos unleashed by the collapse of Communist rule in 1989, then as a correspondent for the *Financial Times*, reporting for the past decade across Central Europe, and most recently as an editor at Politico, still keeping close tabs on Polish politics. All of the profiles of entrepreneurs in the book are the result of my interviews and conversations with them.

The book's start date of 1987 marks the last year in which Poland was functioning as a more or less orthodox member of the Soviet bloc—although the decay of a system that had been imposed on the country by the Red Army in 1944 was already apparent.

1 From People's Poland to the Third Republic

The first thing that hit you about the Poland of 1987 was the smell—a pungent mix of coal smoke leavened with coarse tobacco, a whiff of cabbage and rancid sweat overlaid with clouds of diesel exhaust. It was an odor that coiled and lingered on the streets and alleys of cities, towns, and villages. It was not the smell of a successful or a happy society.

The smell hit me in the southern city of Kraków in 1987, where I was taking a year off from university in Toronto to study in Poland. It was only one symptom of a decomposing country.

At Kraków's Jagiellonian University, the first phrase the Third World students (mostly from Brazil and Argentina) who were studying Polish before beginning inexpensive medical and architecture studies would learn was *Nie ma* ("We don't have it"). They heard it in shops when they tried to buy meat or wine. They heard it in kiosks when trying to buy luxuries like soap and razor blades. They heard it fired at them by surly waiters indicating a lack of almost every item on the menu, from beer to "exotic" dishes like beef cutlets and pork chops (no point in ordering on Monday, as meat was not sold on the first day of the week). At one point I remember tossing aside the menu and telling the waiter, "Just bring me whatever you have."

There was not much point in getting fancy when ordering drinks at the Pod Jaszczurami (Under the Lizards) student club on Kraków's medieval square—all they served was vodka and Pepsi. When one stumbled back upstairs in the late evening after several rounds, the square—which today is thronged with foreign tourists and lined with cafés and restaurants—was almost deserted. Scattered streetlights cast small pools of light on the edge of the broad expanse of Europe's largest town square, but did little to lift the gloom. The few restaurants were shuttered, while shops, all closed in the evening of course, bore imaginative names like "Bread," "Shoes," and "Milk Products."

The city choked under a pall of smoke issuing from the coal-burning smelters of the Nowa Huta Lenin Steelworks. The enormous factory was tied to a planned city built in the 1950s that was supposed to swamp the intellectuals, dispossessed gentry, and professors of Kraków with more socially appropriate working classes. The corrosive smog forced the Church of St. Peter and St. Paul, up the road from the market square, to carve new life-sized statues of the twelve apostles lining the church's front courtyard. The old ones had been eroded down to sandstone stumps by the acid. What the smog did to the lungs of the city's inhabitants can only be imagined.

As a student I would get monthly ration cards for meat, fats, flour, butter, and a card that was exchangeable for chocolate, vodka, or cigarettes (sort of a sin card), which I would hand over to my grandfather, who lived in Kraków, a short walk from the university. The cards were badly printed pieces of paper with little squares that had to be cut out by salespeople and handed over together with cash to make a purchase. The lucky few who owned automobiles got cards with allotments of gasoline. Chocolate was an expensive rarity—the less fortunate having to make do with an ersatz chocolatelike product that was dark and sweet but otherwise bore no resemblance to the original.

I had arrived in Poland with three hundred dollars, at a time when the average monthly salary of a Polish worker came to about twenty-five dollars. That made me rich. My Western university friends and I played poker games in our student residence for enormous piles of almost worthless zloty bills decorated with a mix of Polish communists and national heroes—often to the vague disgust of Polish students for whom the joke money was not all that funny.

Those US dollars were pretty useful at the Pewex shop a few tramway stops away from my residence. There, dollars—or crude coupons issued by the Polish state in paper denominations ranging from one cent to one hundred dollars—could buy you things like chewing gum, canned meat, coffee, Coca-Cola (a Christmas present for a nephew), and even domestically produced cars without the years-long wait forced on people paying with zlotys instead of hard currency.

The defining characteristic of retail life was the queue. Drably dressed people lined up outside food shops, furniture shops, and stores carrying refrigerators and washing machines, often simply on the strength of a rumor that something worth buying or trading for had been "thrown" there by suppliers. Waits stretched into days, with officious line watchers compiling lists of who was where in the queues. Professional line sitters took the spots of people who had to work. War veterans, pregnant women, and mothers with small babies were allowed to scoot to the front of the line—and this set up a roaring underground trade in borrowing babies to avoid interminable waits.

An aunt of mine remembers lining up for almost three hours outside a Warsaw shop with a decent selection of meat. As the hours wound down, she watched the beef disappear, followed by the pork tenderloin and then the stewing pork. She finally left, not unhappily, with a bag of frankfurters.

A couple of the ubiquitous, bitter, but accurate political jokes of the period convey the mood.

> Q: What is seven kilometers long and eats potatoes?
> A: A Polish meat queue.

> General Wojciech Jaruzelski, the country's ruler, is being driven through Warsaw in a limousine when he sees a long queue of people outside a food store.
> He tells his chauffeur to stop, and asks him how long they have been there. "Six hours," the driver replies.
> "This is dreadful," says Jaruzelski. "I will have to do something."
> An hour later, a huge truck arrives outside the shop and delivers two hundred chairs.

This didn't mean that there was no food to buy. The stalls at the farmers' market at Kraków's Kleparski Market were filled with mounds of apples, potatoes and beetroot—not particularly exotic, but a lot better than what was available in the state shops. However, the prices were far above what most people on state salaries could afford. While you could buy eggs at the open-air market, there was no meat. Instead, peasant women would whisper sotto voce that they had pork or veal, often hidden under their coats for a quick sale away from the eyes of the police.

The farmers' markets were one sign of a surviving market economy in a communist system. In the late 1980s, about three-quarters of the Polish economy was in state hands, which was less than in most other Soviet Bloc countries. Because of fierce resistance from the local peasantry, the Communists never successfully created Soviet-style collective farms. This was one of the many compromises (another included a much larger role for the Catholic Church than in the rest of the bloc) that the Communists agreed to as they violently imposed their rule on the country—a process that Josef Stalin once likened to the absurdity of trying to saddle a cow.

Communism wasn't a Polish idea; it was imported by the Soviet troops who pushed through the country in pursuit of the retreating Germans in 1944 and 1945. Once in control of Poland, the Red Army helped install a puppet regime subservient to Moscow that used force to ram through a political and economic system similar to the one that existed in the Stalinist Soviet Union. In the late 1940s and early 1950s, the Moscow-backed Polish United Workers Party used arrests and executions to destroy other political parties and terrify opponents, both real and imagined. They also imposed a centrally planned economy, crushing the private business that had begun to emerge from the ruins of the war, by decreeing crippling taxes, arresting owners, and confiscating factories, farms and shops.

Andrzej Blikle remembers how his father scrambled through the ruins of a destroyed Warsaw in 1945 to retrieve barrels of flour and marmalade—enough to allow him to again start baking and selling to the refugees streaming back to rebuild the Polish capital. He spent the better part of two decades trying to fend off the state from taking over his business, and was one of the very few in the whole country to actually succeed in keeping his own business alive. Almost all other enterprises were either destroyed or made property of the government.

Although the system began to relax its grip after Stalin's death in 1953 and a purge of hardline Stalinists in 1956 following a workers' uprising, the Communist Party never lost its distaste for the private sector. Not coincidentally, the revulsion at markets and business proved to be a key factor in the party's inability to manage the economy through the use of five-year plans implemented by Warsaw-based bureaucrats, and was the long-term reason why the party was forced from power in 1989. That economic maladroitness was apparent from the earliest days of Communist rule, and within a few years it became clear that Poland was slipping further and further behind the West.

In the early years, when the party relied on terror to retain its grip on the country and when travel to the West was almost impossible, it was more difficult to make the comparison with a reviving Western Europe that started its burst of rapid growth in the 1950s. People in Poland were also exhausted after the war, which had killed almost a fifth of the pre-1939 population, exiled millions more, left cities in ruins, and annihilated the country's intellectual and economic elite. Even a poor and repressive government was preferable to the murderous rampage inflicted by the Germans.

But by 1956, long-running fury over increased taxes on the most productive workers set off a round of strikes in the central Polish city of Poznań. The protests initially called for bread, more pay, and lower prices, but quickly turned into an onslaught on the symbols of authority, including an attack on a security police prison. The army killed almost sixty people before order was restored.

After the uprising, pressure began to steadily grow on the government to show some of the material benefits of communism. The government's lack of democratic legitimacy and its micromanagement of economic life also turned every economic protest into a political one. As soon as it tried to right public finances by increasing prices or reducing benefits, workers would take to the streets. That created a dramatic ideological challenge to a party that styled itself as the vanguard of the working class.

Another strike in the shipyards on the Baltic coast in 1970 broke out after the government announced an increase in food prices. More than forty people were killed and three thousand arrested in the army-led clampdown.

In the early 1970s, a spooked party tried to make life easier for its subjects, borrowing massively in an attempt to create modern export industries and placate the people with easier access to consumer goods. The result was a brief consumer boom that many older Poles still remember fondly. Private cars (albeit very badly made ones) became more widely available, it was easier to travel abroad, and basic goods like washing machines and ugly furniture could be bought without too much difficulty. A joke of the time has it that Poland turned into a banana republic, as the country was temporarily flooded with bananas—a rare luxury good and symbol of the good life, Polish style.

The boom also wasted money, with modern equipment intended for never-built factories left rusting in fields, and it saddled the country with crippling levels of foreign debt. When the party tried to fix public finances by raising prices, it set off workers' protests in 1976 and again in 1980.

The strikes in 1980 were the most serious yet, with rebellious workers organizing themselves in the Lenin Shipyard in Gdańsk and refusing to be bought off with quickly broken promises made by party negotiators. Instead, they demanded and got the right to form a legal trade union, Solidarity—an act that set off tremors throughout the Soviet Bloc. The party's battle with Solidarity also plunged Poland into political and economic chaos. Solidarity was crushed in 1981, when the Polish military led by Jaruzelski staged a coup on December 13, imposed martial law, and arrested thousands. But despite Jaruzelski's attempts at enforcing military discipline in a bid to restart growth, it was apparent that the socialist economy was broken. Reform efforts consisting of granting state enterprises more freedom did nothing to help, and by early 1988 strikes broke out again.

I did my first reporting for UPI in 1988, covering a march from the Royal Cathedral in Kraków's Wawel Castle on May 3, Poland's traditional independence day. It was a holiday that had long been discouraged by the party in favor of the communist May 1. The march began with a Catholic mass, the prayers echoing through the dark cathedral past the stone sarcophagi of long-dead Polish kings. Then thousands of people chanting Solidarity slogans streamed down the hill into the narrow warren of cobblestoned streets in the city below. There they were met by detachments of militarized police wearing dull gray uniforms with short black boots. The police took running charges at people, swinging short, flexible, and very painful white batons to break up the crowd. I hid in a doorway, and then fled through side alleys to the haven of the Pod Jaszczurami bar, filing my story by pay phone to Warsaw with a vodka-Pepsi in hand.

Two days later I watched riot police jog thorough through the vast squares of Nowa Huta chasing scattered groups of steelworkers—the remnants of the strike at the Lenin Steelworks that had earlier been crushed by force. The revolt was a response to the government of Zbigniew Messner, which had raised prices sharply in February of that year. Although police had initial success in quashing the strikes, the wave of revolt convinced the Communists that they lacked the political backing to undertake the deep and politically unpopular reforms needed to kick-start the economy.

By the end of that year, Jaruzelski's government was negotiating with Wałęsa and the Solidarity labor union, and in early 1989 the two sides held round-table negotiations allowing for partly free elections in June. The deluded Communists, betrayed by optimistic assessments from their ubiquitous internal security organs, were certain that they still held deep reservoirs of popularity and would win the vote. The plan was that after winning the elections, they would be able to defang the opposition by co-opting Solidarity and creating a government of national unity that would get the economy moving again.

The result was a shock. In the free Senate elections, ninety-nine out of one hundred senators were elected with the backing of Solidarity, as were all 35 percent of the seats up for a free vote in the lower house of parliament. On August 14, the dissident leader Tadeusz Mazowiecki became Poland's first non-Communist prime minister since the war.

A few months later, in January 1990, I stood in a crush of people in the Congress Hall of Warsaw's Palace of Culture, a wedding-cake monstrosity of a building inflicted on the Polish capital by Stalin. While protesters outside yelled "Out with the party," at the podium inside the hall, Mieczysław Rakowski, the party's last first secretary, announced: "Comrades, please rise. Carry out the banner of the Polish United Workers Party."

A ceremonial guard walked to the front of the hall, which was decorated with a shabby "XI" symbol to mark the party's eleventh congress. He picked up the ornate flag that had been a symbol of Poland's political subservience to Moscow for more than four decades, and marched it out of the auditorium.

Polish communism was dead.

The way was open to try something that had never been done before: re-create a market economy out of a socialist one. Adam Michnik, the dissident and intellectual who founded *Gazeta Wyborcza*, one of the country's most successful private newspapers, pithily laid out the scale of the challenge: "We know very well how to make fish soup from an aquarium, but we don't know how to make an aquarium out of fish soup."

The ground that Poland had to make up was enormous. Poland had always lagged behind the wealthier western half of the continent. Just before the outbreak of World War II, Poland had inched ahead of Spain, which was still devastated by its own Civil War, and had become about half as wealthy on average as Western Europe.[1] The bloodbath of the war, followed by more than four decades of communism, left Poland further behind than ever. By 1990, Poland was only about a third as wealthy as Western Europe—its lowest point in centuries.

Although late communist Poland was an economic absurdity, it had laid the conditions for a startlingly strong economic revival once orthodox communist planning was scrapped and business was given space to revive. Poles had long been more open about money than people in other Soviet Bloc countries. I remember taking trains across Central Europe in the late 1980s. While I was on my way to visit Prague or Budapest as a tourist, most of the Polish travelers were on the train to make money. They crammed enormous striped nylon bags filled with goods on their way to sell or trade for cameras and optical equipment in East Germany, clothes in Czechoslovakia, and gold in Romania—a trade lubricated with bribes for the numerous border guards and customs officials. Those travelers with slightly more money would take "tourist" trips to places like Istanbul and Bangkok. No one bothered seeing the sights; they were there to buy leather jackets, jeans, cameras, and Japanese VCRs to sell back home.

Outside most Polish banks in the late 1980s, gangs of men stood ready to change money at the much higher black market rate. Called *koniki* (little horses), these nascent capitalists (or gangsters; the two were easy to conflate back then) accumulated some of the first private fortunes in late communist Poland.

Taxi drivers, especially those in big cities like Warsaw and Kraków, did well, overcharging clients and getting an occasional payment in dollars from visiting tourists—a business not dissimilar from that of the prostitutes who plied their trade in the restaurants and bars of country's few Western-style hotels.

"During communism, if you had your own small business like being a taxi driver, you were a financial god," says Roman Młodkowski, the former head of TVN CNBC, the Polish affiliate of the US business-oriented television channel, who ran a TV program showing Poles how to build their own businesses, from used clothing shops (very profitable and quick to set up) to restaurants (financial disasters, as they tend to be in just about every other country).

The corrupt and imperfect Polish version of communism made people very entrepreneurial. Everyone from children to pensioners became very adept at striking deals. If you held someone's place in line, they would repay the favor by tipping you off to an unexpected delivery of ham at the meat shop. Buying a washing machine could involve stealing something from your factory for the shop clerk. With no normal banks and mortgages, and with business loans unheard of, transactions involved plastic shopping bags filled with bundles of cash, which meant that there had to be a high level of trust that the money would not be stolen.

"The whole of society was in a sense entrepreneurial," says Czarnecki, who made his start setting up one of the country's first leasing companies. "You had to make a deal to get toilet paper, a telephone, a car, a holiday. We had to function like that for two generations—it became part of our DNA."

As communism slowly collapsed through the late 1980s, private markets began to grow—supplying the goods, ranging from jeans to perfume and deodorant, that state shops were unable to offer. "In Poland, market mechanisms were never completely stamped out," says Andrzej Kozmiński, founder of a university named after his father, Leon, that in recent years has become one of Europe's best business schools. "In 1989, about a quarter of the goods on the market came from the private sector. A lot of Poles had traveled as well. They had seen capitalist countries and could foresee what was going to happen in Poland."

That was the case with Dariusz Miłek. When he saw a fruit and vegetable kiosk in the early 1980s while on a bicycle race in France, he was stunned; he had never seen boxes of bananas and oranges simply lying there, waiting to be touched. He was already a budding capitalist. He and his team financed their foreign trips by loading down their dilapidated Fiat 125p car with bags of crystal vases and cameras to sell along the way, making the races a paying proposition.

That makeshift capitalism, conducted on the fringes of communism, ended at the beginning of 1990 with the arrival of Mazowiecki's government and the economic reform program fronted by Finance Minister Leszek Balcerowicz. Balcerowicz moved quickly to cut off financial guarantees for state-owned companies, banned the central bank from financing the budget deficit, made the zloty internationally convertible, and ended the state's monopoly on foreign trade. Suddenly what had been illegal or severely restricted became possible.

I saw it walking the streets of Warsaw in January and February of 1990. Inflation was racing at almost 600 percent a year, there was huge political uncertainty, and industries were collapsing. The economic conditions were certainly more dire than anything experienced in Greece, Spain, Ireland, and the other troubled countries of the Eurozone, or in the United States during the recent global economic crisis.

Some people reacted with terror at the changes, hanging on to their jobs in state factories and offices while watching their salaries being eaten away to almost nothing by inflation. Millions were also trapped in villages tied to government farms. With little education, living far from more dynamic larger cities, they languished. But millions more, driven by a combination of desperation as well as a desire to get rich, opened their own businesses—more than a million within a year of the launch of Balcerowicz's reforms.

Many of the businesses described in this book got their start on the sidewalks of Polish cities, as people started selling everything from shoes to bicycles to porn magazines.

In some ways the Polish transformation could be likened to a Central European version of the Oklahoma rush of 1889, when tens of thousands of land-hungry settlers gathered by the border of the state and then raced to stake their claims on virgin territory. In Poland, the open lands were the ability to start and run your own business and, as in America a century earlier, almost everyone had a more or less equal start.

That was when Zbigniew Sosnowski ditched his job as a car mechanic and looked around for something that would make sense as a business in the fast-dawning new reality. On an earlier trip to Germany he had seen people riding bikes for fun. In Poland bikes were for children, or for people too poor to afford a car, like the farmers slowly pedaling their rusty cycles down country lanes while wearing mud-encrusted boots.

"I saw what bikes were in the West, that they weren't just for transportation but also for recreation, and I decided the same thing might work in Poland," he says.

Sosnowski started selling badly made Polish bikes, but by introducing novel concepts like smiling at customers and treating them politely, he quickly drove the surly state-owned bike shop across the street out of business. Within a few years he had shifted from sales to manufacturing, and now his Kross company is one of Europe's largest bicycle makers.

While Sosnowski made his fortune with bicycles, Miłek made his by clambering off his racing bike and devoting himself full-time to sales. He began selling watches, cheap silverware, glassware, and knockoff electronics at a bazaar in western Poland. His supplies were bought at Vienna's seedy Mexikoplatz, a square that had become a disorderly black market dominated by Poles—to the disgust of the prim Viennese. After one day of selling watches he counted his earnings and thought, "Damn. I made about as much as I would have in a year of riding." Racing became just a hobby; he now owns one of the region's largest shoe retailers and is worth about $1 billion.

"We didn't expect such an explosion of new businesses," says Stanisław Gomułka, an economist and one of Balcerowicz's advisers in the early 1990s. "That first phase of Polish capitalism was impossible to repeat. We haven't seen such rapid private sector growth in any other ex-communist country."

Sitting at a table on a sunny spring day outside his suburban Warsaw villa, Gomułka explains that he was more than just a consultant—he was also a practitioner. He had spent two decades working as a professor in the West, but when the economic changes swept through Poland, his brother wanted to start a construction materials business. He talked Gomułka into selling his London flat to finance the business. It is now a company with a $30 million annual turnover and 250 employees.

In those early months of market freedom, people who had the brains and the gumption could move very quickly to make money.

Although the country was poor, Poles did have dollars and marks earned while working illegally abroad or sent in by foreign relatives; but they had often been unable to spend the money on anything sensible.

Some Poles, like Andrzej Blikle, moved to rebuild businesses that had managed to survive communism. Blikle returned to his family's business and capitalized on the Blikle brand to build one of Poland's first franchise operations, spreading the bakeries around the country.

In those first months, the country lacked everything, from supermarkets to hardware shops to modern soaps, paints, construction materials, cars, buses, coffee, cosmetics, bicycles, and even romance novels. The appetite for goods was enormous, but the problem in communist times had been to find a way to supply that demand. Private factories were largely illegal, especially before the mid-1980s. Borders and customs rules made legal importation difficult.

"In the late 1980s and early 1990s there was almost no competition," says Młodkowski. "It was easy to sell and easy to make money. Later the market became much more mature. A lot of people who had lived well from the border trade or selling in markets didn't prepare for the change by investing, and they stagnated and went bankrupt. Those who adapted did not."

There was a premium for the ambitious and nimble.

Nina Kowalewska, a hyperactive woman with a gift for languages and an innate grasp of the schmoozing that is a crucial part of sales and advertising, started in the late 1980s as a fixer for one of my predecessors at the *Financial Times*, helping him arrange interviews and travel around the country. She came to the attention of the publishers of Harlequin Romances, who were looking to get a foot in the door of the Polish market, where people had spent decades reading worthy Polish and world literature but had very little exposure to pulse-pounding bodice-rippers. Kowalewska was asked to find someone who might be able to open the country for Harlequin. However, she so impressed the publishers during the search that they chose her instead.

By 1991, Kowalewska was running the company's Polish operations. A year later she was launching an edgy advertising campaign in a country where ads were almost unknown. She rented the front of the Palace of Culture, Warsaw's tallest building, and hung an enormous heart on it. She also bought six hours of television time and even got the prime minister at the time, Jan Krzysztof Bielecki, to come on with his wife to talk about their romantic lives—something unimaginable under the dour Communists of the previous four decades. "Nothing like it had ever been done in Poland before," she says. The promotion created a new holiday—despite groans of protest from the Roman Catholic Church, Valentine's Day is now one of Poland's favorite festivals—and book sales soared.

The earthquake that produced the rudiments of a market economy also laid bare huge price discrepancies between Poland and the rest of the world. That opened another possibility to people who had the wit to foresee that Poland would quickly become a normal capitalist country, where prices would not diverge significantly from those in Western Europe. A cousin in Kraków remembers being able to buy an apartment in the old city for about three thousand dollars, the same price as that of a newish Lada automobile. "I bought the Lada because it seemed like the better deal at the time," he laughs. He's not bitter because he still ended up getting into Kraków real estate early enough to make money; but those who moved fast did very well.

Labor costs were just as far out of whack.

Jerzy Wiśniewski, head of PBG, one of Poland's largest construction companies, remembers "the humiliation" he experienced in the 1980s when going to pick grapes in France, where he would earn as much in one day as he would as two weeks as a natural gas engineer in Poland. But cheap labor gave a huge competitive advantage to new businesses. Janusz Filipiak, who had been working as a professor in Australia, came home to start an IT company making management software for Polish businesses. He paid his programmers about $150 a month, a fraction of what the same thing cost his West European rivals. "It was impossible not to succeed with wages like those," he says.

Although the Oklahoma land rush metaphor holds true for the vast majority of the new businesses that were created in the first year after Balcerowicz's reforms, there were some people who had gotten an early start on capitalism (like the "sooners" who had grabbed Oklahoma claims before the other settlers), and this gave them a huge advantage.

Jan Kulczyk, Poland's wealthiest man until his death in 2015, was already rich in 1989. His father, a businessman in Germany who had left Poland decades earlier, gave him $1 million to fund his start in business. Using his excellent connections with the government, Kulczyk made his first spectacular deal in 1991: the sale of three thousand Volkswagen cars to the police. He made his first billion dollars acting as a crucial go-between during some of the country's earliest privatizations of state-owned businesses.

Other wealthy businessmen first dabbled in special foreign trading companies set up in the 1980s (where having close ties to the authorities was a necessity), and then built on their capital and connections to make fortunes in capitalist Poland.

A lot of Communist Party industrial managers also saw the way the wind was blowing, and used their knowledge of how business worked and their access to functioning companies to "privatize" the assets of the companies they were running. Aleksander Gudzowaty used the experience he had gained from trading with Russia while director of a state-owned rail-sector company to set up his own business. He took advantage of those contacts with the East to build a commodity-trading business that made him one of Poland's ten wealthiest men.

However, the people who had actually negotiated the changes that allowed for Poland's transformation tended to do badly. Almost no one from the Solidarity negotiating team became wealthy, and today there is a fund to support destitute former dissidents. On the Communist side, few party hacks did well either; it turns out that the oleaginous back-scratching skills needed to advance up the hierarchy of the Polish United Workers Party didn't always translate well into being an entrepreneur.

Even the businesses that had done best under communism tended to be badly managed, overstaffed, and slow, and did a terrible job when faced with real competition—whether it was provided by new Polish start-ups or by the flood of Western companies moving into the Polish market by the mid-1990s.

The Pewex shops that had been the peak of consumer fantasy in years past quickly lost their rationale for existing under post-1989 conditions, when the state gave up its monopoly on foreign trade. Marian Zacharski, a former spy who spent time in a US prison before being freed in a Cold War spy exchange, was the company's final director. Despite being described as "a leading businessman in Poland" by the foreign press and spinning visions of turning Pewex into a multi-billion-dollar retail empire, Pewex immediately ran into trouble and tried to declare bankruptcy in 1993 before finally being taken over by a French company in 1997.[2]

Zacharski's failure was nothing unusual. Despite the perception among many in Poland that the Communists grabbed a big share of the new economy, party hacks actually did not do that well.

"The real apparatchiks didn't get rich. No minister or member of the government became a wealthy person," says Jerzy Urban, the jug-eared spokesman for Jaruzelski's martial law regime, and one of the few senior men around the general to get rich. Sitting behind an enormous desk in an office decorated with a large painting of a naked woman rolling out of bed, and a smaller print over the door of a banana being unpeeled to reveal a penis, Urban explains that the public notoriety he gained by loudly defending Jaruzelski's regime, along with his decision to open a muckraking weekly called *Nie* (No), attacking the first Solidarity government, made him a millionaire many times over.

Like the Communist Party bagmen, businesses with their roots in the state also proved to be a disappointment. The shipyards which gave rise to Solidarity went bust several times, and now only the one in Gdańsk functions at a fraction of its former capacity, competing against successful private yards. The workforce of twenty thousand has shriveled to only two thousand, and the yard is teetering on the brink of collapse. Coal mines were once the home of the coddled elite of the workforce. In the 1980s they even had their own special well-stocked shops to reward their efforts in supplying one of the few cash-earning exports of People's Poland. But in the last two decades, mines have struggled despite very costly restructuring. The local car industry, which produced terribly built cars for which there once was huge demand because of a lack of any alternatives, is now dead, replaced by foreign manufacturers.

By contrast, the private sector in Poland is one of the most vibrant in Europe. Czarnecki recalls that anyone who had the guts to break with the comfort and security of a state sector job in the early 1990s "was guaranteed to succeed." Sitting in an office at the headquarters of his banking empire, he says, "It was normal to break even after just a month. I don't know a single person who started a business in any sector who didn't succeed. There was enormous demand, no supply, and no competition."

While the initial condition of Polish business may have looked pretty wild, Poland moved very quickly to create legal structure to accommodate a market economy, something that other Central European countries like Czechoslovakia and Hungary did at more or less the same time, but which countries further to the east like Ukraine and Russia did not—with very negative long-term consequences for their later development.

The initial rules for business set up first under Rakowski's final Communist Party government and then by Balcerowicz were minimal, meaning that people could start companies without an enormous amount of red tape. That had already applied under late communism; as long as the company was small, under four employees in most cases, there were really very few rules and almost no taxes. Ryszard Florek, the founder of Fakro, today the world's second largest maker of roof skylights, remembers how tax inspections looked at the time that he was running a carpentry and window-making plant in southern Poland in the 1980s: "The inspectors would come in teams of two. One would walk through the front gate and one would stand out back to catch anybody trying to run out the back door. They would do a quick head count and if you didn't have too many workers, you were OK." In those conditions, it was easy for people to form their own businesses.

The steady accretion of rules, taxes, papers, forms, stamps, and approvals built up through the 1990s, like barnacles gluing themselves to the bottom of a once fast boat, and slowed the creation of new businesses while driving some companies into bankruptcy. But in those early years the government actually did a decent job of setting the legal framework of a functioning market economy. A good example was the creation of the Warsaw Stock Exchange (WSE), an institution that has become the largest capital market in Central Europe.

Wiesław Rozłucki, the founder and first CEO of the exchange, remembers the frenzy of late 1989 and early 1990 as the country rushed through economic reforms and built a modern capitalist infrastructure. Rozłucki, who had studied international trade and spent a year at the London School of Economics in 1979, says he was one of the few people in the country to understand how capital markets worked and to comprehend concepts like hedging and futures. That got him summoned by Balcerowicz to create a new stock exchange. Rozłucki and two other Poles showed up in London's City trying to take a look at a functioning stock exchange. They took most of their technical advice from the Paris Bourse, and replicated existing technical and regulatory structures.

"There was no need to find a third way—we just used what other countries had already done," Rozłucki says.

The work was immense. Even Polish market terminology had to be re-created as prewar terms were largely based on French and German, and new ones had to be made up relying on English. Trading opened in April 1991 on the top floor of the old Communist Party central committee building—the only place in Warsaw that had proper computers available to handle that day's trades, as well as providing "a bit of historical revenge," admits Rozłucki. A friend of his painted a makeshift logo on a bit of board that Rozłucki had stored in the basement of his building. The board was propped up on an easel during the exchange's first day of trading, when volume in the five listed companies came to two thousand dollars. The WSE today has a market capitalization of more than $177 billion and a daily turnover of more than $270 million.

Other Central European exchanges, like the one in Prague, were set up without as many rules and were much quicker about grabbing new listings. Like Warsaw, Prague began trading in 1993 with only seven shares, but the number of new listings soared, thanks to the government's controversial voucher privatization scheme, which gave every Czechoslovak citizen given a stake in state assets.

The poorly regulated Prague exchange ballooned—at its peak it had more than 1,700 companies trading. Instead of becoming a normal capital market, it became a swimming pool for savvy financial sharks who quickly took control of many state companies, leaving ordinary Czechs with nothing. The exchange tried to take back the initiative in 1997 by withdrawing 1,301 listings from trading, but the damage had been done. The Prague exchange now has 25 listings, while Warsaw has 483 on its main market thus showing the advantages of a sensible regulatory structure.

Setting up basic economic rules and unleashing a well educated but poor population that finally saw a chance to get ahead after decades of living in a socialist absurdity unleashed an enormous wave of business creation. In Poland the starter's gun fired at the end of the 1980s, and people raced off in more or less equal conditions; many failed, but a few succeeded, creating companies which moved from small trading operations into companies with national, European, and global reach.

In the decade I spent reporting on Poland for the *Financial Times*, my interviews with these entrepreneurs were the most interesting part of my job. Poland has had one of the fastest growth rates of any European economy over the last two decades, and that is due almost entirely to these people who braved red tape, their own lack of practical knowledge, and very little access to capital to succeed in creating their own businesses. There is a hunger to get ahead in Poland that is almost American in scope, says Młodkowski.

The outcome has been a striking advance in wealth. Poland's economy has grown by an average of about 4 percent a year for almost a quarter-century. Now, instead of being only one-third as wealthy as West Europeans, Poles are almost two-thirds as wealthy as their Western neighbors.[3] Never in its history has Poland been this close to Western Europe—and the gap continues to narrow.

Of course, conditions are now a lot tougher. Profit margins of 50 percent or more are unheard of. A lot of the easier ideas from Western Europe and the US have already been "borrowed" and turned into businesses, and the last twenty years have seen a fair number of failures and bankruptcies—but Poland remains one of the EU's most dynamic economies.

When I showed up in Poland in 2003 to cover the country for the *FT*, I adapted a popular American game called "punch Buggy" for my small sons. In the States it meant that if you saw a Volkswagen Beetle, you were able to give your sibling a punch. As there were almost no Beetles in Poland, I made up "punch Maluch," named after the nickname for the tiny Fiat 126p, cars that Sosnowski had repaired in his garage. I had to call off the game within a couple of days, however, because there were so many of the little cars on the road that the boys were beating each other black and blue.

Today such cars are a rarity, even in the poorest eastern parts of the country, having been long since replaced by used cars imported from Germany. Instead, some collectors are beginning to buy the Fiat 126p for its nostalgia value. The old reality of lines and rude service is now a folk memory. Poland's Institute of National Remembrance, a blend of a historical research unit and a prosecutor's office that investigates totalitarian crimes dating back to 1939, has produced a Monopoly-style board game called "Queue." Players have to recreate the absurdity of living in a planned economy, fighting for place in lines that allow them to buy precious goods like furniture and soap.

Two young journalists have also written a time-travel book, *My*

Little PRL (PRL being the acronym for the People's Republic of Poland). Wojciech Szabłowski and Izabela Meyza spent six months trying to recreate the lives of their parents circa 1981. Szabłowski grew a drooping moustache and drove a Maluch, while Meyza wore drab floral prints and would show up in the well-stocked shops of modern Warsaw, befuddling the polite young cashiers by asking if any meat deliveries were expected. The experiment was amusing, but the difficulty in pretending that meat was a luxury also showed the impossibility of trying to recreate a past of privation, political repression, and empty shelves in a modern, democratic, and increasingly wealthy country.

A recent political cartoon has a father telling his young son, "I remember when there was nothing but vinegar on store shelves."

"Really, nothing but vinegar in all the shops of Galerie Mokotów?" says his young charge, referring to a sparkling luxury shopping mall in southern Warsaw.

Oh, and that distinctive smell of Communist Poland is now found only in the remotest parts of the country—more of a trigger for nostalgia than a cause of disgust.

2 In the Starting Blocks

From 1917 to 1989, communism never retreated; there were no examples of a country moving from socialism back to capitalism. That meant that when Poland's democratic reformers took over the country, there were no models to follow on how to rebuild a market economy. Poland also began its experiment in unique conditions: the Soviet Union was still standing, thousands of Soviet troops were stationed in Poland, the country was surrounded by communist dictatorships, and the Polish Communist Party still controlled the police and military. But the country's economic collapse and the thumping administered to the Communists in 1989 elections meant that there was a window of opportunity to make changes–and the country seized it.

Through the 1970s and 1980s, millions of Poles desperately tried to get out of their failing country and build themselves a better life in the normal countries of the West. Leszek Balcerowicz spent the same period trying to figure out how to turn Poland into one of those more normal countries.

The old saw goes: "Success has many fathers, but failure is an orphan." In the case of the early years of Poland's transformation, there is not much need to conduct a paternity test—Balcerowicz, the acerbic economist with a big ego and no tolerance for people who disagree with him, has his DNA deeply imprinted on Poland's success.

In 1970, Polish soldiers gunned down forty-one people and wounded more than a thousand—crushing protests by shipyard workers on the Baltic coast. The grim prediction of Party rule in George Orwell's *1984*, "If you want a picture of the future, imagine a boot stamping on a human face—forever," seemed to be a realistic prospect for Poland and the rest of the Soviet empire.

At about the same time, a twenty-three-year-old Balcerowicz, freshly graduated with a degree in foreign trade from Warsaw's Central School of Planning and Statistics (as well as being a newly minted member of the Polish United Workers Party), was already beginning to think about the kinds of changes that would make the notoriously inefficient communist economy perform better. Of course, all those plans had to be carefully drafted so as not to endanger either the leading role of the party or Moscow's ultimate control over Poland. By the late 1970s he had gathered a group of younger economists at the Central School (now the Warsaw School of Economics, where he still teaches) who would meet every week to try to work out a politically acceptable reform program. This was at the same time that Poland's experiment with a dose of social liberalism and consumerism, fueled by a binge of foreign borrowing under Communist Party leader Edward Gierek, was starting to come unstuck.

The economists' idea was to create a system loosely based on Yugoslavia's labor-managed firms, but with fewer rights for the Party to nominate managers. That made the group one of the few in Poland to have any kind of a coherent reform program when Solidarity arose in 1980. The union paid a lot of attention to Balcerowicz's ideas, but none of them were implemented by the time martial law was declared in 1981 and Solidarity was (at least temporarily) crushed.

Balcerowicz and his team continued to meet through the 1980s, looking at the success of Asia's tiger economics and at the terrible record of attempts to reform communist economics—not a single such effort had succeeded in more than the short term since 1917. They also studied Ludwig Erhard, who had kick started the German *Wirtschaftswunder* in 1948 with a shock program of liberal changes and a currency reform.

In the spring of 1989, while round-table talks were being held between the government and the opposition, Balcerowicz penned a program for the Polish economy that included rapid and massive liberalization, convertibility of the zloty, and quick macroeconomic stabilization. His ideas were at variance with the conversation around the negotiating table, where communist apparatchiks and trade unionists thought more in terms of finding a "third way" that would preserve the fairness of socialism while injecting a bit of the vigor and freedom of capitalism to prevent the economy from collapsing.

Balcerowicz says that even then, with what in retrospect seem obvious signs of the advanced state of communist decomposition, "For most Polish people in the spring of 1989, it still seemed as though socialism would last through the rest of their lives. So did I."

Just a few months later, Mazowiecki was forming his government and asking Balcerowicz to be his Erhard—to become finance minister and deputy prime minister, to head the effort to return Poland to a market economy.

The task was enormous, even larger than Balcerowicz suspected at the time. Poland was in all respects a basket case. In 1989, GDP per capita in current dollars was only $2,165, just over a tenth of that of Germany.[1] The country was running a budget deficit of 7 percent.[2] The country was also staggering under a growing burden of foreign debt, rising from $20 billion in 1980 to $41 billion by 1988[3]—the result of loans accumulated a decade earlier under Gierek. Foreign currency reserves were close to zero, and the country was having trouble making debt payments.[4] Inflation was hitting more than 50 percent a month. The economy had not really grown at all through the crisis-ridden 1980s. Average monthly salaries in dollar terms at the black market exchange rate had shrunk to a ludicrous twenty-five dollars.

Shops were empty, and there was real fear of hunger in major cities. Polish agriculture was largely in the hands of inefficient small subsistence farmers. Industry made up more than 40 percent of the economy, largely producing useless goods that were difficult to sell both at home and abroad. The service sector was almost nonexistent.

Any thought of slowly edging away from the precipice was "pseudo-scientific nonsense," snorts Balcerowicz. The best idea was to make a dash for a market economy by implementing a broad package of deep reforms as swiftly as possible. "I was deeply convinced that the clearly nonradical approaches were hopeless," he says. "I believed that only a radical strategy could succeed, even though it was risky, as Poland in 1989 was largely on uncharted waters."

Here, the parentage issue does become clouded by a few midwives who did help Balcerowicz.

The first, and probably least remembered, is Mieczysław Wilczek. The diminutive chemical engineer was that most unusual of things: a rich capitalist living openly in a communist country. A member of the Communist Party dating back to 1952, deep in the years of Stalinist oppression he initially worked for Polenna, a cosmetics conglomerate pumping out soaps, laundry detergent, and makeup.[5] His first hit was coming up with a product in the late 1960s that would wash the cheap drip-dry shirts that were part of the uniform of every bureaucrat in the socialist bloc. Existing powders left the shirts gray, while Wilczek's IXI did not. He received the staggering sum of one million zlotys for his invention, at a time when the average monthly salary was about two thousand zlotys.

Although he was a star, Wilczek's independent character got him into trouble with the stultifying bureaucracy above him. He argued with the state institution that set the prices of just about all goods sold in Poland, a practice which he complained was setting the price of Polenna moisturizing cream too low. The official's response was: "The price of the cream should be low enough so that every seamstress in Łódź could smear her ass with it."

"I said, 'If you want to make cream for asses, then do it without me,'" said Wilczek in a 2012 interview. "The next day I quit."[6]

Out on his own, he made his money through his own inventiveness. Reading that guinea fowl eggs were richer in vitamins than the chicken eggs used to make creams, he set up a farm and built his own lab to produce creams—meant not for asses but for export to the Soviet Union. He was so successful that he again ran into trouble with bureaucrats, who shut his company down. Casting about for a new business, he hit on the idea of using offal to make animal feed. Using his own patents and designs, he set up twenty plants around the country, charging each plant one million zlotys to get them running.

With his honestly earned money, Wilczek built himself a palatial residence outside Warsaw with its own stables, swimming pool, and tennis courts. These were unheard of luxuries at the time, and they made Wilczek a magnet for actors, models, and politicians keen to frolic on his property. It was there that he met Mieczysław Rakowski, a journalist and senior Communist Party member who took over the government in September 1988. It was obvious to Rakowski that he would have to bring in deep reforms to save the sagging economy, and he turned to Wilczek, making him industry minister and promising him political protection. Wilczek took to the idea with enthusiasm, appearing three times before the Politburo to explain the need for reforms, and even quoting from Milton Friedman while doing so. General Jaruzelski supposedly blocked his ears so as not to hear his heresies.

On December 23, 1988, Wilczek pushed through a new law on economic freedom.[7] The first paragraph began: "Undertaking economic activity is free and permitted to everyone on an equal basis." The law also allowed for any activity not prohibited by law. Regulations restricting business activity and limiting the number of employees a company could hire were scrapped. The regulations were passed by a Communist government on its last legs and in the midst of a very deep economic and political crisis. That meant that the law did not and could not save the floundering regime, but did set a model for clear and concise legislation that freed people to open their own businesses. Decades later, Wilczek, who died in 2014, was still fondly remembered by Polish business people.

"It was really a golden age; you could do almost anything you wanted to," says wistful bakery baron Andrzej Blikle.

The other midwife of Polish reforms was Jeffrey Sachs, the Harvard (now Columbia University) economist who was a key advisor to both Mazowiecki and Balcerowicz in conjunction with teams of helpers from the World Bank, the International Monetary Fund, and other institutions, as well as a large number of ethnic Polish economists coming back to help their homeland. Sachs had made his name advising Bolivia in the mid-1980s, devising a shock therapy program to stop hyperinflation and liberalize the economy. His success there brought him to the attention of Poland's communists, but Sachs turned down their request for help, saying he worked only with democratic governments. The June 4 elections made it apparent that Poland could be on its way to getting such a government, and Sachs travelled to Warsaw to advise Solidarity.

Sachs tells of sitting in the book-crowded apartment of Jacek Kuroń, a chain-smoking giant among Polish dissidents, explaining Poland's economic situation and the kinds of measures that would be needed to fix it.[8] Sachs carefully spelled out Poland's broken public finances, looming bankruptcy, and fast-approaching hyperinflation, and then his solutions. An enthusiastic Kuroń puffed away while sipping whiskey, and then insisted that Sachs type up his thoughts to be presented to Solidarity the next day.

Sachs was taken to the offices of *Gazeta Wyborcza*, the free newspaper set up as part of the round-table agreement that had begun its life housed in a Warsaw nursery school. There he spent the predawn hours pecking away at an early-generation IBM PC, writing up a recipe for fixing the country.

The resulting ten-page document, printed with a dot-matrix printer, begins: "The economic program of Solidarity will seek to resolve the major economic problems facing Poland through a sudden and comprehensive jump to a market economy. . . . The combination of a shock reforms of prices, stabilization, and marketization will halt the downward spiral of the economy and will restore economic growth, producing a sustained rising trend in living standards."[9]

Bielecki, the former prime minister, remarked about Sachs, "He seemed to be a man who knew what he was talking about. After all, he was an American professor."

Sachs later wrote, "The politicians and the general public understood intuitively that a 'shock therapy' approach was not simply another utopian scheme of economic reform, but rather was a quick route to a relatively clear target. In 1989, that target was Western Europe."[10]

The man to synthesize all those plans and then put them into action was Balcerowicz, though, as he admits, "I had never managed anything larger than a seminar." The legislation was prepared over the autumn, and the program, later called the Balcerowicz Plan, was launched on January 1, 1990. Just days earlier, the Polish constitution was amended to end the provision about the "leading role" of the Communist Party, thus guaranteeing property rights and legalizing trade unions. The sense was that the government had to move very fast to make maximum advantage out of circumstances that could quickly change.

Solidarity's victory and the collapse of the Communists gave the reform program very strong political support. It was helped by the very obvious signs of economic breakdown on the streets; the public and politicians were willing to tolerate a level of pain unacceptable in more stable societies. Other, better managed, Central European countries never faced a Polish-level catastrophe, and so never pushed through the same kind of radical reforms. Balcerowicz argues that, as a result, Poland has seen higher average growth during the past quarter-century. The international environment was also remarkably benign. The Soviet Union was consumed with Mikhail Gorbachev's reforms, and no longer had the energy or the interest to police its Central European empire. The West had long been supportive of Solidarity, and Mazowiecki's government enjoyed an enormous outburst of foreign sympathy.

"I was aware that the political breakthrough in Poland had opened the way for a brief period of what I termed 'extraordinary politics,' when it is easier than in normal times to push through difficult reforms," says Balcerowicz.

The new initiative, formally titled the Economic Transformation Program, consisted of ten pieces of legislation. They freed most prices, ended government guarantees for state-owned companies, forbade the central bank from covering government deficits, ended credit preferences for state companies, imposed draconian taxes aimed at halting steep wage increases, eased regulations on foreign investors and allowed them to expatriate their profits, opened the Polish market to foreign companies, made the zloty convertible, ended state control of foreign trade, and unified the rules on importing foreign goods.

Within days, thousands of Poles raced to Vienna, Berlin, Istanbul, and anywhere else they could to get their hands on the goods demanded back home. They filled bags with leather jackets, socks, and jeans and then waited in queues lasting days on the German border to come home to legally sell their merchandise. Polish farmers slaughtered hogs, cows, and chickens and then sold the produce out of the backs of their cars on city streets. For those wanting a smaller cut of meat, the fur-capped farmer would happily wield his ax on a bloody stump and hack off a choice portion.

"Nobody cared about health and safety rules," laughs Bielecki. "We just wanted to get things moving—and they did. It was a textbook example of building capitalism."

Perhaps the purest expression of the wild side of Polish capitalism became the Tenth Anniversary Stadium, an abandoned 100,000-seat arena on the right bank of the Vistula River, constructed on the heaps of rubble left after the 1944 Warsaw Uprising. After 1989 it became home to Europe's largest open-air market. The cracked concrete risers were filled with Poles, Belarusians, Ukrainians, and people from a dozen other nations selling alcohol of doubtful provenance, ripped off computer programs, cigarettes that had fallen off trucks in half a dozen countries, cheap clothes from China and Vietnam, old books, the occasional firearm, illegally copied CDs, and pornography.

Inflation, clocking in at about 685 percent in 1989, began to decline. A year later, monthly inflation was down from 50 percent to 4 percent.[11]

But the changes also wreaked havoc on the old way of doing things. Although private enterprises started emerging much more rapidly than economic planners had forecast, they were not enough to slow the fall in production from big state-owned companies. The external environment also caused problems, with the collapse of Comecon, the Soviet-run common market, forcing companies to switch exports from the USSR and other communist countries to the much more demanding European market. Poland's GDP fell sharply, down by 11.6 percent in 1990 and by a further 7.3 percent in 1991. Unemployment, almost unknown in communist times, hit 6.5 percent in 1990—a shocking figure to many Poles. By 1994 it was 16 percent.[12]

But by 1992, Poland turned the corner and the economy began to grow again. It was only an expansion of 2.3 percent, but that made it the first ex-communist country to return to growth. Poland hasn't suffered a recession since, making it the only country in Europe to grow for twenty-four years straight. Since 1992, average growth has come to just over 4 percent a year.

Balcerowicz insists that the reason is the comprehensive nature of the reforms, unlike the more timid efforts undertaken by many of Poland's peers. Stanisław Gomułka figures that the reforms undertaken before 1989, including those attempted by Wilczek, played an important role. Those efforts, coupled with the retention of a large class of admittedly inefficient peasant farmers on their own plots of land, left Poland with a significantly larger private sector than in other communist countries.

Meat and jeans appearing on Polish sidewalks was just one of the goals of Balcerowicz's plan. He split his policies into two main areas. The first were aimed at macroeconomic stabilization and economic liberalization. These worked very quickly to bring goods to consumers and to allow new businesses to form. A second batch of reforms was much longer-term, aimed at Poland's institutional transformation. That involved everything from creating a modern and independent central bank to restoring Poland's prewar commercial codex, setting up a stock exchange, and privatizing state-owned companies.

The first flush of business saw a lot of scrappy entrepreneurs who paid few taxes and followed fewer rules. The standard model was to begin with retail sales, often literally on the street. The more successful entrepreneurs quickly built up larger businesses, and the smartest among them ended up moving into production—first on a small scale, then nationally, and in a select few cases, internationally.

That first rush of business creation was something like the aftereffects of a forest fire. The first plants to colonize the burnt-back areas are often weeds with little staying power. It was much the same for many of the new businesses springing up after the conflagration of communism. Many of those early entrants were people who were very well connected to the Communist Party, but saw that the changing economy had opened a future much more lucrative for them than that of being a gray apparatchik.

Just three days after the catastrophic (for the Communists) election results of June 4, Bogusław Kott, a former senior official in the finance ministry, was registering Poland's first commercial bank. The bank, operating with the cringeworthy name of Bank Inicjatyw Gospodarczych (BIG Bank, obviously) had some very high-profile backers. Although it was a private business venture, it received capital from the country's largest state-owned (and Communist Party–controlled) institutions. One of the founding companies was also the Foundation for Maritime Development, created by none other than Kott, together with outgoing prime minister Rakowski and Aleksander Kwaśniewski, an up-and-coming cabinet minister, senior Communist Party official, and future Polish president.[13] One of the first shareholders was Urban, the reviled spokesman of the martial law regime.

Although it started with only seven branches, BIG Bank aggressively bought up much larger rivals, thanks to sweetheart deals with the National Bank of Poland and with left-wing post communist governments. It did do innovative things like introduce the first Polish credit cards, but it also became embroiled in the enthusiasm for handing out mortgages denominated in Swiss francs, which after the onset of the global financial crisis almost caused the bank to collapse. Today the bank, under the more respectable name of Millennium, is owned by Portugal's BCP—part of an inflow of foreign banks into the country. About half of Poland's banking sector is now foreign-owned, one of the highest levels in a large European country—but those foreign banks have brought modern risk assessment and management methods.

Onet, one of Poland's leading web portals, recently came up with a list of what happened to some of the country's leading businessmen from the early 1990s.[14] The list looks a lot like a rogues' gallery.

In 1989, Andrzej Rzeźniczak was one of the richest Poles, thanks to his having set up a pseudobank that offered clients suspiciously high rates of return—in other words, a Ponzi scheme. Similar institutions flourished from Albania to Vladivostok during the transitions away from socialism. Rzeźniczak was bankrupt by 1992, and a year later he was being pursued by the police. He died in prison in 2010.

Lech Grobelny, who had made his first money in the 1970s selling pictures of Pope John Paul II, also set up his own bank, and by 1990s was bust, also with the police on his heels.

Perhaps the most audacious was Kazimierz Grabek, Poland's "gelatin king." Grabek started making glues and gelatin out of animal carcasses in the late 1980s, breaking just about every environmental, tax, and other regulation on the books while doing so. By 1992 he was Poland's second richest man, building his jelly empire on huge numbers of ill-secured bank loans. He became so powerful that he managed to corner the Polish gelatin market and even got the government to block competing imports. His lobbying was so successful that his methods became known as "grabbing," a play on his last name.

But by the late 1990s, Poland's politicians had become much more aware of the risks of entangling themselves with shady entrepreneurs. Meanwhile, Polish bureaucracy and law enforcement had also become substantially more efficient—part of the process of adapting to the prospect of joining the European Union.

Grabek has been defending himself against criminal charges on ecological and financial matters for most of the past decade, but the languid Polish court system has yet to finish any of the pending cases.

While men like Grabek quickly shot to the top, many smaller businesses, often with better records of following laws and tax regulations, rose up in their wake. Those are the businesses that have now grown into the birches and poplars now populating Poland's postcommunist forest.

In those first months of the transformation, Sachs tried to get Poland out from under its mountain of foreign debt, contacting the G7 group of rich countries to explain that loans accumulated under the previous dictatorial regime should not have to be repaid. Western countries balked, but when Bielecki was prime minister in 1991, a large chunk of Poland's external debt was written down. The new government held talks with the Paris Club of nations that had lent Poland money, and with the London Club of private lenders. In the end the Paris Club debt was reduced by a minimum of 50 percent, while the London Club debt was cut by 45 percent—enough not to throttle the reforms with hard currency repayments.[15]

In 1991, Poland also signed an association agreement with the European Economic Community, the precursor to the European Union, and made clear its intentions to eventually join. Two years later, on the symbolic date of September 17, the anniversary of the 1939 Soviet attack on Poland during the first weeks of World War II, the last Russian troops stationed in Poland clambered aboard troop trains and headed east.

Now, instead of being a country trapped between East and West, Poland had made clear that it was intent on becoming a full member of the West. That made it an increasingly attractive destination for foreign investors, attracted by the gelling legal system, the return to economic growth, the millions of consumers still hungry for Western goods, and the large numbers of skilled workers.

Foreign direct investment rose from essentially nothing in 1989 to $109 million by 1990. By 1992 FDI was above $1 billion, and by 1996 it was more than $10 billion. Cumulative FDI was $213 billion by 2015, according to the UNCTAD, the United Nations trade body.

The enormous flood of money has had a huge impact in modernizing the country. Foreigners brought in Western management standards, practices, technology, and equipment, thus forcing other parts of the economy to race to catch up as well. Fiat now runs a huge car assembly plant in southern Poland, while Volkswagen has one near Poznań. As a result, dozens of Polish companies now act as suppliers, not just to the local factories but to the whole of the European car industry. Similar things have happened around electronics, with flat-screen television factories owned by Korea's LG and Taiwan's Compal also creating opportunities for local suppliers.

One good example of how foreign investment can modernize a sector is in Lembork, in northern Poland. There, alongside Route 6, a road running parallel to the Baltic coast, neat white buildings emit puffs of not very dangerous-looking smoke into the blue sky. The factory makes french fries—the brainchild of Ernst Christoph Lehman-Bärenklau, a German businessman who spied an opportunity when the Berlin Wall came down in 1989. At the time he was in the potato and french fry business in Western Europe.

"I said we should go to the East because McDonald's and other fast-food companies will now move into there," he says from his office overlooking the factory.

He scouted for good locations across postcommunist Central Europe, but settled on Poland because it was one of the world's largest potato producers. With his Dutch partners, Farm Frites, he bid on a lease for a 10,000-acre plot of land, a piece of terrain that seemed enormous to the Dutch. However, it turned out to be much too small to supply the $50 million potato-processing factory built in Lembork in 1993. Local Polish farmers with their small fields, low yields, and traditional methods were initially unable to make up the shortfall. Also, the potatoes the Poles grew "were round, like tennis balls, not the right shape to supply long strips to companies like McDonald's," says Lehman-Bärenklau.

In those early years, the factory and the cheap land leases in the area, drew farmers from across Europe. "We had people from Scotland, Germany, Belgium, and the Netherlands who settled around us," he says.

Farm Frites and the new settlers also introduced more modern farming methods to the surrounding Poles, raising their yields from fifteen tons per hectare to more than forty—of the right kind of potatoes. Now, only two of the factory's suppliers are foreign; the Poles dominate. "This has become a real success story of the Polish potato industry," says Lehman-Bärenklau.

The same sort of thing happened across Poland as rapid growth drew in both big foreign companies like Unilever and foreign entrepreneurs who saw Poland as a once-in-a-lifetime opportunity.

Englishman Richard Worthington was in Warsaw in the late 1990s, peddling bakery equipment, when he saw that he couldn't get a decent cup of coffee. Poles tended to drink a swill made by pouring boiling water directly onto coffee, and then carefully drinking the result so as not to end up with a mouthful of grounds. He had the not very original idea of opening Starbucks-type cafés, and they were an enormous hit. His Coffee Heaven chain, with locations around Central Europe, is now owned by the United Kingdom's Whitbread, and is part of its Costa Coffee network.

Luis Amaral, a Portuguese national, came to Poland in the mid-1990s, initially to work for Jerónimo Martins, the Portuguese retailer, which was growing its Biedronka chain of discount shops. He ended up buying Biedronka's wholesaler, Eurocash, and has since turned it into one of Poland's largest businesses. "It was a virgin country," Amaral says of the retail environment he found when he first got to Poland.

The country's economic stability was further reinforced by a new constitution passed in 1997 that set a maximum public debt at 60 percent of GDP. During Balcerowicz's second stint as finance minister, from 1997 to 2000, he pushed through even tougher measures to ensure that public debt did not rise too high. By 2004, Poland had become a member of the European Union, the result of consistent policy from parties related both to the old Solidarity movement and to the ex-communist left. The focus on joining the EU helped ensure that overtly populist ideas that could have torpedoed the economy were kept at bay.

The effectiveness of the EU's open door can be seen by the contrast in neighboring Ukraine, which has never been offered EU membership. While the prospect of membership in the EU united most of the Polish political spectrum around sensible policies aimed at conforming to EU standards, there were no such constraints in Ukraine. With no hope of EU membership, Ukrainian governments were free to despoil their country and turn it into a swamp of corruption. Weak and unable to defend itself, Ukraine has fallen prey to Russia. In 1990, Ukraine was actually slightly richer on a per capita basis than Poland, with well developed aviation and defense industries and an agricultural sector with enormous potential. In 2015, a quarter-century after the end of communism, the average Polish per capita GDP in current dollars was $12,494 while in Ukraine it was only $2,115.[16]

Joining the EU also opened spigots of money from Brussels, powering a wave of modernization. From 2008 to 2012, Poland took in about €67 billion in structural funds, and for the 2014–2020 budget, it stands to get €119 billion in agricultural and structural funds.

The result has been a revolution. EU funds finally saw Poland building modern airports, railways, and highways. In June 2012, Bielecki invited a group of motorcyclists to take a run from Warsaw out to Łódź on the new highway finally connecting the Polish capital to the rest of Europe. We roared out past a sign pointing the way to Lisbon, at the other end of the EU's highway network. People crowded the overpasses, snapping photos of cars driving along the newly opened road.

Inside the Polish capital, the old Tenth Anniversary Stadium and its accompanying flea market are gone. Their place has been taken by an enormous and modern stadium, site of the opening kickoff of the 2012 European soccer championships.

The institutions that Balcerowicz and others set up also proved to be durable. The Warsaw Stock Exchange is now the largest in Central Europe, having overtaken Vienna years ago. Poland's banks, dominated by foreign investors, have proven to be well financed and resilient, despite the waves of crisis starting from the 2008 collapse of Lehman Brothers. In that crisis, Poland ended up being the only

EU country not to fall into recession. That was partly due to good luck—a round of tax cuts kicked in just as the crisis started, and Poland's zloty lost value, cushioning exporters. But a strong central bank and well-run government also helped insulate the country. The result has been probably the best quarter-century in Polish history. Marcin Piątkowski, an economist with the World Bank, calculates that Poland is now closer to catching up to Western Europe than ever before in its history.[17]

"Poland is destined for success," says Piątkowski. "Poland doesn't need a revolution. We don't need to change the model, but only to adapt it gradually."

But the rest of the climb to finally equal Western Europe—something Poland has never achieved in its more than one thousand years of recorded history—is going to be tougher than the first leg.

Balcerowicz believes that in twenty years the average Pole could be as wealthy as the average German. But for that to happen, Poland needs to embark on a treadmill of continuous improvements and reforms. Its court system, now one of the most sluggish in Europe, has to be improved. Its universities, which languish at the tail end of international rankings, have to become significantly better. Its government has to finally come through on its promises to remove the red tape throttling business. Poland also has to become significantly more innovative. That is going to be a problem because it spends only 0.9 percent of GDP on research and development, about a third less than the continent's most advanced countries. That spending is also heavily tilted toward the government, which accounts for about half of R&D expenditures. The private sector still spends much too little. One reason is that foreign companies in Poland tend to have production plants there while keeping their R&D work at home. Most Polish businesses still spend relatively little on innovation.

Added to that is Poland's demographic problem. About two million people left for other EU countries after Poland joined the EU in 2004. Poland also has one of Europe's lowest birth rates. That, combined with a low level of labor participation and relatively low levels of savings, means that future Polish governments will have to overcome a long series of hurdles to make the economy more efficient and so able to complete the country's catch-up.

Poland's new government, which took power in late 2015, is ramping up public spending in what it says is an effort to make it more attractive for people to have children. Mateusz Morawiecki, the development minister, has sketched out ambitious plans to boost R&D, develop innovative Polish companies, and increase savings. He also wants to "repolonize" the banking sector by increasing the number of Polish-owned banks. But there are worries that the populist Law and Justice Party government has made so many expensive promises that it could damage the budget. Just months after the new government took office, Standard & Poor's downgraded Poland's credit rating, citing worries over economic policies. It was also concerned about a serious fight over the country's highest constitutional court that has drawn in the European Union, worried the United States, and sent thousands of antigovernment demonstrators onto Polish streets.

"For twenty years from 1995 we strengthened our rating, which means our financial and economic reputation in the eyes of the world, and for the first time this January we started to slide back," Balcerowicz said in a May 2016 radio interview.[18]

Concern over the new government threatens to derail what Balcerowicz sees as a historic chance for Poland. Sitting at a meeting table near his office at the Warsaw School of Economics, and with a diploma on the wall behind his head proclaiming him to be "the father of Poland's transformation," Balcerowicz is optimistic that Poland can continue to scramble back after three hundred years of losing ground against the West.

"Markets function in every culture if they are allowed to operate," he says, pointing out that there was nothing inherent in the character of the Polish people that made their country more successful than those of their neighbors. "If markets don't function, it's because they were forbidden. I had no doubt that if you liberalize there will be a lot of entrepreneurs."

Those kinds of dramatic changes also leave a lot of losers. That's something that the reformers also knew would happen, but which devastated swathes of the country, especially in the 1990s—and which in part led to the overwhelming 2015 victory of Law and Justice.

3 Shocked by Therapy

It's pretty easy to trumpet Poland's economic successes–they have in fact been remarkable. But there is a darker side to the transformation: the millions of people who were left behind. Living in the poorer and more agricultural east of the country, or working for heavy industry, many of them bore the brunt of the shift from socialism. The sense that they were left out of "Poland's new golden age" rankled and grew, spawning protest movements, and in 2015 it helped the populist nationalists of Law and Justice to take power. Despite the political blowback, the lesson remains: Those parts of the economy with the least state interference have done best.

Andrzej Szypuła came home in 1988. Home was Wiśniowa, a village of less than two thousand named after the sour cherry trees that blossom in the orchards tucked into the foothills of the Carpathian Mountains in southeastern Poland. Szypuła, a music teacher, had grown up in the village, but had decamped for the brighter lights of Poland's larger cities as a young man. Now, with a wife and children, he was back—and the first thing that struck him about the place was just how poor it was.

The main employer was the state-owned farm, employing about a hundred people tending to scraggly milk cows and to fruit production. Those workers lived in a row of decaying three-story gray concrete apartment blocks. They were the kinds of buildings that would normally be seen in scrappy industrial areas of large cities, but which in communist countries were used to house state farm workers. These were peasants converted by the state into workers, with living quarters to match.

Government farms like the one in Wiśniowa were created across

Poland on land confiscated from prewar landowners and on territories that had belonged to Germany before the war. The early idea of Poland's Soviet-backed communist rulers had been to follow in the path of the USSR and completely collectivize Polish agriculture. However, even in the most repressive era of the early 1950s, Party planners hadn't quite figured on the stubbornness of the Polish peasant, who resisted every effort to create collectivized farms and take away his private patch of land.

That meant that government-run farms were a much smaller part of Polish agriculture than in the rest of the Soviet bloc. Those state farms that were created didn't make for a particularly compelling advertisement for the benefits of a socialist economy. They were so inefficient that by the late 1980s, about 50 percent of the government's spending on agriculture went to subsidize them, although they occupied only 20 percent of Poland's arable land.[1] The smaller private plots of land were much better at actually growing food. However, the state farms did provide lots of low-paying but stable jobs.

The squat apartment blocks in Wiśniowa overlook the winding Wisłok River, curling its way through the lush green valley. Just around the curve, along a long avenue planted with towering hornbeam trees, their trunks stained green with moss, looms a palace with a crumbling portico, the home of the last prewar owners of the land, the Mycielski counts—my mother's family.

They had been run off their three-hundred-hectare estate in 1944 by the arriving Soviets. Like other Polish landowners, my uncle Jan Mycielski and his family were then forbidden from living in the same region as their estate, so they moved to Kraków, home to hundreds of other dispossessed landowning families. The house's contents—tables, dressers, swords, paintings, and silverware, all accumulated over centuries, were looted. My grandfather Kazimierz is now buried in the crypt below the red brick chapel adorned with his coat of arms, a downward-pointing arrow under a horseshoe. He never returned to Poland after the war, having emigrated to South Africa. The peasants lived on under the new communist system, which at least initially promised them a fairer shake in life than they had received under the counts.

The Mycielski lands were turned into a government farm, and life, always desperately poor in this part of Poland thanks to the poor soil and steep hills, went on. However, despite the poverty—Szypuła saw his first light bulb in the 1950s—there was a certain stability to Wiśniowa. Almost no one had a car; horses were commonly used to plow small plots of land which people worked in addition to their main jobs on the government farm. People tended to stay put. The old palace was first turned into a school and then allowed to decay. The stables and farmyard slowly sagged into ruin, a scraggly stork's nest topping the old tower gate which had most of its windows boarded up.

I remember showing up to visit Wiśniowa in the early 1970s. My grandfather, Stanisław Cieński—a close cousin of my other grandfather (such are the inbred ways of the Polish aristocracy)—flew into a rage at seeing the estate he had last visited during the war. Furiously brandishing his cane like a sword, the old cavalry officer rushed one of the confused farm workers yelling, "This is no way to run a farm. Don't you people have any idea of what you are doing? Why take this away from its rightful owners and make such an unproductive mess?"

That somnolent, inefficient, and poor, but stable and predictable life was upended by the collapse of the Polish economy in the late 1980s and then by Balcerowicz's reforms. State farms were completely unsuited to dealing with a fast-changing consumer market, and the government funds that they depended on to survive dried up almost immediately, thanks to Balcerowicz's new rules slashing subsidies for state industries. Without a constant flow of cash from Warsaw, state farms like the one in Wiśniowa were doomed. By late 1991 they were abolished.[2]

Szypuła remembers the shock that hit Wiśniowa after the launch of Balcerowicz's reforms.

"The farms started to sell off plows and tractors and the rest of their equipment," he says, "There was no money to pay salaries so they killed off all the animals, all the milk cows, to try to earn a bit of money. It was horrible. That's how the socialist economy ended—in a ruin."

Wiśniowa and hundreds of other state farms around Poland went bust. Hundreds of thousands of people lost their jobs, but remained trapped, with no useful skills, far from the cities where there were some signs of economic life.

"That is when the emigration began," says Jacek Rybczyk, secretary of the local government in Wiśniowa, dressed in a peasant's uniform of a gray suit and shirt with no tie.

People from places like Wiśniowa started leaving in droves, first to historical destinations for Polish migrants like the United States and Canada. Once Poland joined the EU in 2004, many more people moved to Western Europe. They were following a familiar path. From the late nineteenth century, when peasants gained the right of independent travel, thousands immediately fled the poor soils and repressive landowners of southern Poland for North and South America. American cities like Buffalo and Chicago were populated by desperately poor Poles from hard-scrabble places like Wiśniowa, then located in a forgotten corner of the Austro-Hungarian empire.

Szypuła puts out an occasional magazine about Wiśniowa. In one issue, he has grainy black and white photos showing musicians from Wiśniowa playing in Carnegie, Pennsylvania; Canada; and Argentina.

That river of people again burst its banks in 1990, a time when it was already easier for Poles to travel abroad. In 2004, when the UK, Ireland, and Sweden allowed citizens of the EU's new member states to legally work in their countries, many more emigrated. In all, about two million Poles left the country in its first decade as part of the EU—many of them fleeing no-hope villages like Wiśniowa.

"I tell the same thing to my music students," says Szypuła. "I tell them to run away as far as you can from this place, even though it really pains me to do so because I love this place."

His daughter now works in a supermarket in Ireland, coming home only for holidays.

"She would love to come back, but to what?" he says sadly. "There is no work here."

The best and the brightest have left—some to Polish cities like Warsaw and Kraków, but many more far beyond the country. The likelihood is that very few will ever permanently return. Many of those who remain are uneducated and unambitious. A half dozen sit outside the local shop on the outskirts of Wiśniowa every morning, sipping on half-liter brown bottles of cheap beer. The same scene is repeated in hundreds of poor villages across the country.

It wasn't just state farms that were hit by the shock of Balcerowicz's plan. Whole branches of the economy, often those most closely tied to the communist ideal of brawny industrialization, were hollowed out or destroyed by the rapid arrival of market capitalism in Poland.

Jacek Kuroń, who had watched Jeffrey Sachs put together an outline of the reform program in his apartment, became the social conscience of the Solidarity movement. As minister of labor and social policy, he was the one who worried about the human consequences of the reforms he had supported. His office was besieged by increasingly desperate people with no way of keeping themselves alive in the hostile new conditions of a market economy. The charismatic chain-smoker appealed for a national movement of soup kitchens, later dubbed *kuroniówki* or Kuroń's Soup, to feed the destitute, something he did himself in open-air kitchens. The term *kuroniówki* later was used to mean benefits paid to the unemployed. Kuroń's generosity and obvious concern for those hurt by reforms provided much-needed political cover for Mazowiecki and Balcerowicz in the early days of shock therapy.

"Kuroń's soups became famous," he later wrote, "and people who, out of kindness, out of their hearts, helped others in this way and in others suddenly felt themselves included in an important national matter—a matter important for Poland."[3]

Kuroń later became a bitter critic of the neoliberalism of the initial reform program.

Poland has become obviously less equal since Balcerowicz's

reforms. Under communism, even the elite didn't really manage to break away from the gray lives of the masses. The most widely used measure of inequality is the Gini coefficient, with zero being Karl Marx's dream of perfect equality and everyone having the same income, and 100 being a state in which all the income is earned by one person. Poland jumped from 26.7 in 1992 to 32.32 a year later, a level that has remained more or less constant since then.[4] That makes Poland a little less equal than Germany and the Czech Republic, but more equal than Russia and the United States.

The turmoil unleashed by Poland's return to a market economy did more than wreak havoc on the land. It also wrecked the very place that had given birth to the Solidarity labor union: the Gdańsk shipyard.

The shipyard had been one of the key export industries of communist Poland. About eighteen thousand workers clad in dark blue overalls scrambled like industrious ants over the enormous hulks of cargo vessels, largely meant for export. Massive green cranes, visible from across the city, turned and bobbed as they lifted gargantuan rust-colored sections of steel hulls into place. Like all socialist enterprises, the Lenin Memorial Shipyard in Gdańsk was hugely overstaffed, with the yard also responsible for financing recreational facilities, medical care, daycare, and all the other gravy of socialist well-being. However, unlike many other large Polish factories, the Gdańsk shipyard was actually making useful goods with some sort of a market value—although in this case it was paid more often in convertible rubles than in dollars for its production.

It was in this place, the heartland of the proletariat, which saw the outbreak of a wave of strikes in 1980 that led to the formation of Solidarity. While the movement they created helped bring down European communism a decade later, the workers themselves had little understanding of how they wanted to change the system, especially when it came to economics. The basic model they were aiming at was a version of Yugoslavia's friendlier communism, in which workers had a greater say in the affairs of their factories. Both Poland's geopolitical realities, with thousands of Soviet troops stationed permanently in the country, and its decades of communist propaganda had made the idea of capitalism foreign, even terrifying, to many of the striking workers.

Their dreams for a fairer future and an exit from Poland's economic crisis were exemplified by their twenty-one strike demands. With the demands hand-written in red and blue ink, and hung up by shipyard gate no. 2 during the strike as a way of making the appeals public, the two sheets of wood have since been recognized by UNESCO as part of the world's cultural heritage. They betray a mindset that could not survive in a truly capitalist economy. Demand number nine calls for the indexation of salaries to cost increases—a sure recipe for hyperinflation. Demand number ten says that exports should only be allowed once all domestic needs have been fulfilled. Number fifteen calls for a reduction in the retirement age, while demand number eighteen wants three-year paid maternity leaves.

That same kind of social-democratic way of thinking was part of the negotiating strategy of many of the economists on the opposition side during the 1989 round-table talks with the Communists. Balcerowicz later joked that the only true capitalist taking part in the talks was Wilczek—the minister and businessman who deregulated business—and that he was negotiating on the side of the Communists.

The shipyard had one of the most difficult transitions to capitalism of any Polish company—a shift that, a quarter-century after Poland's transformation, it has still not succeeded in fully completing. The first shock came in the waning months of Communist rule. Even while the regime prepared for talks with the illegal Solidarity labor union in 1988, Rakowski's government was moving to liquidate the shipyard. The explanation was that the yard wasn't making solid returns—a reason that was immediately questioned, as the yard that year was actually having one of its few good years. The true cause for liquidation was almost certainly ideological. "I decided on that because in Poland only a shock can switch matters onto a different track," Rakowski said at the time.[5]

Rakowski's decision was only the first blow in what was to turn into decades of failure and humiliation for the iconic yard as its history ended up playing as important a role in its survival as its profit, or more usually loss, statements. Liquidation was immediately challenged by Solidarity, which charged that Rakowski was acting out of antipathy toward the union that had humbled the Communist Party, and not basing his decision on the shipyard's business case. Still, no matter how he came to the decision to shut the shipyard, the past decades have actually tended to bear out Rakowski's thinking as to the enterprise's dubious economic merits.

Just days before the June 4, 1989 elections, Wałęsa and his top advisers were in Gdańsk trying to rescue the shipyard, and the savior was to be Barbara Piasecka-Johnson, the world's richest Pole—admittedly a not particularly demanding category at the time. Piasecka-Johnson, then simply plain Barbara Piasecka, had been one of the millions of Poles who had left communist Poland to make a better life for themselves in the West. Many were hugely over-qualified for the often menial jobs they found there, and Piasecka, an art historian, was no exception. She ended up working as a chambermaid for the family of Seward Johnson, an heir to the Johnson & Johnson fortune.[6]

Piasecka's indifferent cooking meant that her duties as a maid only lasted a few months. Smitten, the cosmetics and pharmaceutical magnate married her in 1971. His death in 1983 left her one of the world's wealthiest women. After a bruising court battle, she was worth $350 million—an unimaginable fortune in Poland. That money, all held in the hands of a patriotic Pole, made the heads of Solidarity leaders swim. The plan was for Piasecka-Johnson to inject $100 million (small change to someone so rich, they felt) into the shipyard in return for a majority stake and a chance to turn it into a viable business. This was all dreamt up at a time when there was no law on privatization and when the whole Polish legal system was in complete disarray.

Together with Wałęsa, Piasecka-Johnson even made the cover of *The New York Times Magazine*, where she was called "Lech's American angel."

The problem was that she was careful with her money. The auditors she hired combed over the shipyard's books and studied its prospects, and reported back in 1990 that the massive 15-acre production hall on an overall shipyard territory of more than 350 acres—together with the whole assembly of docks and cranes, all the welding equipment, all the screws, bolts, hammers, stores of steel, and everything else—was little more than junk worth only about $7 million.[7] Piasecka-Johnson also held out for non-strike guarantees from the powerful labor union, and wanted permission to slash the workforce—not at all the kind of capitalism Solidarity had been hoping for.

Wałęsa was furious. "So, Mrs. Johnson, it was supposed to be $100 million, and what? You're taking it for that, or else good-bye."[8]

She didn't take it.

By this time the yard was in serious trouble. The collapsing Soviet Union canceled its shipbuilding orders, leaving the yard with three unfinished vessels that had been destined for the USSR. Instead of reforming the shipyard, the state together with the workers ran it in a 60–40 split, a procedure that smacked of Yugoslavia and was about as effective.

By 1996 the yard was formally declared bankrupt, although ship production continued. Again, the yard's historical status as the cradle of Polish liberty kicked in. Radio Maryja, a right-wing religious network founded by Tadeusz Rydzyk, a charismatic priest who has more of the American televangelist about him than of the Polish parish vicar, started a national fund-raising campaign to save the shipyard. In his appeals he compared the collapse of the yard to Poland's eighteenth-century partitions. The idea was for Rydzyk, at the head of his pious legions, to buy out the government's share of the shipyard for 100 million—though this time it was zlotys, not dollars.[9]

Others saw hope in Zygmunt Solorz-Żak, a Polish billionaire who had ordered a ship in 1997. Nothing came of that, although he did earn the gratitude of powerful Solidarity politicians for his help.

In the end, the government bundled the bankrupt Gdańsk yard together with its rival in the neighboring port city in Gdynia. Rydzyk never accounted for the money he raised, and has since been desultorily probed by Polish prosecutors unwilling to annoy one of the country's most powerful religious figures.

The shipyard was being used for lower-end production by Gdynia, but it continued to excite political imaginations. Though it had only a couple of thousand workers, its union leaders quickly became national figures because of their association with Solidarity's birthplace, and they were able to command outsized attention due to the place and not its business potential. Union leaders found that for them it was easier to push management to agree to higher salaries and fewer layoffs than it was for their union counterparts in other failing Communist-era companies—thus making the situation of the shipyard even worse. The yard's historic nature has also made it a magnet for journalists, giving it a titanic hold on both national and international attention. I've been up there a half-dozen times to do stories of its impending demise.

Additional problems came when Poland joined the EU in 2004. The financial lifeline of government aid that had kept the yard working through the 1990s was no longer allowed. The European Commission launched an investigation of state aid given after 2004—eventually allowing it, but only at the price of dramatically slashing the shipyard's output in order not to disturb EU competition rules.[10]

In 2005, the twin Kaczyński brothers, Lech and Jarosław, leaders of the Law and Justice party, made the separation of the Gdańsk yard from Gdynia one of the key points of their national election campaign. They won, and they did split off the Gdańsk shipyard, again making it an independent company—although it was still not a viable business. Desperate to save the yard, and fearful of the public fallout in case it failed, the government frantically looked for an investor. It found one in the Industrial Union of the Donbass, a steel conglomerate from eastern Ukraine owned by oligarch Sergei Taruta.

In Ukraine, one of the most corrupt countries on earth, a high-profile investment being shepherded through by the most powerful politicians in the country means that there will be a lot of support and that the investment will not fail. In Poland, a member of the EU, it doesn't have to mean anything at all—and in the case of the shipyard, it didn't.

"We were invited into this whole thing by the government because of the symbolism of the shipyard," says Jarosław Łasiński, a stout and bespectacled man who until 2017 was chairman of the board of Gdańsk Shipyard Group, the Ukrainian company that owns 75 percent of the shipyard.

The new owners had optimistic plans to revive the shipyard by broadening its product range to include towers for power-generating windmills and steel constructions, thus evening out the cyclical nature of ship construction. Every time I visited the yard under its new management, I was taken out to see where workers were welding the enormous circular drums that form windmill masts. But the new owners quickly ran afoul of the EU's tough state aid rules, and got into an enormous fight with the ARP, the government's industrial development agency, which owns 25 percent of the shipyard. The shipyard has been late in paying worker salaries and is running large losses, and Taruta has warned that it faces another bankruptcy.

"We are slowly failing," says Łasiński,

The mood outside his office is grim.

Employment at the shipyard is down to about 1,800 people. I stood by watching them stream out of the yard on their way home from work. No one wanted to talk.

"We're sick of reporters coming up here to write about us," snarled one older man dressed in the shipyard's dark blue overcoat uniform. The rest stared straight ahead as they filed out the main gate, walking past three towering crosses, a monument commemorating the 1970 massacre of workers by the Communist government.

The shipyard now only controls a fraction of the territory it did in 1990. The European Commission demanded in 2009 that the property be split up and sold, leaving only a rump portion under the ownership of the Gdańsk Shipyard Group. Many of the most talented workers left long ago; Norway needs highly skilled welders, and pays them a lot more than they were making in Gdańsk. The whole shipyard feels like a postindustrial ruin. Its internal roads are lined with derelict brick buildings—only a few of which are being used. But the symbolism still tugs on Polish heartstrings. In its successful return to power in 2015, Law and Justice again called for the revival of Poland's big shipyards.

Other key parts of the Communist-era economy have been pummeled just as badly as the Gdańsk shipyard.

The sooty coal miners who toiled deep underground in Silesia were seen as the country's proletarian vanguard. The region had special shops that were accessible only to miners, much to the frustration of nonminers. They were fawned over by Gierek, himself a former coal miner, albeit in France before the war. He even built the country's only four-lane road (it would be a bit excessive to call it a highway), running from Warsaw to Katowice, the Silesian capital.

Coal, along with ships, was one of communist Poland's few viable exports. But those industries were saddled with the same inefficiencies that bedeviled every other part of the communist economy. They were hugely overmanned and technologically backward, and they depended on a steady flow of government subsidies to keep operating. After 1990, the government tried to fix the sector. It amalgamated the mining companies into seven groups, and tried to cut production and decrease employment. However, powerful unions prevented much change. Finally, an ambitious program launched in 1998 ended up spending about $9 billion in forgiving old mining debt, closing inefficient mines, and paying for early retirement, redundancy, and retraining for thousands of miners.[11]

There has been some progress. The number of working mines has been cut by more than half, from seventy in 1990. The number of workers has also plummeted. In 1990, coal mines employed 388,000 people. Now, just over 100,000 work there. Most of the redundant miners managed to find work elsewhere, although they tended to have training limited to the mining sector. Thousands more miners took early retirement. Like the jobless former state farmworkers, many of these older miners sit drinking beer breakfasts outside the dilapidated redbrick apartment blocks in down-at-the-heels Silesian cities like Bytom.

But like the shipyard workers, coal miners are well organized and politically powerful. That has allowed them to fight the deeper restructuring that would actually have a chance of making the state-owned coal companies profitable; the mines tend to only briefly emerge from the bath of red ink that has been their natural habitat for decades.

The miners showed their muscle in July 2005. Thousands of burly workers, many bearing ax handles and waving Solidarity banners, stormed the grounds of the Polish parliament. Dozens were injured and arrested in the melee with police. They heaved chunks of coal and bottles at the authorities, who responded with water cannons and tear gas. The miners got what they came for. Terrified MPs, who were gearing up for national elections later that year, voted through an amendment setting up a special pension scheme for miners that allowed them to retire earlier than other workers. Adding to the unfairness, miners do not contribute enough into the social security system during their shorter working lives to fully fund their pensions. That means that other workers have to kick in to cover their generous benefits.[12] Politicians have been trying to change the system for a decade. But thousands of well-entrenched miners, mining pensioners, and their families have made it political suicide to do so.

The new Polish government is still trying to rescue the sector. In 2016 it created a new mining company that took the best mines from the ailing state-owned Kompania Węglowa, but the effort still has to pass scrutiny with the European Commission.

The special coddling reserved for politically powerful workers was also doled out to retirees during the very first stages of the transformation—despite the later myth that the old paid the highest price for market reforms. Part of the original package of reforms led to a rapid increase in pensions coupled with easier access to retirement as a way of helping people who could not find jobs in the new capitalist economy.

Farmers also got a gift from the state: a separate pension scheme of their own, which reformers have spent decades trying and failing to change because of the political power of rural Poles and the parties that represent them in parliament.

"It's a myth that there were lots of protests," grumbles Balcerowicz. "These protests were not from the poorest, but from the best organized."

The dissatisfaction and fear created by Balcerowicz's reforms very quickly turned into a political movement. The first bizarre iteration was Stan Tymiński, a Pole who had made his fortune in Peru and Canada and then came home to challenge Wałęsa in the 1990 presidential elections. Stunned by the depth of the country's collapse, Poles were swayed by the man of mystery who had struck it rich in the West and come home speaking Polish with an exotic-sounding foreign twang. Tymiński ran a computer company in Canada and an eclectic array of businesses in Peru, where he had traveled to gain Amazonian spiritual enlightenment. He ran on a campaign largely built around attacking Balcerowicz.

"When I registered as a presidential candidate in 1990, Leszek Balcerowicz was my handy 'whipping boy' from the very beginning of the campaign," Tymiński wrote after the election, claiming that Balcerowicz's reforms were a "swindle" that had devastated the country.[13] Traveling the country with a mysterious briefcase that he claimed was filled with documents that would compromise Wałęsa as a secret police informant, and touting his own twenty-one-point program modeled on the one of Solidarity from a decade earlier, Tymiński struck a chord with voters bewildered by the sudden changes around them. He shocked the political establishment by defeating Mazowiecki in the first round of elections, taking 23 percent of the vote. Wałęsa handily defeated him in the second round, and Tymiński retreated to Canada, but he had broken the ground on a model of building a populist movement based on opposition to Balcerowicz and to liberal economics.

A successful exponent of that strategy was Andrzej Lepper, a crafty peasant politician and former state farm director who started leading farmers' protests against economic reforms in 1991. Lepper had actually been a fairly innovative farmer, raising buffalos and ostriches on his own land in the 1980s. Like many other farmers he also went into debt, but in the 1980s loans were easy to repay. That changed after Balcerowicz's reforms, when banks imposed positive interest rates, strangling thousands of indebted businesses—including Lepper's.

"The payments grew and grew," Lepper later recalled. "I decided that we wouldn't make enough to even cover the payments. That made me furious. My wife cried and couldn't sleep."[14]

Enraged, Lepper jumped into politics, leading bands of disgruntled farmers who attacked grain transports and dumped wheat out onto railway tracks, also occasionally beating up political opponents. Lepper, a former boxer who characteristically sported a cable-knit sweater over his bulky frame, led his peasant forces with the war cry of "Balcerowicz must go!" Years later, his body squeezed into a designer suit and his white hair pomaded into a pompadour, he led his legions into the Polish parliament in 2001 and even rose to the rank of deputy prime minister from 2005 to 2007. He was destroyed by his unreliable coalition partners from the Law and Justice Party (which first ruled the country from 2005 to 2007), and he committed suicide in 2011. But by then, the anti-Balcerowicz mantra had been taken over by the Kaczyński twins.

Ironically, both the Kaczyński twins had been strong supporters of the Mazowiecki government and of the initial market reforms. However, the size of the disgruntled electorate makes populism a potent attraction for politicians. There is no doubt that the devastation unleashed by the reforms was widespread. Unemployment went from almost nothing to 6.5 percent by the end of 1990. It peaked at 20 percent in 2003, the year before Poland joined the EU. However, the country's strong economic growth, its inflows of foreign investment, and the creation of thousands of new businesses have lifted the living standards of just about every Pole.

"People talk about the social costs of reform, but what about the social costs of not reforming?" asks Balcerowicz. "Without reforms it would have been incomparably worse."

But the counterargument is an easy one to make, especially to people like those in Wiśniowa and similar villages scattered across Poland who feel they've lost out on the transformation. During the dual 2015 presidential and parliamentary election campaigns, Law and Justice railed against the unfairness of the economic transformation. They also denounced Wałęsa as a traitor, alleging that he had been a secret police informant in the 1970s. These were techniques that echoed Lepper's appeal.

Law and Justice took special delight in caricaturing the "lemmings," a term used to describe the thousands of middle-class strivers living in the suburbs of the country's big cities, commuting daily to work to earn the money to repay their expensive mortgages (which often were denominated in Swiss francs).

But while the politics of denouncing the transformation has paid dividends for Law and Justice, the reality is that even some of the worst-affected industries are seeing a turnaround—albeit usually only once the state backs away and gives the private sector a chance.

A new rival has grown up in the shadow of the Gdańsk shipyard. The private—and profitable—Crist shipyard uses the facilities left by the bankrupt Gdynia yard to build vessels that service Baltic and North Sea oil and gas wells. The Crist yard employs more than one thousand workers, many on controversial temporary work contracts that lower costs but infuriate unions. The owners started their business in 1990, initially making small elements to be installed by the shipyards in Gdańsk and Gdynia. As the larger yards ran into trouble and started to shrink, Crist grew. It is now a key element in the government's plan to recreate a viable shipbuilding industry in Poland.[15]

Coal has seen the same sort of evolution. While the two biggest coal companies—Kompania Węglowa and Katowicki Holding Węglowy—are both owned by the state and regularly lose huge amounts of money thanks to high costs, falling global coal prices, and rising imports from cheaper countries like Russia and South Africa, another coal company is doing much better. In Lublin, on the other side of the country from the very deep mines of Silesia, the coal mining company Bogdanka is turning a profit and investing in future production. The company was privatized by the government in 2009 (albeit restored to government control in late 2015).

There is also a turnaround of sorts in Wiśniowa. The low-slung apartment buildings built for the government farm workers are still ugly and tattered. But the village has new sidewalks and a new sewage treatment plant. Before, heavy rains would send raw sewage flooding out onto the main road. The village is still a place to leave for anyone with drive and ambition, but for those who decide to stay, the standard of living is up sharply from 1989. Every family has a car—often used ones that began their lives in Germany, but still much better than feet, horses, or the poky little communist-era cars owned by the fortunate few prior to the reforms. The government has built a new school. Fields that had lain fallow after the collapse of the state farm have been leased to farmers who now run larger commercial enterprises.

"When we joined the EU, the largest farms did the best," says Rybczyk. "Small farms had to fulfill EU sanitary norms and so they were pushed out of the market—but the big ones did well. It all depends on whether someone is well organized or not."

Still, the village has a bit of a dependency culture. Aside from the few successful farmers, most people live off the government or from remittances sent from family members living abroad. There are no investors, and no prospects of any ever showing up to set up a gleaming factory overlooking the Wisłok. About a fifth of the villagers are officially jobless, but many more survive on tiny plots of land as subsistence farmers and are not part of the formal economy. What jobs there are pay the Polish minimum wage—about $560 a month.

"My life and my neighbor's lives are better," says Rybczyk. "The roads are a lot better. We all have telephones, not to mention cars. But there is no work here. What fell apart fell apart when the state farm closed. Since then, the little private shops that people opened have mostly gone out of business when the chain stores showed up a few years ago. As for investors, we had a few take a look around here, but then they went to better places. They won't come back."

With no pretty lakes, and not much in terms of historical interest except for the Mycielski palace, there is also not much of a tourist trade. As for the palace, it actually looks better that it did when my ancestors were running the place before the war. Black-and-white photos on my wall show a square neoclassical building in graceful neglect, peopled by cigarette-smoking aristocrats lounging near the stairway. The Mycielskis were always more interested in culture than in profit, and with 750 acres there really wasn't enough income to give the place a frequent lick of paint.

The EU has changed that. The local government, which owns the palace, has gotten money from Brussels to refurbish the main building. The collapsing farm buildings have also been renovated. Out of a total cost of $1.5 million, the EU stumped up $1.3 million—a sum completely out of the reach of local authorities. In 2013 I climbed through a broken doorway and roamed the rubble-strewn interior of the stable, careful to avoid falling though the floor into the cellars below. Since then, the building has been turned into a sixteen-room boutique hotel. The stork's nest still sits above the main gate, now repainted a cream color.

"This is a completely different Wiśniowa," admits Szypuła. "This place was so poor that no one could help us, not the Austro-Hungarian emperor, not the Mycielskis, and not the communists. Maybe not until we joined the EU in 2004."

4 The Survivors

The communists were pretty terrible at building but excellent at destruction. That's why after four decades of their rule they had successfully eliminated just about every single larger private restaurant, factory, and shop. A few businesses hung on over the forty-five years of Communist rule–and in the early years of economic transformation, used their traditional business knowledge to become significant players. However, almost all have since been overshadowed by larger foreign or homegrown companies.

Poland may have been a fairly blank slate when communism crumbled in 1989, but there were still a few faint scratches left over from the previous era—a handful of family companies and doughty entrepreneurs who had hung on to traditions of private enterprise through the war years and then decades of communism to emerge blinking into the light of a free economy.

Poland was not always the economic absurdity that it became under communism. In past centuries it had a normally functioning economy, although it had lost its political independence at the end of the eighteenth century when the Polish Commonwealth was carved up by Russia, Austria, and Prussia (later Germany), disappearing from the map of Europe for 123 years. Warsaw, the fourth largest city in the Russian empire, had a stock market. Banks and credit unions arose in all the territories controlled by the partitioning powers. Łódź, a village on the western fringes of the Russian empire, became one of the driving motors of Russia's industrialization. By the mid-nineteenth century it hummed as a central European Manchester. Colossal redbrick factories (one recently revamped as a modern shopping center, another turned into fancy loft apartments) housed thousands of Polish, Russian, German, and Jewish workers, while ornate palaces in the center of the city celebrated the businessmen who became rich off the global cotton trade.

But a twentieth century of wars, border changes, and ideologies harrowed Poland's business classes and left very little commercial tradition when the country moved to recreate a capitalist economy in 1989.

Jews made up 10 percent of the country's population before the war, and they formed a crucial part of Polish economic life. Jewish businesses ranged from large factories to craftsmen like jewelers and tailors and to the thousands of tiny shops on the country's eastern marches supplying peasants with shoes, hoes, thread, and cloth. Almost all their owners were murdered in the Holocaust. In Łódź, renamed Litzmannstadt by the Germans, only about eight hundred Jews out of the more than two hundred thousand incarcerated in the city's ghetto survived the war. Across Poland, the few remaining Jews who tried to return after the war often found their property appropriated by hostile Poles who had no intention of returning it, and so the vast majority of them left Poland. Today, only about ten thousand Jews remain.

German businesses in the west of the country were also destroyed. German land was handed to Poland after the war in compensation for the vast swathes of its eastern territory it had lost to the USSR. Millions of Germans were deported west, leaving factories and shops with no owners. What wasn't looted by the Red Army was taken over by the Polish state.

That left Poles as the only business owners after the war. They quickly ran into problems from the newly installed Communist government, formed in 1944 under the aegis of the Soviet Army, which was unwilling to allow the re-creation of a market economy. One of the new government's first acts was to strip landowners of their property—anyone owning more than fifty hectares of land lost it without compensation.

Factories and shops were next.

In 1946, the government confiscated mines, oil wells, sugar mills, and other strategic assets, as well as any business that employed more than fifty people, though theoretically the owners were entitled to some compensation.[1] The government then moved to confiscate all private property in Warsaw, and justified it by the need to rebuild the destroyed city from the ravages of the war. A year after seizing factories, the Communists took on private shops, declaring a "war on trade."

Hilary Minc, the party's chief ideologue, laid out the stakes during a gathering in 1947: "The question is this: either the state power of the people's democracy and the growing economic power of the state are able to control the market, and then our industry will steadily become completely socialist, or else the market will not be controlled and the power of the capitalist market will become dominant."[2]

The balcony of my *Financial Times* office in central Warsaw looked out at the building of the Jabłkowski Brothers department store. Built in 1914, it was Warsaw's toniest shop in the interwar period. My grandparents would make a point of stopping in when they traveled to the capital. The building was damaged during the 1944 Warsaw Uprising, but as it was built out of reinforced concrete, the bulk of it survived. The family was back in business by 1945, selling from the ruins.

"Everything that could be transported was sold in two or three days," remembered Feliks Jabłkowski in his memoirs.[3]

By 1948, the department store was making about half as much money as it had before the war, while only using two of its floors for sales. But as the Communists tightened their grip, the Jabłkowski Brothers store faced increasing difficulties in supplying itself; state-owned shops grabbed most of the available products on the market. They also faced extortionate taxes for "wartime profits," an arbitrary category designed to ruin private businesses. On May 15, 1950, the experiment with trying to run a department store under Stalinism came to an end. Two Citroën cars pulled up outside the front doors, and a group of men wearing long black coats clambered out. They summoned the shop directors. Eighty-eight-year-old Józef Jabłkowski slowly made his way down the ornate stairs. Once he got to the bottom, he was told, "You have no more access to the building. Please leave immediately."[4]

His son, Feliks, was arrested and questioned by Julia Brystigier, an ardent Communist who was called "Bloody Luna" for her brutal interrogations. "We have decided to eliminate the owners as a class," she told him. "The only rescue is to liquidate the company."[5]

"My father didn't want to be liquidated as a person, let alone a class," says Felik's son Jan Jabłkowski, a distinguished man with a gray beard. "He signed the paper."

Special teams came to take inventory of the store. Then inspectors put ludicrously low prices on most items—for instance, by categorizing furniture as firewood—the better to easily loot the store's contents.

What happened outside the Warsaw shop was just one small skirmish in the much larger battle against the private sector. "There must have been hundreds and thousands of incidents like this around the country," says Jan Jabłkowski.

Without the store, Jabłkowski's mother got a job in a museum. Feliks tried small businesses raising rabbits and mice for laboratories, before starting an international trade company. Unfortunately, it was successful, so it was quickly confiscated. In 1990, following the end of communism, the family started legal proceedings to try and regain their building. The family won case after case, and by 2010 they were written into the title deed. But the building had since been handed over to a trade association, which in turn had leased it to a businessman who had subleased it to a bookshop. No one paid the Jabłkowskis any rent, and the tenants refused to move out. Finally, court officials allowed the reactivated Jabłkowski Brothers company to retake control of the building, but the old tenants are still fighting, slowing efforts to redevelop the space.

Still, despite their long battle, the Jabłkowskis were lucky. They had something to fight for. Few other Polish businesses survived the depredations of communism in any form at all.

The so-called war on trade carried dire consequences for shopkeepers and tradesmen who violated the new policy. In a campaign run by the ominously named Special Commission for Battle with Economic Excess and Damage, owners could be jailed for five years if they were found to be overcharging, or they could even be sent to labor camps.[6]

Private business—known by the regime under the derogatory term "privateers"—also faced ruinous taxes and malevolent levels of red tape.

Andrzej Bartkowski remembers the losing battle his family waged in the 2006 book, *Privateers 1945–1989*, which describes the crisis of Poland's private businesses. "All the privateers—now only small-scale privateers—had to spend hours waiting for the raw materials needed for production. The time needed in departments to handle 'class outsiders' was so viciously layered that one department could only handle one matter. The whole thing started to become dramatic. We lost our last apprentice. Maybe it's unbelievable, but we, in the food business, began to starve. The repayment of old debts as well as the payment of high taxes and the lack of raw materials turned into a barrier that we could not overcome."

The clampdown on business led to a dramatic shrinkage in the number of private shops, falling from about 130,000 in 1947 to only 50,000 two years later.[7]

Those who didn't get the message ended up in court, or in jail—or dead.

The government's antipathy toward people it described as "privateers," "speculators," and "market gardeners" continued for the next four decades. The final case that resulted in the death sentence for economic crimes—the so-called "meat affair"—took place in 1964, when several hundred people were charged with stealing meat, and one was executed.[8]

The level of control slowly eased over the years. In 1956, three years after Stalin's death, Poland's era of political terror ended. Each subsequent decade saw a further loosening of the rules, as an increasingly desperate Communist Party tried to fend off cyclical worker revolts by ensuring that at least some goods were available. By the 1980s, small shops stocked with things like clothes, radios, and cassette tapes were common—but the state was always wary of allowing large-scale private business.

The result is that true multigeneration family firms are exceedingly rare in Poland. Only a handful of owners had the toughness and the luck (unlike Jabłkowski) to hang on to their businesses through war and communism. One of those was Jerzy Blikle, of the third generation of a family firm that ran a café and sweet shop on one of Warsaw's best streets. His grandfather, Antoni Blikle, had founded the A. Blikle cake shop in 1869. Jerzy expanded the business between the wars and it became a favorite Warsaw haunt, attracting the likes of Charles de Gaulle, who was just a French colonel advising the Polish military during its successful war against the Soviet Union in 1920.

When war came in September 1939, Jerzy Blikle left his very pregnant wife, climbed in his car—still something of a rarity in what was quite a poor country—and drove to join the army. He handed the car keys over to the military and joined his unit, a horsedrawn light artillery regiment stationed in the east of the country. There he first fought the Germans attacking from the west, and then, after September 17, the Soviets invading Poland from the east. By September 24 his unit commander gathered his men and told them that they had fulfilled their oaths. Those who wanted to leave could take off their uniforms and go home as honorable men.

Jerzy Blikle did, walking all the way back to Warsaw through a country that had been ravaged by war. He had made a good choice. The Red Army took those who stayed in uniform with their units as prisoners of war. In the spring of 1940, almost all Polish officers in Soviet hands—about 22,000 men—were executed with a bullet in the back of the head and buried in mass graves.

Back in Warsaw under German occupation, Jerzy reopened his restaurant, and even added a summer garden in the back. One reason was to give jobs to the scores of unemployed who now roamed the streets of the Polish capital. The other was to deal with the explosion of business caused by the German occupation as thousands of people who had lost their jobs subsisted on trading and wheeler-dealing—all best done while sipping a coffee at a café table.

Andrzej Blikle, Jerzy's son, points to a back-and-white photograph hanging on the wall above his head at the Blikle café, showing wartime waiters standing by crowded tables. I dig into Marshal Mannerheim's breakfast, an egg and lobster confection named after the father of Finnish independence—a frequent visitor to interwar Warsaw and a Blikle customer—while Andrzej Blikle tells the story of his family business.

Because of his military background, Jerzy Blikle had close ties with the Polish underground, and in the summer of 1944 he saw the warning signs that an uprising against the Germans was imminent. Soviet armies were steadily pushing the Germans back, and Warsaw was convulsed by rumors that Red Army tanks were near. Jerzy took his wife and small son out of the city, riding back to his café by bicycle every day. The outbreak of the uprising on August 1, 1944, found him outside the city with his family. They watched from a distance as the Polish capital held out against the Germans for sixty-three days. The Soviets did eventually reach the right bank of the Vistula, but did little to help as their erstwhile Polish allies were crushed by the Germans. The heroic but futile rising killed more than 200,000 people, and left most of Warsaw a bloodstained sea of ruins.

The Blikle family, like thousands of others, was left with nothing. Jerzy hired himself out as a baker; his salary was two loaves of bread a day, and that was enough to make him an object of envy for many. In January 1945, when the Germans were forced to retreat westward, he walked back into the city. Nowy Świat Street, one of the capital's grandest thoroughfares, had been destroyed. Collapsed buildings spilled bricks and rubble into the road. Jerzy got to the site of his café and scrambled through a window into the basement. There he found two barrels of flour and two of marmalade—enough to restart the business.

"He came back to us with the barrels loaded onto a horsedrawn wagon," recalls Andrzej, who was five years old at the time.

Living in the southern Warsaw suburb of Konstancin, which had been spared the destruction unleashed on the capital, Jerzy would pull a wagon along the street loaded with baked goods, his small son sitting on top.

"That's how we started to rebuild," says Andrzej.

Jerzy first got a new spot for his shop in one of the few buildings that had survived the war. In 1947 he was able to get a bank loan; banks were still functioning on a more or less normal basis in those very early years of communism.

"For the first three years after the war, prewar Poland was reborn," says Andrzej. "People rebuilt their companies, and then what they had rebuilt was confiscated."

Jerzy took the money from the loan and rebuilt the original building that had housed his bakery. Part of what he built was confiscated in 1950 for the Union of Hunters. Hunting had become a very popular recreation among the leaders of the proletariat, aping the lifestyle of the landed gentry, a social class destroyed by the Communists. Many other small business owners were browbeaten into handing over their businesses, subjected to constant tax inspections, and even threats of violence.

"My father said, 'I'll never hand it over to them; they'll have to take it from me by force,'" says Andrzej. "He would have died without his own company; he was completely unfit to work for anyone else."

The Communist Party didn't take his business—in part because the people in charge of crushing private enterprise ate Blikle pastries. The end of Stalinism in 1956 made life slightly easier for the tradesmen who had survived, but the war and its hardships left a deep impact on Jerzy. When he was building himself a new house in Konstancin, he made sure to build a tiled garage (this at a time when private cars were almost unheard of)—the reason being that if another war were to come or his business were confiscated, he could set up a new bakery in his garage. Stunned by the loss of everything he had owned before the war except for the flour and marmalade, as he rebuilt and began to earn some money, he quickly bought his son a medal and a belt buckle made of platinum.

"The idea was that I would be able to sell them if war came again," says Andrzej.

By the 1960s Jerzy had the largest private business in Poland, with forty-two employees, thanks to the popularity of his cakes with government departments and foreign embassies. That didn't mean that keeping the business was easy. The café was subjected to frequent controls. Inspectors would come in through all three doors at the same time, physically tear the telephone from the wall, and then proceed to check the books. A favored technique was to find an error in the accounts and then rule them invalid, which meant that the business had been operating illegally. The penalty was the confiscation of all assets and punitive taxes.

"My father would fight and eventually win; we'd get an inspection like that about twice a year," says Andrzej.

At one point Jerzy was arrested for having bought fifteen eggs. Faced with constant shortages, the bakery would buy orange peel from its customers in order to make *pączki*—the jam-filled Polish pastries that had become a Blikle calling card. With chocolate available only on ration cards, Blikle had to go to hard-currency shops to buy Western chocolate bars to use in his desserts.

The final brutal control came in 1966. Jerzy Blikle suffered a massive heart attack during the inspection and had to be rushed to hospital. He demanded that the doors of the bakery be sealed. Once out of hospital, he went to the government ministry in charge of trades and demanded—and, more amazingly, got—permission to have a flat-rate tax levied on his turnover. The minister, fearing that the years of needling would mean the end of what was a fairly high-profile business, gave way. Every year, Communist bureaucrats would calculate the tax based on production, not sales (because this was a system that valued production more than profits). And even then, the accountants made a hash of their calculations.

"We survived because we were quite small and because my father was enormously determined," says Andrzej. "It was a really heroic battle."

It was also a battle that seemed to have no foreseeable end.

"Neither my father nor I thought we would see the end of communism in our lifetimes," he says. Instead of following his father into the business (despite having obtained a baker's license), Andrzej became a mathematician. His father died in 1981, the year that martial law was declared and the Solidarity labor union was crushed. A cousin took over the bakery.

But the system fell a lot faster than anyone expected. In January 1990, just months after Poland emerged from forty-five years of Communist dictatorship, Andrzej Blikle was faced with a problem. There was no snow in the traditional mountain resort town of Zakopane, so instead of skiing he spent the holidays in Warsaw poking around the family bakery to see if he could turn it into a going concern. He chose the bakeshop over skiing.

"For me it was a calling. It was my second youth," says Andrzej, who still has something of the smartly dressed continental professor about him as he sits in his wood-paneled café. "I didn't know anything about business; I taught myself everything."

The shop was a hit, with long lines snaking out the door and a separate counter for big orders by newly opened businesses to feed sweet treats to their workers. Despite the high inflation and chaos on the streets, the environment was actually very favorable for new businesses.

"Whatever was not forbidden was allowed," says Andrzej, referring to the regulations passed by Wilczek. Blikle quickly took stock of the shop, and realized it had to expand if it was to stay alive. "I saw that it was profit or perish," he says.

The first new business opportunity presented itself thanks to an entrepreneur from Łódź who had heard of Blikle's *pączki* and was determined to sell them in his home city. Every day he would load the buns into two taxis, which would make the eighty-mile run to his house. He would sell out in two hours, pocketing a 40-percent markup. At the same time, Andrzej was organizing a loan—at what was then an unremarkable interest rate of 45 percent—to expand the business, and his banker told him about the idea of franchising.

"I had no idea of what that was, so the banker's wife bought me a book about franchising in London," he says. "I read it, and the man in Łódź became my first franchisee."

Rebuilding entrepreneurial traditions didn't come without missteps. At first, Blikle decided to choose franchisees who were just starting out in business, but it turned out that each venture was more successful if the franchisee had enough money to immediately build a bakeshop or café that emulated the original one in Warsaw. Switching to franchises run by people who were already successful in other businesses didn't work either, because they tended to run their Blikle cafés through managers and not by themselves.

"Franchises are best run by families," says Andrzej, adding that more than a dozen franchises had to be closed over the years while he perfected his model. Today, the family retains total control over quality, baking all its goods in Warsaw and trucking them daily to locations around the country.

Andrzej also saw that he would have to upgrade the pokey bakeshop on Nowy Świat. He got a fright when he strolled over to a nearby Christian Dior showroom that had just opened in Warsaw.

"I saw that we would have to be the same if we were to survive," he says. Competition was also increasing rapidly. In communist Poland, cakes and pastries had been among the few treats that were broadly accessible, and all were bought in small bakeries or restaurants. But within a few months of the end of communism, new grocery shops were also edging into the cake market.

"I saw that we would have to compete on quality," says Blikle.

He needed serious money to rebuild the shop and add a restaurant. He started talks with the Polish-American Enterprise Fund, a US initiative started in 1990 and backed by more than $200 million to invest in developing a market economy. It has since become one of the region's largest private equity firms. The fund showed Andrzej the arcana of how to keep track of his cash flow, a level of financial sophistication that his father never had to master. In the end he balked at taking money from the fund, fearing that it would mean a loss of control of his business.

The problem was that he had already ordered expensive Swedish baking machines and had no money to pay for them. Bankruptcy loomed. He was talking about his problems to a friend—one of the businessmen who had made a fortune running what was called a "Polonia company" in the 1980s. These were firms which were ostensibly run by foreigners—usually from the Polish diaspora, called the "Polonia"—and which were especially active in providing consumer goods in the 1980s. Most of them went bust in the 1990s when they were faced with real competition from Western companies. But at least in the early years of transformation, businessmen associated with those companies were the first people in Poland to have accumulated any stock of capital—thanks in large part to the insatiable demand for consumer goods from people starved of choice by decades of communist ineptitude. Andrzej's friend was no exception, saying he would lend the money.

"I showed up at this rundown building the next day," says Andrzej. "My friend wasn't there, but one of his workers handed me a plastic bag stuffed with cash. They didn't bother counting it or even asking for a receipt—it was all done on the basis of trust. I took out my briefcase and filled it with stacks of bills, just like in a gangster movie."

The money went to rebuild the bakery, to open a restaurant next door, and to open one more location in Warsaw. Bags of cash were a not unusual feature of early Polish capitalism, when banks had not yet figured out how to operate in a capitalist economy.

"The new building was being built by a team of two brothers who turned out to be lawyers. When I saw the contract and how much they were earning, I understood," says Andrzej of the topsy-turvy environment in the early 1990s. In a mark of how Poland had changed in just a few months, one of the assistant bricklayers was a Russian astrophysicist who was in Poland to earn dollars—the kind of thing that Poles had been doing for decades in Western Europe and the United States.

Returning to his business heritage has made Andrzej something of an apostle of capitalism. He started with no knowledge of business, and taught himself by reading business books—the most influential being Brian Joiner's *Fourth Generation Management*, one of the bibles of total quality management.

"What a phenomenal book," he says. "It was a revolution, and I decided that I wanted to manage like that."

In the early 1990s, when skilled managers were very difficult to find, he bought an overhead projector and began to give lectures on his own experiences. "It was expensive to train people, and I thought, 'I'm a professor, I can teach.' Now I have more than one hundred people who attend my lectures. I've sort of returned to academia through the back door."

When he took over the business, it had only forty employees in its one historic location, and was worth about $60,000. Now, after an investment of more than $1.5 million, it has twemty-one cafés, a mix of fully owned and franchises. "My vision is of us as a niche company," says Andrzej. "We don't want to be on every street corner."

Andrzej has also become very involved in the growing issue of company succession, an increasingly important subject for first-generation entrepreneurs trying to decide whether to sell their businesses or hand them off to their children. Andrzej first chose his son Łukasz to run the company, but in the end, control was given to a professional manager. "Sometimes a choice has to be made between being a workplace for children or a company that has to be managed professionally," says Andrzej. "My father always told me, 'You can't sacrifice your reputation for gain.' Reputation was what allowed him to get back on his feet after the war and got him that loan in 1947. Reputation was also what got my first loan and allowed me to expand the business."

Andrzej now spends much of his time running a foundation aimed at propagating family companies and of helping them plan sensibly for the handover from one generation to another. "Our business has been around for more than 130 years, and we want it to be around for the next 100 years," he says.

Paradoxically, Andrzej's undeniable skill at lecturing about business has not always translated into a similar talent at running his family firm. Blikle has lurched into and out of financial trouble over the last two decades, and has now been reinforced by outside investors and professional managers, with the family playing an increasingly marginal role. The new management is also pushing for an aggressive expansion, building new wholly owned and franchise operations to take advantage of the company's still very strong brand name. The idea is also to start selling products like frozen pastry and ice cream in supermarkets—breaking with Andrzej's earlier determination to keep Blikle as a more exclusive luxury goods chain.

The problem for Blikle is that Poland's surging economy has attracted very large food companies, including the homegrown Coffee Heaven chain (now part of Costa Coffee) as well as entrants like Starbucks. Despite its reputation and its early start, Blikle has remained a niche product. It might have had the chance to become a large national and even international chain had Andrzej been more aggressive in the early 1990s. Now, the competition is much fiercer, and the new managers have a much more difficult task in growing Blikle, which still has almost all of its locations in and around Warsaw. But Andrzej has few qualms about not selling *pączki* from Moscow to Manchester. Sipping on a coffee in his historic café and looking back on his transition from an academic to a capitalist returning to his family's commercial roots, he says he has only one regret: "That my father couldn't see this, couldn't see that the business would survive and I would be involved and my son after me."

Blikle shares its status as Poland's most historical family business with the Kruk dynasty of Poznań, whose member Leon Skrzetuski started a jewelry shop in that western Polish city in 1840. Poznań had been taken by Prussia when Poland was dissolved at the end of the eighteenth century, and the city acquired the mercantile habits of its German masters. Even today the people of Poznań are seen as harder-working and more entrepreneurial than people in the other parts of the country.

"In Poland, there are only two family companies: Blikle and Kruk," says Wojciech Kruk, a distinguished-looking man with a clipped salt-and-pepper mustache. Kruk's father, Henryk, took over the family business in 1928, and managed to hold on to the shop through the depression.

When Germany invaded in 1939 it annexed Poznań and renamed it Posen, incorporating the city as an integral part of the Reich. Poles with possible German roots, like the Kruks, were asked to sign the Volksliste, a register of ethnic Germans living in formerly Polish lands. Those who did not sign paid a steep price. Some were exiled, others sent to concentration camps, and some were killed. Henryk Kruk refused, and was deported to the central part of Poland. His shop was confiscated and put under German management. and he spent a year in a German jail. In 1945 he returned to Poznań, once again a Polish city, to try and rebuild his business. But a shop with hired employees selling bourgeois articles like gold chains and fancy watches was unimaginable after the Communist takeover. The family shop was confiscated in 1950 as part of the "war on trade," and Henryk Kruk landed up in jail for ten months after a search of his basement revealed a seventeen-kilogram sack of sugar.

Stalin's death in 1953 and the end of political terror in 1956 opened the door a crack for private business, and Henryk again edged into private enterprise—setting up a small workshop in his basement to produce jewelry, although he was not allowed to use gold and was limited to hiring only one worker.

"Those were the times when you got into trouble if you were even slightly above average, but it didn't matter, my father refused to work for anyone else," says Wojciech Kruk. "After 1956 there was no more danger of arrest unless you got involved in politics, and my father's principle was not to be showy or ostentatious."

That tattered legacy was enough to set the younger Kruk apart from his peers. In a society where the state crushed any bourgeois pretensions and made enormous efforts to promote people with the appropriate background—children of dirt-under-the-fingernails workers and peasants—Kruk stood apart by haughtily proclaiming his heritage a scion of Poland's gentry and merchant classes. "I was raised to be the owner of a jewelry shop," he says while tucking into a dinner at Dyspensa, one of Warsaw's finest restaurants.

Although Henryk Kruk was limited to making silver and plastic ornaments and did not produce under the family brand, what he managed to sell was enough to put the family in a significantly better economic position than that of most other Poles. When Wojciech headed off to university in the late 1960s to study socialist economics, he owned his own car—an unheard-of luxury in those times. In the evenings after attending classes, Wojciech would sit in his father's workshop and make jewelry—more slowly and clumsily than the four trained employees working for his father. He hit on the idea of making commemorative ashtrays—which did not require as much finesse as brooches and earrings, but were a big hit with local shops.

In 1974, a twenty-seven-year-old Wojciech Kruk took over the business, and within four years he opened the family's first shop in almost thirty years, a 130-square-foot store on a Poznań side street. The shop quickly became an enormous hit in a country that was starved of anything attractive to buy. Kruk really launched the business when he managed to acquire a modern Western ear-piercing pistol—the only such piece of technology in the city of more than one million. He became a speed piercer, puncturing forty ears an hour—each lobe quickly decorated with a Kruk earring. "Never have I earned so much with so little financial or intellectual effort," he says.

His big break came in 1981. Both Wojciech and his father had always carefully studied changes in the law—ensuring that their business was fully legal, but taking advantage of any available loophole. In the late 1970s a new law had appeared granting privileges for master artists, and as a jewelry designer Kruk qualified. By 1981, with the economy flat on its back following the imposition of martial law to crush Solidarity, master artists got a particularly juicy business privilege. They were allowed to keep half of any hard-currency earnings instead of being forced to convert them to zlotys at the usurious official exchange rate. Kruk saw his chance and began to make jewelry with amber—commonly found on Poland's Baltic coast—for export.

By 1988 he earned $1 million in sales, half of which he was allowed to keep. These were enormous sums in Poland at a time when the monthly salary was about twenty-five dollars. When the communist system crumbled in 1989, most other Polish entrepreneurs were starting their adventure in business by selling goods in open-air markets. But Kruk was already rich, and better positioned for a quick launch than almost anyone else.

"I had the capital to develop my business," he says. "I still had to build the company from zero. We only had the one small shop and I had to turn that into a chain of shops at a time when almost no one in the country had any experience with jewelry."

Kruk was one of the country's richest men, wealthy enough to dabble in politics as well as business. He was elected to the upper-house Senate in 1991, where he became one of the most vociferous advocates of a liberal free market in parliament. But politics meant that he had less time to expand the business, which in the early 1990s continued with the tradition of selling wholesale jewelry to other retailers. "I lacked the desperation of a first-generation businessman," he admits. "I come from a merchant-gentry background. I underestimated the value of having our own shops. That was a result of me not spending more time in the West when I was younger, where I could have seen how businesses there worked."

In order to get the capital for expansion, Kruk got $3 million for selling a majority stake in his company to the Polish-American Enterprise Fund, since renamed Enterprise Investors. By 2002 Kruk had an initial public offering on the Warsaw Stock Exchange. Kruk now had a 28 percent share in the company that bore his name, but was still the president of the board and generally set the company's direction while continuing to be involved in politics. The chain, named W. Kruk, was growing quickly, with fifty-three shops around the country as well as a second chain called Deni Cler, which sold Italian clothes.

That easy existence ended in 2008, when the rapid development of Poland's capital markets and an increasingly modern investor class caught up with the stiff-backed conservative senator. In May of that year Rafał Bauer, the CEO of Vistula & Wólczanka, an upmarket clothing chain which had recently made a splash in the market by hiring Irish actor Pierce Brosnan to star in a commercial, dropped a bomb. He was making an unsolicited bid to take control of W. Kruk. Bauer's idea was to combine his brands with those of Kruk to create Poland's first luxury good chain—sort of a minor copy of France's LVMH to cater to the growing wealth of Poland's nascent middle class. Kruk was stunned by what was one of the first hostile takeovers in modern Polish history.

"I thought it inconceivable that someone would try something like that against the will of the family," he says, becoming visibly angry as he sips a glass of wine. "The company was increasing its profits by 30 percent a year. It was paying good dividends and I thought I had peace and quiet for the next three generations. In other countries, in companies like Gucci, the founding families are treated like golden eggs. That wasn't the case here."

Bauer had a reputation as a cold-eyed visionary, ruthless with the bottom line. "The numbers should decide, not emotions," he said at the time of the bid. Known for racing around Warsaw in Italian sports cars, Bauer was the antithesis of Kruk's more genteel approach to business.

Kruk saw that he was unlikely to be able to defend himself. He was certain that investment funds that held a majority stake in W. Kruk were ready to sell, as Bauer was offering them a 10 percent premium on the current share price and the bidders were acting within the law.

Kruk scrambled to find a rescuer, but failed. Fearing that the deal would go through and that he would be left holding a useless rump of his own company, he agreed and sold off the company his family had founded in 1840, and in return pocketed 100 million zlotys ($30 million). His stake in W. Kruk dropped to only 5 percent.

The move stunned Bauer, who had apparently counted on Kruk hanging on to his shares and agreeing to be a figurehead chairman in return for a lavish salary. But the two failed to come to any meeting of the minds: Bauer seems to have been offended at Kruk's haughty patrician manner, while the older man was put off by Bauer's cutthroat capitalism. "It was a clash of two ways of doing business," says Kruk.

Initially, Bauer seemed to be a winner—taking a 66 percent stake in Kruk and joining the venerable jeweler with his brasher brands. But as the share price sagged following the deal, Kruk did something unexpected. He joined forces with Jerzy Mazgaj, a rough-talking bullet-headed businessman from Kraków who had built up a series of very successful luxury businesses, and the two started buying shares in Vistula. Once they had acquired a combined 9 percent of the company, they joined with other shareholders and unseated Bauer, taking control of Vistula. "I don't think they expected that," says Kruk with a grin. "I had to make a decision to defend the family wealth, and I was not ready to retire; it's not in my character."

Kruk had become a business star—the first example of a reverse takeover in Polish capitalism. But the Kruk-Mazgaj honeymoon didn't last long. Mazgaj (whose story appears later in this book) is much wealthier than Kruk and, like Bauer, an example of the more ruthless modern sort of Polish capitalist. Ostensibly a partner, Kruk quickly saw that he had really lost control of his family company, which was tightly incorporated into Mazgaj's luxury business portfolio. He was sidelined on the board of W. Kruk, and quit in 2012.

But almost two centuries of family business tradition are difficult to ignore. Kruk is now bankrolling the efforts of his two children, Ania and Wojciech Jr., who are building their own chain of jewelry shops, named Ania Kruk, and carefully eschewing the sales of gold, silver, and luxury watches to steer clear of legal trouble from Mazgaj. The chain already has ten outlets, a fraction of W. Kruk's more than seventy, but it is growing quickly. Production, designed by Ania, is aimed at a young and hip consumer, not the same audience as that of the more staid lineup at W. Kruk. Wojciech Kruk still has his eye on his inheritance, making occasional grumbling comments about his hopes to buy back W. Kruk from Mazgaj and again take control of the business that bears his name.

Kruk started in 1989 as one of Poland's wealthiest businessmen, and he has since long been eclipsed by younger and more aggressive men. But the taste of failure awakened something atavistic in the retired senator: sometimes the hunt for revenge and the family name is at least as powerful as the urge to get rich.

Blikle and Kruk are not the only Polish family businesses with roots dating to the nineteenth century. The traditions of Zbigniew Grycan, dubbed Poland's ice cream king, stretch back to the regions of eastern Poland that were lost after the war, when Poland was forced to cede about a third of its territory to the Soviet Union and in return acquired lands in the west taken from Germany. There, in the small and largely Jewish town of Buczacz (the birthplace of Simon Wiesenthal, the Holocaust survivor and later Nazi hunter), Grycan's grandfather and father opened their ice cream business. Their main competition was a Jewish ice cream shop. Buczacz today lies about 150 miles east of the current Polish-Ukrainian border, and in 1941, when Grycan was born, it was the scene of hellish torment. The Germans murdered about ten thousand local Jews, most of them shot outside the town and the rest killed in the Belzec death camp.

Poles like the Grycans survived the Soviet occupation in 1939, then the German invasion in 1941 and the Soviet reoccupation in 1944, much of the time living in terror at the ethnic cleansing campaign being conducted by Ukrainian nationalists. Grycan's father spent most of the occupation in hiding, and the business was shuttered.

The family's situation became untenable after the war, as the Soviets—with the agreement of Poland's British and American allies—agreed to shift Poland westwards. More than a million Poles were resettled. Leaving behind homes, farms, and businesses, they were packed into railway cars and taken west. The Grycan family, like many other deportees, went all the way west to the lands taken from the Germans, settling in Wrocław, or Breslau as it had been before the war. Millions of Germans were in turn shifted farther west, freeing up thousands of homes for the resettled Poles. Breslau had been one of the final resistance points for the German army against the Soviets. Turned into a fortress, or *festung*, on Hitler's orders, the city only surrendered in May 1945, a few months before the arrival of Polish refugees from the east.

The Grycans and thousands of other newly arrived Poles found a city in ruins. But in the winter of 1945, Józef Grycan was back to harvesting ice off local ponds and storing it in the burned-out wreck of a German school. Many of his workers had made the same journey west from Buczacz, and he found them in western Poland. They had to make the rounds of nearby farms and carry milk and cream back to the city on their backs. But by the spring of 1946, Grycan was selling his ice cream in a shop and through street sellers.

As the communist state began to consolidate its political and economic control over the country, business for Grycan began to be tougher than simply sourcing impossible-to-find raw materials and then selling to hungry but very poor customers. Tax inspections and increasingly rigorous bureaucratic controls were aimed to shut him down. Zbigniew Grycan remembers coming home from school in 1953 to get free ice cream—a magical ability that had gained him an enormous circle of friends—only to find that the old sign over the shop had been changed. "No ice cream for you," said the salesgirl, who the day before had worked for his father but was now an employee of the state cooperative that had taken over the shop.

"My father tried to fuss a bit, but they locked him up for a month," says Zbigniew Grycan.

When the ideological winds again shifted over allowing small shops, Józef Grycan reopened his business and his son was determined to follow in his footsteps. "My father was a *prywaciarz* (privateer). He had spent his whole life working for himself and it was the same for me," says Grycan.

At the age of fourteen, Grycan was sent to Warsaw to train at one of the few decent hotels in the Polish capital, and in 1962 he opened his own shop in western Poland. "I didn't want to work directly for my father, so I opened my own shop," he says. "My aunt was moving to Britain and she had sold her apartment. She gave me some money and I rented a hole-in-the-wall shop for my first business."

Although Silesia in the early 1960s was a poor and dingy place, it was a market that was terribly served by state shops. This meant that anyone producing goods of decent quality was swamped. "It was a producer's market, not a consumer's market," says Grycan. "The trick was to produce—once you did that, it was easy to sell."

In 1980, he bought Zielona Budka (Green Cabin), a single ice cream shop in Warsaw. The shop was a huge economic success, and it still exists today. It also gave Grycan the economic base and brand to make a fast start after 1989. While competitors were taking their first baby steps in business, and before foreign companies really had the Polish market in their sights, Grycan was opening his own ice cream factory in 1991 and striking distribution deals with shops and supermarkets. The company had more than thirty thousand branded fridges in retail points around the country.

He put almost 200,000 miles on his car in those years, often sleeping in it instead of hunting for hard-to-find hotels as he drove from shop to shop around Poland. He also made hops to Italy to visit small ice cream manufacturers there, to get a sense of how the industry worked in the West and to buy more modern equipment. The sight of a rumpled Pole showing up in northern Italy as a businessman, not a hired worker, was a bit of a surprise. "They were a little suspicious of me," says Grycan. "I had no credit. Everything I bought was for cash."

But that effort paid off.

"Maybe I survived because I was tougher," he says. "I was also used to having money and not spending everything I earned. A lot of people had 'hot money' that they spent very quickly." That made a big difference in the early 1990s, when almost every new business was a winner. Those who had taken the leap and started their own company did extremely well—but a lot of that early money went for cars, houses, and shopping trips. Grycan, instead, kept plowing his earnings back into the business and building his brand.

"The trick is not to skimp on quality," he says. "People can taste, and if you do it well they'll keep coming back."

By the mid-1990s, when foreign companies moved into Poland with mass-market products and modern advertising campaigns, Zielona Budka had already become a recognized brand. But selling ice cream out of a small shop is very different from running a fast-growing company in an increasingly competitive environment. Grycan is a micromanager, even occasionally getting involved in mixing batches of ice cream, and delighting in showing up incognito at his own shops to gauge his customers.

His first problem came from Poland's notoriously unpredictable tax authorities, who in 1997 alleged that he had not paid VAT and had confiscated money from his accounts. Grycan eventually won in court, but development of his business had been delayed.

He fended off takeover offers for his company, but was then hit hard, first by the Russian economic crisis of 1998, which pummeled his Russian operations. Zielona Budka had been selling ice cream as far afield as Siberia, a market that, despite its foul weather, is one of the world's keenest for ice cream. Then the Polish economy slowed dramatically in 2000 and 2001. Ill and unable to keep tabs on the day-to-day operations of his business, he finally decided to sell a controlling stake to Enterprise Investors, the same fund that had bought Kruk's jewelry chain and had almost bought out Blikle.

Grycan remained on the management team, but increasingly chafed at being part of a company he did not control. The biggest friction came over the fund's focus on the bottom line, a business model that earned profits through volume sales, but which he felt undercut the chain's tradition of selling high-quality ice cream at low margins.

"I didn't really agree with the way they were running things," he says. "The financial director would try to cut costs as much as possible. I've always been concerned about having a good product."

His wife kept operating the original Warsaw shop, but the two then did what any sensible and wealthy pensioner would do: they started traveling the world. He quickly ran out of enthusiasm, and, driven by what he saw was a slump in quality in the brand he had built, decided to jump back into the business. In 2004, after the expiry of a do-not-compete clause, he was back to making ice cream, this time under his own name: Grycan—Lody od Pokoleń (Grycan—Ice Cream for Generations). His friends thought he was insane to get back into an industry that was very different from what it had been in the past—having become much more similar to fast-moving consumer goods markets of the West.

"People warned me not to start this business because there was a lot of competition," he says. "They said I was crazy to get back into the same business, but we did manage to find a space for ourselves in the market."

The second time around he took a different approach, focusing much less on supermarket sales—which account for only half of his turnover—and much more on building up an own-branded chain of cafés and ice cream shops—the same niche where Blikle once had a clear shot at becoming a dominant player. The company does not reveal revenue and profit figures, although Grycan says it has just under 10 percent of the Polish ice cream market, which is worth about 1.2 billion zlotys ($375 million) in total annually. So far the company undertakes almost no advertising, relying instead on having a good presence in the new shopping malls that have sprung up in the country's largest cities, and on Grycan's personal reputation as Poland's ice cream magnate.

This time, Grycan is determined to retain much closer control of his eponymous company than when he owned Zielona Budka. Although he is conscious of costs, he devotes just as much effort to coming up with new flavors such as spice cake, poppy seed, and melon, and to keeping an eye on quality. "I have the final say in the company," he says, sitting at a Grycan café in central Warsaw. "All the fruit we use is real. If the ice cream is mango, then we peel mangos in the factory."

An elderly woman at the next table overhears Grycan and interrupts. "I just want to congratulate you on your success," she says to a beaming Grycan. "This is a fantastic company."

Asked if he might list the new company, Grycan rolls his eyes and shakes his head. Grycan has abandoned most franchising, after finding that franchisees did not maintain the standards he wanted. Now his only franchisees are his twin daughters, Magdalena and Małgorzata. He charges them market rates, and hopes that the experience of running their own operations will prepare them for eventually taking over the whole business. "I want them to know everything from the ground up. You can only learn by doing," he says. Małgorzata, who is a graduate of Poland's leading business school, is his "right hand" in running the business with his wife.

Grycan's is also a cautionary tale about the onrush of modern culture into Polish life. While he has built a business with his own name as its brand and has stressed quality as its hallmark, his daughter-in-law and two granddaughters have taken the family name in vain. Known as the "Grycanki," a diminutive form of his last name, Marta Grycan and her daughters Weronika and Wiktoria have become celebrities—showing up at top Warsaw restaurants, hobnobbing with musicians, and taking part in plus-size fashion shows. Poland's top tabloid, *Fakt*, even had an internet page devoted to their exploits, which may not reach Paris Hilton proportions—one stunt had them serving fish in a supermarket—but which do make them local luminaries.

Grycan reacts with distaste when asked about his relatives, whose plush size acts as a warning about the consequences of eating too much ice cream. But they have no role in his company—their own efforts at getting into the ice cream business have sputtered, and an attempt at creating a television show had to be canceled due to a lack of capital. Granddad was not on hand with his wallet to keep the venture going.

Grycan's insistence that his family business be handed on to the next generation (his less showy daughters, not the children of his estranged son) is part of a broader trend among Polish family companies. From 1939 to 1989 there really wasn't much worth handing on to the next generation, with the exception of a work ethic and book knowledge. Men like Blikle, Grycan, and Kruk were rarities, people who had traditions and business practices inculcated from their earliest years—and, in Blikle's case, who had an actual business to run. However, building a business on nostalgia and a sense of noblesse oblige hasn't always worked out well in the cutthroat world of renewed Polish capitalism. Blikle and Kruk's more genteel ways may have made them icons of an earlier prewar business tradition, but they missed their chance to become truly large companies two decades ago, when they started to race to riches far ahead of their competitors. They lost out to tougher entrepreneurs, people who had to build their businesses with no capital, experience, or tradition, but who in the end scrambled further than the few people whose business roots had survived the five decades since German tanks smashed through Polish border crossings on September 1, 1939.

5 Oligarchs?

Poland has rich people, even very rich people, but none of them are wealthy enough to qualify as oligarchs. That's made an enormous difference in the country's development. Unlike Russia, Ukraine, or even the Czech Republic, Poland's magnates haven't been able to seize control of the country's political system.

For most of the world, the go-to figure for unimaginable wealth is Bill Gates. In Poland, the embodiment of riches beyond measure was Jan Kulczyk.

A couple of years ago I was walking with him through the medieval market square of Wrocław, and the sight of the unprepossessing man with designer stubble and lank hair growing down to his collar was enough to turn heads. "Great to see you. Are you planning to buy up half the city?" joked one man as he saw Kulczyk approaching.

But although Kulczyk was long the richest Pole, the way he came by his money and the role played by him and his fellow billionaires atop the country's economic pyramid are very different from the methods of the oligarchs who dominate many other postcommunist countries. Those differences help explain why Poland has been one of the postcommunist world's biggest successes.

Although there was no denying that Kulczyk was rich, he wasn't nearly the dominant presence that true oligarchs are in other excommunist countries. Kulczyk, who was born in 1950 and died during a botched heart operation in 2015, was worth about $3.8 billion at his death, according to *Forbes* magazine's ranking of the wealthiest Poles for 2014. However, the richest Pole was only a tiddler compared to other Central Europeans bestriding their respective richest lists. Kulczyk's fortune gave him about 0.6 percent of Poland's GDP, slightly better than the 0.45 percent of US GDP controlled by Gates, but only a fraction of the corresponding percentages controlled by other regional tycoons.

In the neighboring Czech Republic, Petr Kellner got his start running an investment fund during that country's controversial voucher privatization program. He now runs an empire worth $11.4 billion—mainly in banking and insurance. That gives him 5.5 percent of his country's GDP. In Ukraine, Rinat Akhmetov, the country's leading oligarch, had a fortune of $12.2 billion before Russian-led rebels devastated eastern Ukraine in 2014, where his steel and coal holdings are concentrated. That gave him 7 percent of Ukraine's economy in 2014, though by 2016 that had diminished to 3 percent.

Overall, Poland has one of the lowest levels of wealth concentration of any of the region's excommunist states. Looking across the region, toting up the number of dollar billionaires as compiled by *Forbes*, and dividing by GDP makes Poland stand out from the rest of the postcommunist world. As of 2016, Poland, a country of almost 38 million people, has only four dollar billionaires, including Kulczyk's two heirs. In total, they have $7.9 billion, or 1.6 percent of the country's economy. Their Czech counterparts account for 8.5 percent of the Czech economy. In Ukraine, Europe's most corrupt and arguably most dysfunctional country, the local dollar billionaires account for 7.8 percent of the economy. Russia's seventy-seven billionaires control 21.6 percent of the country's GDP.

The reason for the discrepancy dates back to Poland's 1989 transformation. The big question for early reformers was how to re-create a capitalist class while reducing the role of the state in the economy. The debate was part of a broader shift away from government ownership happening in countries from Chile to the United Kingdom and the United States. Some advisers wanted postcommunist governments to sell assets to the highest bidder. But because local people were poor, this meant that key state companies would end up being owned by the few locals with any money—either well-connected apparatchiks, people with ties to the security services, or the often shady businessmen who had made their fortunes in the murky legal climate of late communism. Foreign investors were unlikely to be enticed by the prospect of owning clapped-out communist-era factories. Others called for factories to be handed over to their workers, but that raised issues of fairness. Why should small groups of workers end up owning valuable assets while millions of teachers, postal workers, and others would be left with nothing? That led to a call for every citizen to get a share of the wealth that had been created under communism—an idea called voucher privatization.

Balcerowicz and his team were early enthusiasts of the idea. "I was convinced from the very beginning that we have to go beyond the traditional methods of privatization applied in Western countries in order to accelerate this process," he says, sitting at a conference table around the corner from his office at the Warsaw School of Economics.

Here, Poland was saved because of its divisive politics. As the Solidarity camp splintered into opposing factions in 1990 gathered either around Wałęsa or Mazowiecki, the privatization program ended up languishing in parliament. When it was finally passed in late 1995, it was much smaller in scope than the reformers had originally hoped for. "The original idea was to do a voucher privatization, but I'm proud to say that I helped block it," says Bielecki, a wiry little man who served as prime minister for most of 1991.

While hundreds of thousands of small shops quickly changed into private businesses, big state factories and utilities were privatized more slowly and, in comparison with other postcommunist countries, more honestly. The result was that it was much harder for the rich and well connected to steal state assets, as they ended up doing elsewhere in the region.

That hasn't stopped Jarosław Kaczyński and Law and Justice from denouncing privatization and accusing Polish business of being founded on corruption and theft, but that charge isn't true.

Czechoslovakia was an early enthusiast of the idea of voucher privatization. Every citizen had access to vouchers that could be traded for shares in state-owned companies, something that started to happen in 1992, a year before the country divided into the Czech Republic and Slovakia. However, most ordinary citizens had no knowledge at all about the companies they were bidding on, and little sense of the value of the vouchers that they held. The same was not true of the sharks who quickly saw they could make a killing out of the process. More than four hundred investment funds, some started by banks and others by managers (some with close ties to the country's communist-era StB secret police) started vying for vouchers.[1] The classic example of the criminal nature of Czech voucher privatization was Viktor Kozeny, who set up a fund called Harvard Capital and Consulting—named after his alma mater, but with no ties to the university. Enticed by ludicrous promises of returns of more than 1,000 percent, many Czechs signed over their vouchers to Kozeny—later dubbed "the Pirate of Prague." Harvard Capital soon controlled billions of dollars in Czech companies, but much of the money was diverted to foreign shell companies. Kozeny, who lives in the Bahamas and has been fighting extradition, was sentenced in absentia to ten years in prison by a Czech court in 2010. Czech authorities are still trying to recover $410 million in assets from him.[2]

Kozeny was the most brazen fund operator, but a little digging into the fortunes of the wealthiest Czechs and Slovaks reveals many lucrative brushes with voucher privatization. The deeply criminal process even created a specific term in Czech: *tunelování* or tunneling, under which insiders would shift assets and property from a listed company to a privately held vehicle, leaving the clueless shareholders holding stock in a valueless shell while the managers scampered off with the goods.

That concentration of wealth of dubious provenance has also had an effect on the political systems of both the Czech Republic and Slovakia, which are significantly more corrupt than in Poland. Transparency International, the anticorruption watchdog, puts Poland at 30th place globally in the 2015 version of its annual Corruption Perceptions Index, while the Czech Republic is 37th and Slovakia is 50th. Russia is 119th out of 168 countries, while Ukraine is a dismal 130th.

By the mid-1990s, Russian reformers followed the Czech model of voucher privatization. That—combined with massive corruption, occasional violence, and easy access to cheap bank loans by clever "entrepreneurs"—saw nickel mines, oil and gas fields, and other assets sold off for ridiculously low prices. A similar process led to the rise of many of Ukraine's oligarchs.

Poland was different. First, aside from coal and copper, it didn't have many mineral assets worth stealing. Those two resources are still largely state-owned. Secondly, Balcerowicz's initial reforms ramped up interest rates. That meant that well-connected businessmen could not get cheap loans to buy up state assets. Finally, when the government's delayed privatization program did start in 1995, it was much more carefully done than in the Czech Republic and on a much smaller basis, affecting only 512 companies. Poland only set up fifteen funds to take part in the process.[3] It was a good thing that the scale was small, because the Polish funds also proved to be a disappointment. Buying often loss-making companies and then restructuring them before selling them on the open market is an expensive business requiring the kind of know-how that was largely lacking in Poland in the mid-1990s. Instead of earning through exits, as happens with private sector funds, the Polish managers made their money by squeezing their funds for high fees. Although their performance was lackluster, it did not result in the wholesale corruption of the economy, as happened elsewhere in the former Soviet bloc.

"Observing the economic performances of the Czech Republic and Poland some ten years into the transition, it is hard not to conclude that the early promise of voucher privatization was misplaced and that the delay in individual participation in investment decisions was the wiser choice," wrote Barbara Katz and Joel Owen in a 2001 comparison of the privatization experience of the two countries.[4]

Being slow off the mark and limiting the scale of voucher privatization meant that Poland dodged the bullet that hit Slovakia, the Czech Republic, Russia, and other post-Soviet countries. In those countries, the quick grab for state assets was the surest route to enormous wealth. Most Polish billionaires acquired their wealth through work and ideas, rather than by relying on corruption and connections. That is not to say that Poland was free from corruption and unhealthy connections between government and business. Insiders dealing with government tenders for infrastructure and telecoms contracts in the 1990s say that kickbacks of at least 10 percent and envelopes bulging with cash were the rule of doing business. That helps explain why relatively few US companies were big players at that time—the US Foreign Corrupt Practices Act made it significantly more dangerous for Americans to do those sorts of deals than for their European counterparts. But the relative rarity of Polish billionaires has also meant that the country has developed in a more entrepreneurial and less corrupt fashion than many of its peers.

A couple of the richest Poles became rich because they had an earlier start than anyone else—and Jan Kulczyk fit nicely into that category. At the dawn of Poland's transformation, some people were legging it far down the track while other would-be entrepreneurs were still shuffling up to the starting line. To go back to the Oklahoma analogy, the "Sooners" were the handful of people who managed to stake their claims on choice land early. Kulczyk attainted his wealth by operating as a Polish "Sooner." He joked that he hadn't needed to steal his first million because his father gave it to him.

Henryk Kulczyk, a veteran of the wartime resistance Home Army, left Poland in 1956 after running into trouble with the authorities while building a wool business. He set up shop in West Germany where he started importing Polish mushrooms, berries and other agricultural products, and afterwards selling German agricultural machines back to Poland. It was a business that made him hugely valuable to the cash-strapped communist authorities, and one that demanded excellent contacts with the apparatchiks running Poland, as well as with German business.

Henryk Kulczyk headed a Polish-German business association. "My father had an easy way of making contacts and gaining trust," said Jan. "Being the chief of these organizations automatically meant that he had to have super connections." It was that talent for building and keeping top-level contacts that the father passed on to his son.

Jan Kulczyk, holding a newly minted law doctorate, moved to Germany in 1977 to learn how to do business from his father. Although Kulczyk wasn't a politician and had never been interested in holding any office, he had the gifted politician's talent for turning the full force of his attention on the people who mattered to him. I crossed paths with him many times over my decade in Poland, and he always lavished attention on a reporter who had a hugely valuable resource in his hands: space in pink pages of the *Financial Times*.

By the end of the 1970s, the connections that the two Kulczyks had made both in Germany and in Poland would allow them to start making serious money. By then, the cash-strapped Polish government had swallowed its ideological qualms about the evils of capitalism and started to slowly open the country to companies owned by ethnic Poles living abroad. The Kulczyks were one of the first in, opening a company in 1981 called Interkulpol. (The "inter" and "pol" prefixes and suffixes were frequent tags for the hundreds of such businesses that sprang up in the 1980s).

Kulczyk told the story of his swift rise to become one of the country's wealthiest men in a hushed meeting room in his Warsaw offices. Behind the gray sofas stood a single painting on an easel: the interior of Antwerp's cathedral, by Flemish Renaissance painter Pieter Neefs. Beautiful office assistants with long hair and longer legs floated past the open door.

Interkulpol started out making wooden houses, then branched out into everything from agricultural machinery to car batteries, lipstick, deodorant, and cologne—most of it produced in state-owned factories. Their hit product was BHP, a soap paste used to remove oil and paint stains.

"The greatest thing was that the market absorbed everything," said Kulczyk. "This was the first island of capitalism in Poland."

The foreign Polish companies—called Polonia businesses—balanced on the edge of the Communist Party's ideological tolerance. While they provided an injection of cash, as well as consumer goods that state factories simply couldn't produce, they were also an unwelcome reminder of communism's economic failure.

That cozy way of doing business ended after 1989, when the tawdry western knockoffs made by the Polonia companies faced the full force of Western competition—first in the form of consumer goods bought in Vienna and Berlin and sold by individual traders on Polish streets, and within a couple of years by foreign companies setting up operations in Poland. Almost all of the Polonia companies went bust, but those that survived ended up forming a core of the Polish elite. Zygmunt Solorz-Żak, who vied with Kulczyk for the status of richest Pole, also launched in the 1980s, starting a shipping company in Germany that sent packages to Poland and then importing used cars to Poland.

The two wealthiest Poles were strikingly dissimilar—with different paths to success, and different backgrounds, heritage, and interests. They also favored different social circles. However, both men scrambled to the top of the Polish economic pyramid thanks to a couple of remarkable sweetheart deals—including one spun from an initial investment of about $6.6 million that within a decade was worth over $1 billion.

Kulczyk was smart enough to see that the political changes of 1989 would end the old order. "I realized that we were starting to be normal, and soon there would be normal cars, normal houses," he said.

Abandoning lipsticks and deodorants, Dr. Jan (as his underlings were required to call him) became the Polish importer for Volkswagen. That was not a role open to the average Pole. Kulczyk had looked around to see his fellow wealthy Poles snapping up the rights for Renault, Mercedes, and other Western car brands. However, he had an "in" with Germany's largest carmaker. Earlier, during a trip to Poland by German Chancellor Helmut Kohl, Kulczyk was part of the Polish group taking part in the meetings. There, he ran into his German partner in the agricultural machine business. His associate, who was also the brother of future German President Johannes Rau, introduced him to a senior Volkwagen executive who was also along on the trip. This meant that when Kulczyk approached Volkswagen, he was talking to friends. "When I later turned to them, he knew me and knew that I wanted to become an importer for Volkswagen," said Kulczyk. With those connections, he helped Volkswagen win a contract to supply the Polish police with three thousand new cars.

"The police contract was important because it was the first such prestigious contract for me as a beginning investor," Kulczyk says. It also helped him make a final break with the shoddy world of Polonia companies.

The deal happened because the Polish government only wanted to import cars from automakers willing to invest in the country. Kulczyk brought in two of Volkswagen's top executives, Carl Hann and Ferdinand Piëch, who flew into Warsaw on their own airplane—something beyond the imagining of luxury for Polish businessmen. "Mine today is fifty times better—a jet," avers Kulczyk. "But for us in the 1990s, it was a shock."

He took the Germans to see a decaying factory in Poznań that was making two hundred stolid Tarpan vans and light trucks a year. "There were some twenty to fifty guys standing there and whacking away with their hammers to make the Tarpans. I said, 'Look, it's handmade.'"

Kulczyk captivated his Germans with his optimistic spin of using the massive but half-empty factory halls to produce Volkswagens, showing them the contract for three thousand police cars if the deal went through. The Germans went for it.

Kulczyk's later business contacts with Germany were made easier by his personal ties to Hanna Suchocka, the Solidarity activist who served as prime minister from 1992 to 1993, and who had coincidentally been Kulczyk's friend at university. "Everyone knew we were friends," he said. "Let's just say it straight: that made an impression everywhere. Not only in Poland, but out in the world. When I would go with Hanna on official trips . . . I wasn't some poor relative from Poland. I was in the right place, the place where decisions were made."

The prestige and financial security provided by Volkwagen—he was selling eighty thousand cars a year by the early 1990s—plus his excellent connections gave Kulczyk the boost he needed to swiftly grow his empire. In 1993, using his access to cash thanks to Volkswagen, he successfully bought a government owned brewery, Lech Browary Wielkopolskie, for just over $6 million. The auction was only open to Polish business, as the government wanted to boost local capitalists. Kulczyk promised to build a Polish brewery business and float it on the Warsaw Stock Exchange. But looking at the Polish expansion of Carlsberg and Heineken, he decided he needed help to compete. He began to cast about for a foreign strategic partner, something that later caused him significant grief in Poland. He settled on South African Breweries (SAB), as it was then looking to expand its international operations.

With SAB as a partner, he took part in the 1996 privatization of another brewery, Tyskie, and spun that into a deal that rocketed him from being merely rich to being Poland's leading billionaire. The Polish government was very keen on selling Tyskie, a decrepit brewery with a historical roots dating back to 1629. It was located in Silesia, the heart of Poland's industrial beer belt, where Germanic traditions of downing a foamy lager after a day of mining coal were still strong. The government had already more or less come to an agreement with Heineken to sell the brewery to the Dutch company for about $125 million, Kulczyk said. Instead, Kulczyk struck a deal with SAB creating a joint venture in which his stake in Lech would be worth 60 percent, and Tyskie would make up 40 percent of the final company. The full pricing would depend on the price paid for Tyskie—if the deal went through.

After hearing that the Dutch had the inside leg on the race to buy Tyskie, he pressed the South Africans to calculate their own price. They also came up with a value of about $125 million. Kulczyk pushed them to recalculate. "I told them, 'If we want to win, then we couldn't give $5 million more. We have to put down $200 million.' They thought I had fallen on my head. I told them the market was growing and there were interesting perspectives, but they said, 'Jan, there is no way our board would accept that. Even though we want this and we want to get our money out of South Africa.'"

Kulczyk added, "It was important for me to get them to pay as much as possible for Tyskie, because if that 40 percent was worth more, then my 60 percent stake would also be worth more. I did what I could to make it expensive."

The South Africans flew home, still mulling the offer. In the end, growing worries about South Africa's post-apartheid political stability prompted SAB to agree to the deal as a way of shifting assets from South Africa to the safer confines of Central Europe. The stunned treasury ministry took the cash, and Kulczyk saw his stake in Lech soar in value to $300 million. Despite the price, the South Africans were well pleased. Their fast-growing Polish business has paid annual dividends of about $300 million, making the original purchase price inconsequential. The two breweries were combined into a single company called Kompania Piwowarska. In 2009, Kulczyk exchanged his stake in the Polish joint venture for a 3.8 percent holding in SABMiller worth more than $2 billion.

Being the middleman in very lucrative privatizations was the model for some of Kulczyk's other big deals. He was so conveniently placed in so many important transactions that he acquired a nickname, "Kluczyk"—a play on his last name, meaning "little key."

Aside from the beer business, his other signature—albeit not particularly profitable—deal was that of taking part in the controversial privatization of TP SA, the Polish telecoms monopolist. Governments in the mid-1990s had considered the idea of selling off a significant stake in TP SA. Telecoms operators from both France and Italy were keen. However, nothing came of those efforts. Instead, the treasury floated a 15-percent stake in the company in London and Warsaw in 1998. The treasury tried again at the end of the millennium, and this time the French were ready; they had Kulczyk join them in a consortium.

Kulczyk's political connections were legendary, but he always denied that they granted him special favors. "As well as meeting with business people, I also know a lot of politicians, as well as people of culture, science, and the Church, not only in Poland but also abroad," Kulczyk told a parliamentary commission investigating practices at Poland's state-controlled oil company, PKN Orlen, in which he was a significant shareholder. "These people often ask for my opinion, and I tell them my assessment of the economic situation from the point of view of the business sector. I have never used my contacts with politicians to further my own interests."[5]

The new duet of France Telecom and Kulczyk swayed Treasury Minister Emil Wąsacz, who agreed to sell 35 percent of TP SA to the partners: a venture in which Kulczyk held a one third share and the French the rest. In the end, the consortium took 47.5 percent of the telecoms company, paying the government about $4 billion—the largest privatization in Polish history.

The transaction quickly became very controversial. The new French owners ramped up tariffs, squeezing more profits out of TP SA while it held on to its telecoms monopoly, which would end a year before Poland joined the European Union in 2004. Kulczyk backed out of the partnership with the French, earning only $50 million for his role in helping the transaction go through. The funds to buy his share of TPSA had been borrowed on international markets with the help of France Telecom.[6]

In 2012, Polish prosecutors charged two of Kulczyk's senior executives, Jan Waga and Wojciech Jankowski, with acting against the interests of the company during the TP SA transaction.[7] The case against them has been crawling through the lethargic Polish court system ever since.

As the 1990s wound to a close, many of the biggest Polish privatizations were completed. With the Warsaw Stock Exchange growing in size and liquidity, there was also a preference for the politically less controversial option of the treasury selling its stakes through IPOs. That created less need for intermediaries, and forced a change in Kulczyk's business model. Kulczyk, meanwhile, was building his Volkswagen car importing business, which he ended up selling to the German carmaker in 2012. He also helped build key segments of Poland's A2 east-west highway, running from the German border to Warsaw.

Another of Kulczyk's signature transactions involved buying shares in PKN Orlen, the state controlled oil refiner. Kulczyk Holding, his investment vehicle, began buying Orlen shares on the open market in 2000, eventually accumulating 5.6 percent of the company, which gave him just over 10 percent of the vote at shareholders' meetings. Kulczyk's plan was to use his influence to push through a merger of Orlen with MOL, the Hungarian refiner, and Austria's OMV. But the plan fell apart due to political resistance at giving up control of Orlen, which was seen as one of the crown jewels of Polish state capitalism and a provider of lots of lucrative jobs for the politically well connected. It also ended up entangling Kulczyk in a sprawling political scandal.

Although the treasury directly and indirectly owned 28 percent of Orlen, Kulczyk's stake, coupled with his high political profile, gave him enormous authority over the company's direction. The idea at the time was for Orlen to buy up a smaller state-owned refiner, Lotos, after a mooted sale of the Lotos refinery to Russia's Lukoil fell through. The idea of a Russian oil giant gaining an important share of the Polish fuel market was politically unpalatable.

Kulczyk had spent about $100 million on his shares, hoping to triple his money within a few years. But Orlen was a deeply politicized company. When the center-right government lost power in 2001 to former communists under the leadership of Leszek Miller, the new administration wanted their man atop one of the country's most important companies. Their clumsy strategy for getting rid of the incumbent CEO was to stage a very public arrest in 2002.[8] Two years later, the treasury minister at the time declared publicly that the arrest had been politically motivated. The ensuing scandal demolished Miller's already crippled administration, which had just suffered through an agonizing inquiry into a convoluted influence peddling scandal.

Parliament created a special commission to investigate, but the main target turned out to be Kulczyk, and the accusations were for trying to strike an electricity deal that had nothing at all to do with Orlen. During the commission's probe, it started looking into rumors that Kulczyk had actually been trying to sell Orlen off to the Russians—something he strenuously denied. The investigation also dug up that Kulczyk had been at a Vienna meeting with a former KGB spy, Vladimir Alganov. In one of his other ventures, Kulczyk had been looking into the idea of importing cheap electricity to sell in Poland. One of his associates organized a meeting for him with a senior adviser to Russia's energy ministry, who turned out to be Alganov. During the July 2003 meeting in a Vienna restaurant, Kulczyk chatted with Alganov about electricity issues. Once back in Warsaw, Kulczyk reported the meeting to Miller and then gave a statement to the government security agency.[9]

A year later, Poland's richest man had become the main focus of the parliamentary investigation. He failed to show up for one hearing, staying in London due to ill health and what he said were fears for his safety in Poland. When he did finally arrive in Warsaw, his presence sparked a media frenzy. Kulczyk spent hours testifying before the committee, insisting that he had done nothing wrong in meeting Alganov and had no part in the arrest of Orlen's CEO. But the high-profile investigation, which dug up controversial material about Kulczyk's meeting with Miller and President Aleksander Kwaśniewski to discuss oil company issues, turned Kulczyk from the key to making high-profile deals in Poland into a toxic brand. Politicians steered clear of him, and even his fellow tycoons gave him a wide berth.

At a time when two center-right parties were gearing up to win the 2005 parliamentary elections, largely around a platform of combating corruption and sweetheart deals for insiders, Kulczyk came to symbolize everything that had gone wrong during the first phase of Poland's return to capitalism. Kulczyk pulled in his horns. The shares in Orlen were quickly sold, and he shifted the bulk of his business interests to London. I talked to him a few years later in his opulent office in London's Mayfair district. There, as he reclined on a couch embroidered with golden thread, Kulczyk talked of how he was changing his focus to ventures like hunting for oil in Brunei and embarking on investment ventures in Africa.

The Polish model of tight connections with decision makers cannot be replicated in the wider world. Instead, Kulczyk turned his exemplary social skills to his fellow tycoons. He boasted of the quality of his yacht and private airplane, and of how he punched in the same division as the world's other billionaires. His first African venture was done in tandem with Indian billionaire Lakshmi Mittal.

However, being a bit player on a global scene obviously was not enough for Kulczyk. In 2010, he took a stab at buying Enea, Poland's third largest power generator. A 51-percent stake in the utility was valued at $5 billion. This was going to be the final step in creating a private national energy champion. I sat talking with Kulczyk in his Warsaw offices as his team scrambled to finalize the contract with the treasury ministry over the last weekend in October 2010. Kulczyk, confident that he had the deal in the bag, gave me a few minutes of his time to spell out his vision. He wanted to become the "Richard Branson of Central European energy," setting up a private power company to compete with sluggish state-controlled utilities. I got a strong sense that the deal would be a way for Kulczyk to remake his legacy—to turn from wheeler-dealer to industrial tycoon.

But at the last moment, and to widespread surprise, the treasury ministry backed out of talks with Kulczyk and abandoned the deal. There were apparently a few problems with Kulczyk's offer, the most important being financial. Kulczyk had said he had the cash on hand to buy the treasury's 51-percent stake in Enea, and that he had financing lined up to buy the rest of the company that had been floated on the Warsaw Stock Exchange. However, the treasury was very cautious about the level of debt that Kulczyk would have to take on, and about what could happen to Enea in the event that he ran into trouble and banks stepped in to take over the utility. But Kulczyk's past was even more of a hindrance. The memory of his earlier promises to keep his businesses Polish and then selling them to foreigners still smarted in the treasury's headquarters. The fear was that he would end up doing the same with Enea.

The final problem was political. Kulczyk's brand was a potential problem for the centrist government of Prime Minister Donald Tusk as it prepared for parliamentary elections in 2011. A high-profile transaction that saw Kulczyk take control of a key part of the economy would have opened Tusk to uncomfortable attacks from the right-wing Law and Justice Party opposition.

Kulczyk later tried to put a positive spin on the whole experience, saying that he had offered the treasury twenty-six zlotys a share, and that Enea (still controlled by the state) was now trading at significantly less. "God was watching over me," he said. But there is no doubting that the Enea decision was a blow. He shifted back to focusing on investing in Africa. But when Tusk visited Africa in 2013 in an effort to improve Polish economic contacts there, Kulczyk was not along for the trip. Instead, Kulczyk's son Sebastian went. Even then, Tusk was not present when Sebastian Kulczyk made a presentation to Polish business on Africa's business prospects.

But the lure of again proving himself in Poland was too strong to overcome, as was his traditional method of making deals on government privatizations thanks to intimate contacts with politicians and top officials. Kulczyk dipped back into Polish business in 2014. A Kulczyk Investments subsidiary, KI Chemistry, bought control of Ciech, a leading chemicals company in which the treasury held a 38-percent stake. Again, the idea was to build an industrial conglomerate that would make Kulczyk a builder and not a dealer. But the transaction immediately attracted controversy. The issue was the price paid by KI Chemistry. The company offered thirty-one zlotys per share, below market analysts' assessment of a fair price of thirty-three zlotys. KI Chemistry ended up buying 51 percent of Ciech, taking the treasury stake and another 8 percent held by PZU, a state-controlled insurance company. The government watchdog agency accused the treasury of selling its shares too cheaply. In 2016, anticorruption investigators raided Ciech and Kulczyk Investments looking for documents related to the sale.

In late 2015, illegal recordings surfaced that had been made in the Amber Room, the plush restaurant in the headquarters of the Polish Business Roundtable Club. The recordings were of Kulczyk discussing the Ciech acquisition with a PR specialist and with the head of the government watchdog agency. Other recordings had him chatting with Paweł Graś, Tusk's closest adviser, about removing the editor of a newspaper that had published unfavorable stories about Tusk's children.

Kulczyk's untimely death removed him as a potential target for the Law and Justice government. His children, Sebastian and Dominika, have since retreated to London, far from Polish prosecutors. "Kulczyk escaped their clutches," said a close adviser. "It would be dangerous for the children to stay in Poland under the current government."

Although Kulczyk long topped Poland's rich list, he never exerted the kind of political control that true oligarchs in the rest of Eastern Europe enjoyed.

Petro Poroshenko, elected Ukraine's president in 2014, is one of his country's richest men. A tycoon who built his fortune on chocolate and sweets, but who has additional interests in cars and media, he also has been a politician for almost two decades. He served as chief of the powerful National Security and Defense Council and as foreign minister under former President Viktor Yushchenko, before becoming trade and industry minister under his rival Viktor Yanukovych. Other rich Ukrainians, like Yulia Tymoshenko, the former prime minister and two-time presidential candidate, also dominate the top of that country's politics, while oligarchs were pressed into service in eastern Ukraine to stop Russian encroachments in early 2014.

In the Czech Republic, Andrej Babiš, that country's second wealthiest man, created his own political party, ANO, and romped to second place in 2013 parliamentary elections. He became finance minister in the new government.

Kulczyk's Polish peers have less influence over Polish politics than do their counterparts in other Central and East European countries. The Poles also have a much better record at creating real businesses than do other regional tycoons.

While Kulczyk and some of his peers from the 1980s Polonia businesses had a rather gilded start, other denizens atop the wealthiest-Poles list had much more hardscrabble beginnings. And the further one travels down the rich list, the weaker the shadow cast by the communist era. Kulczyk's smooth ascent to the top of the Polish business pyramid, combined with his frequent media appearances, made him a favorite target of right-wingers who see Poland's post-1989 transformation as being largely shaped by people with murky pasts tied to communist-era secret services.

Although Kulczyk had intimate links with senior politicians, he was never tarred with charges of agreeing to inform for the communist-era security police. The same can't be said for his longtime rival for the crown of richest Pole.

Kulczyk may have been handed his chance in life by his wealthy father, but Zygmunt Solorz-Żak became a billionaire despite his roots in a very poor working-class family in the central Polish city of Radom. His father was paralyzed, and his mother earned money by unloading coal. Unlike Kulczyk, who made his fortune by cooperating closely with foreign companies coming into Poland, Solorz-Żak has battled foreign investors from the very beginning. Both men continued to follow different business models for decades after their first successes.

In Solorz-Żak's vaguely hagiographic 1994 authorized biography, *Utopić Solorza* (Sinking Solorz, written to improve his tarnished public image in the early 1990s), his business origins hark back to the early 1970s, when he apparently sold votive candles outside Radom's main cemetery to mourners decorating family graves—a Polish tradition. His name was different then—Zygmunt Krok—but he was already displaying a nose for the bottom line that would become a hallmark of his later business career.[10] In an interview with the *Gazeta Wyborcza* newspaper, Solorz-Żak remembered taking his monthly earnings of 350 zlotys and using them to travel to East Germany (it was significantly easier for Poles to travel around the region than it was for other denizens of the Soviet bloc). There he would stuff his suitcase with women's blouses and lollipops, and cart them back to Poland for a quick profit.[11]

In 1977, driving a rattletrap Polish car bought from his trading earnings, he decided to take a gamble and break out of the penny-ante Radom blouse and lollipop market. Traveling to Bulgaria with friends, he stopped by the Polish embassy in Bucharest, Romania, to announce that his identity card had been stolen. The embassy issued him a passport good for travel anywhere in the world and valid for fourteen days. Solorz-Żak and his friends managed to drive across Europe, stopping at a refugee camp for Poles in Austria. In Austria, he identified himself as Piotr Podgórski (the name of a childhood friend), and told the local police that his papers had been stolen. The Austrians issued him valid documents.

He then crossed into Germany, and by 1981 he was running an import-export business. There he met and married his first wife, Ilona Solorz, and took her last name as his own. Traveling back to Poland in 1983 to straighten out his legal status, the budding businessman with the complicated past quickly became a target for the security police. He was an attractive mark at a time when the communist authorities were trying to mop up the remnants of Solidarity, as well as hoping to penetrate foreign networks of Poles. Solorz had been organizing the transport of food and other aid for the Polish Catholic Mission from Germany to a destitute Poland still under martial law. The mission was based in Munich, also the home of Radio Free Europe, one of the pillars of the anticommunist broadcast media. The secret police in particular preyed on anyone who was facing potential legal difficulties—a status Solorz easily met. They approached Solorz, persuading him that he would only be able to untangle his paperwork with their help. He was registered as a secret informant under the alias "Zeg."

By all accounts, Zeg was a very poor agent—as was the case with many of the people recruited through SB ruses. The secret police were hoping for juicy details about émigré organizations in Munich, but largely got dodging and weaving from Solorz. The spooks ended up crossing him off their list of active agents as "not useful." However, the taint of being in any way associated with the security services continues to hang over Solorz-Żak (Żak was the last name of his second wife). When information from his old SB file was made public, he explained. "I was young and scared, afraid that they could put me in handcuffs at any time."[12]

Just as Kulczyk made his fortune with a surprisingly lucrative deal with the state, Solorz-Żak's astonishing good luck came in broadcasting.

He had been involved in importing used cars into Poland in the 1980s and early 1990s—largely German Trabants, the two-stroke horrors that East Germans were racing to replace with much more solid West German cars like the Volkwagens that Kulczyk was busy importing for better-heeled Poles. Solorz-Żak turned the import business into an enormously profitable venture, taking advantage of the turmoil around East Germany's adoption of the West German mark at a time when the transfer ruble, the USSR's international trade currency, was still a valid means of exchange. That allowed him to get ludicrously favorable exchange rates.[13]

As Solorz-Żak's business interests in Poland grew, he surrounded himself with a group of loyal confidants from his old haunts in Radom, and then began to scale the ladder of Polish society, getting to know politicians and bureaucrats (many of whom ended up appointed to the boards of his companies), as well as senior prelates. His political contacts tended to be with the post-Solidarity figures from the old anticommunist opposition, while his most useful bureaucratic contacts were the old apparatchiks plugged deep into the regulatory system.

In 1992 he hit on the idea of buying time on a satellite and setting up an office in the Netherlands, which allowed him to begin broadcasting despite the lack of proper Polish permits. Aiming at middle- to lowbrow programing, an enormous market segment that Poland's public television was too sluggish to target properly, Solorz-Żak's new station, Polsat, proved an immediate hit. The new broadcaster was famously tightfisted. Legends circulated about him inquiring why reporters could not also film their own material, and why he had to pay for studio lighting when broadcasts could simply use daylight.[14]

Polsat was one of 235 applicants for a new terrestrial broadcast license being issued by Poland's telecommunications regulator. Solorz-Żak's capital of $10 million was significantly less than that offered by competing bids, but his company was already broadcasting and, more importantly, it was all-Polish. In the same way that Kulczyk's Polish passport ended up being the deciding factor in his Tychy bid, Solorz-Żak's lack of foreign ties gave him a boost at a time when regulators and many politicians were increasingly concerned that Poland's nascent capitalism was being swamped by foreign investors. This was a particularly sensitive issue in broadcasting, with many on the political right, especially the Church, worried that an opening to the West would swamp Poland's distinctive Roman Catholic culture. Whatever could be said about Solorz-Żak, it was clear that he was a Polish small-town boy on the rise.

Despite the rumors about his past cooperation with the secret police that were already circulating by the early 1990s, Solorz-Żak's ramshackle start-up was granted the license on January 27, 1994, edging out companies like Time Warner, CNN, and Reuters. Within two hours, a furious President Wałęsa moved to fire Marek Markiewicz, the head of the communications regulator, raging: "Was there no way to find a person with one passport and one last name in a country of forty million?"[15]

Markiewicz later ended up hosting his own show on Polsat.

Solorz-Żak had made lofty promises about upholding Poland's moral fiber in his programming—something that appealed to powerful clerics. In fact his fare was dominated by TV quiz shows, contests, crime dramas, and soap operas. Solorz-Żak has said that his model is Rupert Murdoch, and that his shows are aimed at "simple people." That formula made Polsat one of Poland's largest and most lucrative broadcasters.

However Solorz-Żak got the license, Polsat became the core of his empire, and he became one of the most successful and ambitious broadcasters in the region. The cash spun off from television launched him into insurance, banking, and other businesses. The poor boy from Radom had become one of Poland's richest men. He was also one of the best connected. Although he has long denied it, he did have sway over some areas of Polish politics, creating what one former prime minister told me had been dubbed the "Party of President Solorz." This was a cross-party grouping of MPs who had financial or personal ties with companies from Solorz-Żak's sprawling web of businesses.

In a 1993 interview, Solorz-Żak did acknowledge that he had very good contacts with the former nomenklatura. "I'm not interested in what someone was doing before they started working for me," he told *Sukces* magazine. "On the margin, not everyone was born in 1989 and not everyone slept on Styrofoam [the bedding used by Solidarity-era strikers]."[16] In the same interview, he stressed how he had not taken on debt to build his businesses.

I crossed paths with Solorz-Żak in 2005, when he was showing his capitalist claws in another business deal. A year earlier, he had taken over Elektrim, one of Poland's original conglomerates. It had been one of the earliest companies to be traded on the Warsaw Stock Exchange. The sprawling company, making everything from yogurt to chicken feed and power generation equipment, had run into increasing trouble. However, it did have a couple of assets that made Solorz-Żak pay attention. One was the ZE PAK electric utility, a large brown-coal-fired generating station in central Poland. Another was a 48-percent stake in Polska Telefonia Cyfrowa, one of Poland's three main mobile telephone operators.

Elektrim's investment in mobile telephones was again the result of

Poland's official preference for local capital. Deutsche Telekom (DT), the German operator, could not take a majority stake, so in 1999 Elektrim became a partner. But the Polish company brought in another partner, France's Vivendi, despite fierce protests from the Germans. The Germans took the issue to arbitration, and in a convoluted 2004 decision the tribunal found that the original transaction with Vivendi had been flawed, and that the shares had always belonged to Elektrim.

Under Solorz-Żak's leadership, Elektrim switched allegiance and, together with DT, got the decision of the arbitration tribunal approved by a Polish court. The French investment of more than $2.4 billion appeared to be completely lost. Elektrim and DT appointed a new board of directors and moved quickly to install their own security guards at the mobile operator's Warsaw headquarters. Jon Eastick, the chief financial officer of the old board, sat fuming in his lawyer's offices a few blocks away waving sheaves of banking documents that he said proved that the coup would fail.

"The French were fully aware of the risks they were taking," said a grinning Solorz-Żak, seated at his enormous desk in the headquarters of Polsat, a gold-colored office tower far from downtown Warsaw on the unfashionable right bank of the Vistula River. There was a definitely a wolflike delight in Solorz-Żak's eyes as he described how he had bested Vivendi.

The telecoms drama had many twists and turns before it was resolved in 2010. Vivendi ended up getting $1.7 billion and the Germans took control of the mobile operator, while Elektrim was able to exit from bankruptcy, repay bondholders, and leave Solorz-Żak with a majority stake in the profitable ZE PAK power facility—one of the country's largest—as well as with valuable Warsaw real estate.

Solorz-Żak's next leap was his 2011 acquisition of Polkomtel, another of Poland's leading three mobile operators. The idea was to combine his broadcast properties with Polkomtel and launch one of Europe's first high-speed internet mobile LTE networks. The idea of marrying content with a carrier is one shared by cutting-edge communications companies around the world. It put Solorz-Żak on a par with some of the world's most ambitious corporations, a big break with the usual Polish tendency of ducking expensive innovation and simply copying Western models.

Solorz-Żak also had to abandon his long-held principle of avoiding debt—a proclivity for borrowing had driven many of his fellow tycoons into bankruptcy in the early 1990s, when Polish interest rates soared. But to buy Polkomtel in an eighteen-billion-zloty leveraged buyout, the largest in CEE history, Solorz-Żak had to load up on about fourteen billion zlotys in debt. In this deal he was competing against big European private equity funds like Apax. He ended up beating their offering price by about one billion zlotys. That made his feat a first for Polish business: going head-to head against top Western rivals and beating them, not partnering with them. Now, in order to make the gamble pay off, Solorz-Żak is slashing costs at his subsidiaries and refinancing debt to lower repayment costs. He is also racing to install the expensive LTE network across Poland.

Both Solorz-Żak and Kulczyk took advantage of the disarray in Poland in the early 1990s to build their business empires, using knowledge and financial assets earned by working in Germany in the 1980s. This gave them an enormous head start when the state was doling out resources, from privatizing state-owned companies to broadcast licenses. In that era, there were fewer barriers to businessmen trying to influence politics. Both the threadbare post-Solidarity politicians, who had spent the 1980s wearing patched pullovers and worn corduroys, and their apparatchik counterparts, more used to ill-fitting suits and short fat ties, were easily swayed by the glamor of new money. At that time there was nothing unusual about politicians hobnobbing with business elites.

But by the 2000s, with entry into the European Union approaching, ties between politics and money became much more toxic for politicians. A series of high-profile corruption scandals, particularly the bizarre 2002 Lew Rywin affair, soured politicians' taste for business. In that scandal, Lew Rywin. the film producer who had worked on films like *Schindler's List*, apparently offered a $17.5 million bribe in order to change a draft law preventing print media from owning broadcast platforms. The resulting "Rywingate" scandal set off a parliamentary inquiry (followed quickly by the unrelated "Orlengate" probe), and made corruption and ties between business and politics into the burning political issue of the day. It also led to the 2005 electoral victory of the Law and Justice Party, largely on a program of rooting out corruption and of exposing the "web" of nefarious contacts between business, communist-era spies, criminals, and politicians. Not much came of those investigations, largely because most such links were more myth than fact, but they did force politicians to steer clear of business.

Unlike in the Czech Republic, where the country's second richest man is finance minister, or in Ukraine, where an oligarch is president, politics in Poland is remarkable for its absence of successful entrepreneurs.

Both Kulczyk and Solorz-Żak were indebted to the unique conditions of the transformation for their rise. They had that in common with business leaders across the postcommunist world. Soviet mathematicians, Czech fund managers, and import-export companies from across the region were quick to scramble to the summit of the new economic order.

A few years ago, I led a panel where the guests were Kulczyk; Zdenek Bakala, a former Czech investment banker who had become a coal baron (and whose coal company went bankrupt in 2016 due to the collapse in coal prices); and Sandor Demjan, the founder of Hungary's Trigranit, one of the region's largest real estate developers. I asked them if they could have succeeded to the same degree if they had been doing business in California instead of in Central Europe during the once-in-a-lifetime conditions of the transition from communism to capitalism. All insisted that they had been born with the knack for rising to the top, no matter the system. I doubt that. But all three did manage to seize the moment and profit from it.

It bears repeating that in Poland, the scale of the enrichment of the country's elite is smaller than in most other excommunist countries, both because Poland was poorer than its neighbors with fewer lucrative assets to grab, and because the government did a better job of setting the initial conditions of the transformation. The lack of true oligarchs who could twist the political system and the business environment to their own purposes has created much healthier economic conditions, allowing a business model dominated by small and medium-sized companies (similar to Germany's, albeit on a significantly smaller scale) to take root.

6 White Socks and Dark Suits

THE POLISH QUEST FOR LUXURY

Some of Poland's first fortunes were made in catering to long-suppressed tastes for good food, fine clothes, and cosmetics–the symbols of an affluent Western lifestyle that was an abomination to the communists and a source of yearning for deprived Poles.

Luxury is a relative concept. For people living in rich Western countries, a true luxury is enormously expensive or hard to get, something that provokes appropriate awe from the less well-to-do and a knowing glance from peers. That may be a Rolls-Royce, hand-tooled leather luggage, a well-crafted Swiss watch, or a Donald Trump–style golden toilet. In Poland in the 1980s, the finer things in life for most people meant getting enough gas to fill their car, finding some meat, and using raspy toilet paper instead of newspaper.

Forty years of communist propaganda had tried to drum in the idea that luxury was anathema, and four decades of communist economic policies had made such goods impossible to produce in the country and very difficult to import. But Poland's rapid return to economic normality recreated a market for opulence, and a host of Polish entrepreneurs were savvy enough to see that there would be a demand for everything from perfumes to Italian suits, makeup, cigars, decent wines, and ritzy dinners. They built their own fortunes around that narrow but fast-growing niche.

Although the Poland of 1989 was a place of almost no luxury—where the only wine was Sofia, a tonsil-curling plonk in plastic-corked bottles from Bulgaria, and Coca-Cola could only be bought in hard currency boutiques—historically Poland was not a place where indulgence was a foreign concept. In centuries past, the Polish nobility had been noted across Europe for their ostentatious displays of wealth, even if their taste made some West Europeans cringe. One of the most startling examples was Jerzy Ossoliński's bling-filled entry into Rome in 1633 to take up his post as the Polish Commonwealth's ambassador to the Holy See. Huge crowds gathered to watch as Ossoliński, clad in gleaming armor and a fur cap topped with a peacock feather, a ruby-encrusted sword swinging at his side, rode into Rome preceded by hundreds of servants, velvet-covered camels, and horses shod with golden horseshoes.

Even today, the crumbling ruins of palaces and manor houses strewn across the Polish countryside show that at least some Poles did have the means to develop a taste for luxury.

Before 1939, Poland had been a deeply unequal society. The vast majority of people were trapped in poverty, on the land as peasant farmers or in big city slums. For many, shoes were something to be worn on Sunday or during winter, and the goal was to find enough money to survive. Those who could not do so ended up drifting to the larger cities. There are stories of peasant girls from the Carpathian foothills selling themselves for something to eat.

However, there were people who had enough money to follow the fashions of Western Europe, and there was also a Polish luxury goods industry in everything from bespoke suits to handmade shoes, engraved shotguns, and delicatessen foods. Some people had money dating back centuries—people like my ancestors, landowners from old noble families who used the money generated by their estates to maintain a fantastically high standard of living compared to that of the rest of the country. My grandfather, Stanisław Cieński, owned an Austro-Daimler ADM limousine, which came complete with an Austrian chauffeur, Josef, who tripled as a traveling companion and as a mechanic to fix the car when it got banged up by traveling on the potholed, unpaved roads of southeastern Poland. The two men drove together as far as Barcelona, stopping in northern Italy and the French Riviera to see friends along the way.

Further down the economic ladder came the bourgeoisie—Polish and Jewish—swelling cities like Lwów, Warsaw, and Wilno. It was to these people that the Jabłkowski brothers aimed their new department store in central Warsaw and a second one in Vilnius (then in Poland, today the capital of Lithuania). In eight catalogs sent out over the course of the year, often decorated with pictures of fashionable flappers, the store presented the latest styles from Paris, tweeds from Great Britain, porcelain and mechanical toys from Leipzig, modern printed textiles from Lyons, and winter sports gear from Vienna. "Everything you buy from us is fashionable," the leaflet accompanying the catalogue assured customers.

While the wealthy nobility was touring the Mediterranean coast and hobnobbing with Italian counts, the Polish middle and upper middle classes were taking holidays on the Polish Riviera, the eighty-five miles of coastline carved between Germany proper and East Prussia on the Baltic Sea after World War I. There, new guest houses and villas catered to vacationers along the white sand beaches and the frigid waters of the Hel Peninsula—not far from where the German battleship *Schleswig-Holstein* fired the opening salvos of World War II in the early hours of September 1, 1939.

The resulting war destroyed the luxury market. The main goal of every Pole was simply to stay alive. Those who did emerge from the six-year bloodbath of the war were destitute. My grandfather, severely wounded in 1939, earned money by pawning family jewelry in postwar Kraków. When the money was completely gone, my grandmother would reach for a roll of wide silk sashes embroidered in gold and silver thread that were worn as belts in the traditional outfits of the nobility, unroll one of the heirlooms, and hand it over to my grandfather to sell. Their rapid descent into penury was mirrored by the rest of Polish society. Most of the prewar aristocracy fled the country. Almost all of the Jews had been murdered, and the majority of the handful of survivors escaped Poland to get away from postwar pogroms. The few remaining industrialists and retailers had their properties confiscated.

The new communist authorities conformed to the Soviet model, in which ostentatious consumption—at least that which could be seen by the proletariat—was frowned on. One of the few brighter lights came from longtime prime minister Józef Cyrankiewicz and his second wife, actress Nina Andrycz, who lit up postwar Warsaw with a bit of glamor. But that was an exception. Color was washed out of Polish society, replaced by the ashen gray of concrete and dirty snow. The deadening grayness of communist rule stamped out every appearance of good taste, even among the Communists themselves. The Communist-era cabinet expropriated a nineteenth-century French-style castle, Jadwisin, located on a lake less than an hour's drive north of Warsaw. Despite having the resources of an entire country at their disposal, they remodeled the interior of the palace to look like a low-budget American hotel. "Look at this mess," grumbled Prince Krzysztof Radziwiłł, the son of the last prewar owner, as he stomped along the cheap red carpet covering the main hallway of his old home. "These idiots had absolutely no imagination. They could have done anything, and they did this."

Occasional luxuries did exist, such as earrings and rings supplied by private shops like the one run by Wojciech Kruk. Kraków kept its culture of cafés and pastries, part of its heritage as one of the leading cities of Galicia, the region of historic Poland that formed the northern rim of the Austrian Empire. Poles, like other members of the Soviet bloc, displayed a keen appreciation for the dubious fashion merits of jeans and jean jackets. The privileged classes, like apparatchiks and miners, had access to special shops and to so-called "G" cards—"G" for the miners, or *górnik* in Polish. Those cards allowed miners to buy video recorders, washing machines, and other goods that were almost impossible for normal Poles to find.

The true temples of consumption were the Pewex hard currency shops. There, precious items like Lego blocks, Western jeans, Nescafé coffee, and Polish cars could be bought for hard cash and no waiting. "Pewex was like a lost paradise" noted a book about the retail life of communist Poland.[1] "On the shelves were Wild Musk perfume, Omo washing powder, knitted sweaters, real jeans, and canned ham. Anyone could buy them, provided they had the money." Those who could not afford such finery contented themselves with putting on appearances by carrying about a Pewex plastic bag.

The economic collapse of the 1980s further scrubbed Poland of any attempt to break free of the coal-smoke-begrimed reality of late communism. The streets of the Polish cities were filled with dour people dressed in drab clothes. But it was also the time when Jerzy Mazgaj saw his chance at creating a luxury market in Poland.

Mazgaj is a beefy man with close-cropped hair whose formidable bulk makes him look rather like a nightclub bouncer, until one sees he is wearing a beautifully cut Ermenegildo Zegna suit set off with a Rolex watch. Mazgaj foresaw that, although Poles were poor, the odds were that they wouldn't stay that way forever, and that a fortune could be made selling them fashionable goods. "I thought there had to be some sort of a change," he says of the dismal 1980s. "The shops were empty; it couldn't last."

Mazgaj, born in 1959, grew up in the soulless ranks of concrete apartment blocks built for workers in Tarnów, a nowhere town of one hundred thousand, with a strong chemical industry sector, in southeastern Poland. He ran for the bright lights of Vienna as soon as he could, escaping from what he calls the "sleepy Galician town where nothing ever happened." In Vienna he saw a wealthy and cosmopolitan city, a world away from parochial Tarnów. He also made his first money, selling newspapers and distributing leaflets, all while perfecting his German. The language came in useful when he returned to the Austrian capital as a university student, leading Polish tour groups through the city. But while tourists from wealthy countries would marvel at the glories of imperial Vienna—St. Stephen's cathedral, the Schönbrunn and Hofburg imperial palaces, and the opera and symphony—the Poles had altogether more down-to-earth interests. They wanted to be taken straight to Vienna's Mexikoplatz, the huge open-air market where they scooped up electronics, coffee, and everything else in short supply back home. They packed their purchases into enormous bags and headed home to make a profit—as much as two hundred dollars from a single trip.

By the early 1980s, Mazgaj had spread his wings far beyond Vienna. As a guide for Orbis, the state tourism monopoly, he was taking tour groups to Singapore, India, and elsewhere in Asia. Again, the Polish tourists he was shepherding were much more interested in turning a profit than in seeing the sights. Mazgaj also traded, buying high-tech toys like VCRs in Singapore and selling them for a fat return back home.

While traveling in India, Mazgaj got a close look at a society on the brink of enormous change. In 1985, the government of Prime Minister Rajiv Gandhi was attempting to shake the country out of its socialist torpor by liberalizing the economy. Those reforms ended up stalling before a second bout of much deeper changes in 1991. But they did have a galvanizing effect, as a new group of entrepreneurs suddenly arose, and with them a demand for whiskey, decent cars, and the other baubles of economic success. "I saw the very quick creation of a luxury market," says Mazgaj. "I thought that a similar thing would happen in Poland, because people of success want to differentiate themselves."

That may have seemed like an improbable intellectual leap in the sullen atmosphere of post-martial law Poland, but Mazgaj was convinced that change would have to happen in Poland as well. If and when such a transformation took place, the egalitarianism imposed by the communists would start to fray—just as it had in India when the Nehruite socialists saw that their policies were a failure. "After a few decades of life in communism, where a professor and a worker had the same ration cards for the same terrible meat, they would want a breath of fresh air and to look like people in the West," says Mazgaj. He was not the only one to see that Poles were exhausted with communism, and that there was money to be made in catering to long-suppressed consumer needs.

Irena Eris, a handsome woman who favors big necklaces and an even bigger smile, left her secure job in state-owned Polfa, a pharmaceutical company, in 1983 at the age of thirty-three, determined to start her own cosmetics company. "The job at Polfa was very ossified and bureaucratic. They didn't use young people with energy. I dreamt of doing something for myself and then taking the satisfaction from it," she says, sitting in a meeting room at her company's headquarters and factory in Piaseczno, a rundown suburb south of Warsaw.

With a PhD in pharmaceutics and an interest in cosmetics dating to her own youthful battles with acne and allergies, Eris was convinced there would be a market for private cosmetics in Poland. "Polish women had always had a good sense of how to care for their skin," she says. "In a planned economy, of course, no one thought of fulfilling market needs, and there were always shortages of creams. They weren't of bad quality, but there was no motivation to improve them. As a woman, I knew there was a lot of room to make new products. I had a vision."

That vision started with renting a five-hundred-square-foot apartment in Piaseczno and mixing up batches of her new product in a single pot. Then, with the help of her one employee, they used a spatula to slather it into tubs. Her husband, Henryk Orfinger, would then load up the family's Polish Fiat and tour private shops around the country, encouraging them to stock this new product bearing his wife's name (her true last name was Szołomicka, but Eris had more of a ring to it), complete with the imposing title of "Doctor."

State shops were indifferent to the charms of Dr. Irena Eris.

"There were no products on the market, but state stores were staffed by people who were happiest when they didn't have any customers," she says. "Slowly, the clients who bought the product liked it and began to tell their friends. That is the most powerful form of advertising."

The whole venture was financed by her mother, who lent Eris the equivalent value of six Polish cars—an enormous sum in the 1980s. Not content to make just one product, Eris plowed her profits back into the business, formulating new cosmetics, buying a packaging machine, and trying to make her labels eye-catching. Her name became a brand—one of the first such examples in postwar Poland. By the late 1980s, retail and commercial customers lined up outside her small factory, waiting to get their hands on cosmetics as soon as they came off the production line.

At the same time that Eris was setting up her facial creams business, Wojciech Inglot was quitting his job at Polfa. Soon after the end of martial law in 1983, Gen. Jaruzelski decreed that state companies had to sell off unused equipment; it was one of his periodic attempts to kick-start the lethargic economy by encouraging smaller businesses. In Inglot's case, it worked. He borrowed money from his sister and bought machinery he used to make cleaner fluid for cassette players. But his true ambition was far more colorful. He had visited relatives in the United States in the late 1970s to earn hard currency, and there saw a proper consumer market. He was bedazzled by the enormous variety of cosmetics and nail polishes—a riot of shades and variation completely foreign to a monocolor Pole.

Confident that Polish women would eventually follow in the footsteps of Americans, Inglot decided to take a costly gamble. In 1987 he bought a ticket to New York, booked a fantastically expensive room at the Waldorf Astoria, and showed up at a cosmetics convention. There the gregarious Inglot, a heavyset rumpled man with glasses and a big grin, charmed the Americans, who gave him crucial contacts and information. They saw the young Pole, from a country wrongly known in America mainly for sausages and hefty women, as something of a curiosity, not sensing that he would eventually grow to become a competitor.

With the knowledge he gained at the trade show and through later contacts, Inglot returned home and, often using American ingredients, began to mix premium nail polishes. His launch surprised Polish shops both with his high prices and with the quality of his product. "When martial law ended, I was certain that Poland would turn into a normal country," he said in 2012 as we sat in an upscale shopping mall in downtown Warsaw, drinking South American red wine at a bistro overlooking hundreds of well-dressed shoppers. Inglot died suddenly in 2013; the company is now run by his sister, Elżbieta Inglot-Kobylańska, and Zbigniew Niziński, a longtime Inglot executive.

Because the consumer market was so starved of goods, Poland in the late 1980s was actually an easy place to do business. Mazgaj, Eris, and Inglot quickly saw their fortunes multiply. The enormous changes unleashed in 1989 would challenge their management skills but also allow them to grow far beyond their roots as cottage companies.

When Poland opened itself to the rest of the world, the luxuries for which people had spent days waiting in queues, or had pulled every imaginable string to get, suddenly seemed tawdry and ridiculous. A brown roll of toilet paper or a Polish-made Frania washing machine, complete with a hand-operated roller to wring the water out of sodden clothes, didn't seem like much of a find in a world where BMWs and Swiss watches were accessible—for a price. Under communism the gateway to status products had been political position and connections; in post-1989 Poland the crucial factor was the same it was everywhere else: money.

Although Poland was still an impoverished country, affluent people did exist there. Some had earned money abroad, while others—even at that early date—had managed to scramble ahead by creating their own businesses, generating the first substantial amount of disposable wealth in the country's postwar history. Mazgaj quickly saw that he could provide a very useful service: advice on how to sensibly spend some of that cash. He had invested his profits from his tours of Asia into two buildings in the medieval center of Kraków—a location which today costs millions but in 1987 cost a few thousand. He didn't quite know what to do with the buildings, but wanted them to earn their keep, so he went into retail, stocking them with clothing, off-season odds and ends picked up from Thai clothing factories.

Mazgaj then hit on the idea of selling premium brands. In 1988 he took a trip to Metzingen, the headquarters of Hugo Boss. He figured that the upper-end but not ridiculously expensive German clothier would be a good fit with up-and-coming Poles. His first hurdle was persuading the Germans that he was serious. Despite his command of the German language—"I was even able to add literary flourishes," he boasts—he had a difficult time convincing Hugo Boss executives that there was a market for two-thousand-dollar suits in a country where the average worker earned the equivalent of a couple of cases of beer a month. Eventually Mazgaj's enthusiasm swayed them to take a gamble on the young Pole.

Mazgaj got his suits, and his potential customers got a case of sticker shock. In Poland's rapidly depreciating currency, a Hugo Boss suit cost millions of zlotys. "People thought that I had added too many zeroes," he laughs. "Some of them were angry that they couldn't afford what I was selling. But there was a group of rising people who understood that in a properly cut wool suit you make a decent impression."

Polish businessmen were no longer content to wear acid-washed jeans and look like provincial rubes when meeting with their Western European and US counterparts. These were not people with roots in the prewar elite. The heirs of Poland's old ruling classes tended to live in small flats decorated with black-and-white photographs of vanished bourgeois life amid mismatched furniture and chipped sets of porcelain. Many of them had taken the lead in doing battle with the Communist regime. In their world, books were more important than clothes—thus creating the archetypical bearded opposition activist clad in a rumpled blazer pulled over an old sweater. Instead, Mazgaj's customers were much like him: people who had no family tradition of wealth and style, but who had built their own businesses and suddenly had significant sums of money to spend on consumption.

"The first clients were not intelligentsia, but raw new money who had to be taught not to wear white socks with their new suits," he says. "These were people who were willing to pay for success and the brand so that everyone could see that they were successful."

Brand was key. Mazgaj admits that he had to import branded products because he had no idea of how to create his own clothing company. For his customers, a top foreign brand also served as a quick identifier of their status and wealth, and nothing that Mazgaj could have done on his own would match the cachet of established Western consumer goods.

But not everyone was content to piggyback on a foreign name.

Irena Eris had already gained renown in the final years of communism. Now, as the state cosmetics sector wilted under an assault by L'Oréal, Nivea, Dove, and Estée Lauder, her little company was prospering because she had managed to create a brand. "After 1989, companies that had no brand, which were unconcerned about quality because of constant shortages, ran into real trouble," she says. "We were flooded with products that until then had been forbidden. They weren't expensive, and they were properly packaged. I survived with no problem because the brand was known. Our clients knew and trusted us."

Pollena, the state cosmetics giant with fourteen factories producing not only for Poland but for other Eastern Bloc countries under the Soviet-run common market, ended up seeing most of its plants sold off to foreign companies keen to grab a foothold in the virgin Polish market. Faced with her first serious competition, Eris moved upmarket. She plowed about 4 percent of her revenues into research and development, set up her own laboratory, and moved to develop a much wider range of products. Her business published the results of its research in cosmetics journals, and joined the international trend of making facial creams and cosmetics as scientific-sounding as possible by adding ingredients like vitamin K and folic acid. She also diversified. In the mid-1990s she opened her first cosmetics institute, where women get pampered and dosed with top-end lotions administered by an on-site dermatologist. "The client has to feel that the entire world revolves around them," she says. "They should come out beautified both physically and psychically."

With that in mind, Eris's company built two five-star spa hotels, one in the Polish mountains in the south and another in the Masurian lake district north of Warsaw. "When the rat race began, people were stressed and they needed a place to relax," she says. Building an empire ranging from cosmetics to spas and even including golf contests (a favorite pastime of Poland's new elite) has proven to be an enormously successful formula. Eris and her husband Orfinger are worth about five hundred million zlotys, making them one of the country's wealthiest couples.

Eris's cosmetics are now available in forty countries. But the company still has a lot of work to do to become a true international brand. There was an attempt to sell her products through Britain's Boots pharmacy chain, but the effort did not go well—in part because Eris did not shy away from labeling where her products were made. "Poland is a little-known country and was often badly perceived," she admits. "Cosmetics are best seen if they come from France. We didn't really have the money to aggressively penetrate the UK market."

However, national origin has been much less of an issue for Poland's other eponymous cosmetics company. Inglot now has a presence in eighty countries, which gives it Poland's second largest international footprint, trailing only Pope John Paul II, who visited 129 countries during his papacy. The company's products are labeled "Made in Poland. Made in EU." "We see no problem with the name at all," Inglot said. "Sometimes Polish phobias are overdone. We don't wrap ourselves in Polish flags and eagles, but we don't deny that we're Polish."

Inglot also faced a wrenching change when Poland freed up its markets in 1989. He first rushed to improve the quality of his packaging. Then he allowed women to test makeup before buying—something of an innovation in the Polish market, where sales were still dominated by the old "no handling" approach of customers being served from behind a counter by a clerk. As Polish customers began to be allowed to browse shelves for themselves, Inglot faced another problem. His wide range of colorful nail polishes fought for space with much better-funded foreign companies. Inglot's polishes were ending up close to the floor, and he was only able to show a small part of his product line. Relying on customers to stoop low to get cosmetics not being advertised day and night on television and in fashion magazines seemed like a sure recipe for failure.

"It was almost impossible to place our whole collection," Inglot said. He recognized that he didn't have the financial muscle to go head-to-head with the powerful marketing teams from big cosmetics companies. "You needed a special relationship to get shelf space, and we didn't want to have a kicking contest with that horse."

In the early 1990s, he took the radical decision of pulling his products from the shelves of more than three thousand shops and pharmacies. Instead, he set up his own retail operations inside the shopping malls that were starting to open in larger Polish cities. There, often putting up "islands" in the middle of crowded walkways instead of renting more expensive shops, Inglot was able to control space and display. It also led directly to his enormously successful international expansion. A Polish-Canadian businessman was wandering through a Warsaw mall and stopped to admire the Inglot collection—a company he had never heard of. He approached Inglot about opening a similar shop in Montreal in 2006. There, a businessman from Dubai noticed the first foreign Inglot franchise, and he decided to open a shop in his own country.

The unusual way in which Inglot broke out of Poland threw the company into the deep waters of foreign business much faster than other Polish companies. The traditional way Polish businesses grow is to first reach a large size in the friendlier confines of the country's domestic market, and then tentatively set up operations in neighboring countries like the Czech Republic and Germany before daring to move further afield. Inglot's rapid foreign growth turned that model on its head. He was present in Abu Dhabi, Australia, and South Africa before opening in Germany or Russia. Each new country demanded reams of paperwork, as cosmetics and the ingredients that go into them are very differently regulated. "We now understand the whole world," he said. "Once you understand a certain country, then future growth is easier."

As the business grew, Inglot created an innovative model. The company tended to own the outlets in English-speaking countries outright, relying on the generally more transparent laws in those countries, and their easier regulatory environments. Elsewhere, the company grew through franchises. Inglot stuck with his factory in his native Przemyśl, a town of sixty-five thousand hard by the Ukrainian border and probably the Polish town most redolent of old Galicia, with its baroque churches and cobblestone streets. There, his workers make all the company's cosmetics, as well as counters, furniture, and even the brochures and posters for shop displays. When a new franchisee signs on, Inglot packs a container full of cosmetics, furniture, and all the other supplies needed to open an outlet, and sends it to the new location complete with a Polish crew. They set up the shop in twenty-four hours, spend a week training the new shop staff, and then return home—leaving the retail operation on its own.

Although it might be cheaper to manufacture in Asia, Inglot (and his successors) have stuck with Przemyśl, partly out of patriotism and also because it is easier to keep an eye on quality closer to home. It also makes it possible to rapidly change production to suit fickle customer tastes, something much more difficult to do on long-term production contracts with factories in China or Vietnam.

Before he died, Inglot spent almost all his time in the air, jetting from France to Argentina and Morocco talking with possible new franchisees and keeping an eye on existing operations. When I met him for the interview, during which we polished off two bottles of wine, he had just come back from a trip through New York, Los Angeles, and Hawaii, again to New York, and then back to Warsaw. He was planning to fly again a couple of days later.

At his death he had succeeded in making Poland a presence in the cosmetics industry. An Inglot ad often flashes over New York's Times Square. The company's initial success came from Polish women who wanted to be treated as valuable customers. They were the harbingers of a broader trend of people demanding to spend their money on luxuries, both big and small. One of the easiest and most ostentatious ways to show off for Poland's new post-communist elite was at restaurants, and restaurateurs were among the first businesses to realize there was money to be made in aiming high.

Piotr Adamczewski, one of Poland's leading food journalists, sits over an espresso at the Wedel café, located in one of the few prewar buildings to have survived the 1944 uprising that left the bulk of the Polish capital a smoking ruin. He waxes nostalgic about the intricacies of traditional Polish fare.

"People who say Polish cooking is potatoes with fatty sauce and pork are wrong. There is much more to it than that," he says, and launches into a description of an intricate eighteenth-century dinner menu of Madame de Pompadour, the mistress of France's Louis XV. Part of the menu included a *poisson à la polonaise*, pike in broth with batter and eggs. Polish cooking also relied heavily on game—the wild boar, deer, and duck that the nobility spent much of their free time hunting, then dragging back to the kitchens of their manor houses for servants to prepare.

But most of that tradition was lost after the war. Some restaurants did survive, but there were few quality ingredients, wait staff were generally hostile, and cooking was aimed at being fast and filling instead of good. The nadir of that trend was the creation of milk bars: tacky canteens where indifferent cooks would serve doughy pierogies, cutlets of unidentifiable meat, and gluey mashed potatoes, all washed down with sickly sweet fruit compote containing almost no fruit. It was food as fuel for the working classes. The classic, albeit slightly exaggerated, depiction of a communist milk bar is from the cult 1980 Polish comedy film *Miś*, in which the hero is yelled at in a milk bar and then has to slurp his soup with a spoon chained to the table to prevent theft. The country's rulers also saw little need for the fripperies of fancy foods. Official banquets often centered on dishes like chicken Kiev, grated carrots, and cabbage on the side, accompanied by sulfurous mineral water and bottles of warm vodka

After 1989, the shortages that had made running a restaurant almost impossible suddenly ended. It was in this environment that Madga Ikonowicz came back to Poland after a life spent abroad. She had lived with her father, a reporter for the Polish Press Agency, in countries like Bulgaria and Cuba. "We made dinner receptions for Fidel Castro, who would come by our house," she recalls. She then lived in Spain, where she had taken formal cooking classes, and watched its transformation from a repressed dictatorship under Franco to a fashionable European country, complete with a vibrant national cuisine. She came home to Poland at the age of thirty-six after her husband's death—and was astonished to discover that the stories from her mother about the richness of Polish cooking were completely untrue. "I would tell Spaniards that Polish cooking was the best in Europe, but when I came here, I saw there was nothing," she says, sitting in an alcove at U Fukiera, her restaurant on Warsaw's old town square, an intimate eatery decorated in the overblown rococo style which has become her trademark.

In Warsaw, she fell in with the Gessler family, a clan with restaurant traditions dating back to most of the twentieth century, who had opened one of Warsaw's few aspiring eateries. Ambitious, enormously self-confident with billowing blonde hair, fluent in seven languages, and with the sheen of foreignness then so desirable to Poles, Magda Ikonowicz swept into the life of Piotr Gessler, who was running the family restaurant together with his wife, Marta, and his brother Adam. The resulting romantic and social tensions created the tangle of Piotr with his new girlfriend, Magda, taking one shift while Piotr's wife, Marta, and Adam handled the other.

By 1991, the arrangement had become impossible to sustain. The brothers, who by then owned three restaurants, split their assets, leaving Piotr and Magda (now married) with U Fukiera. Magda, now carrying the Gessler name, came into her own. Her magnetic personality turned the restaurant into a favorite haunt of the country's post-communist power elite, with people ranging from the editor Adam Michnik to Jacek Kuroń all regular guests. Poland's opening to the world created rapidly changing fashions for foreign food, starting with Vietnamese cuisine, and then falling for an imitation of Italian before passing on to sushi, which is still popular. Today, delayed by the inevitable few years needed for a trend to move from New York and London to Poland, fancy burger bars are now the hot fashion. Gourmet food trucks are also starting to appear.

Gessler stuck with her vision that Polish cooking was something the country's elite would eat. She catered to the nostalgic Polish hankering for the vanished life of the iconic manor house and the long-disappeared nobility—a bizarre but resilient element in the consciousness of a nation with overwhelmingly peasant roots. The cover of almost every Polish home and garden magazine, and vast swaths of the suburbs ringing Polish cities, are sprinkled with kitschy copies of old Polish residences, whose defining element is a peak-roofed columned veranda over the front entrance. "I looked for dishes from aristocratic Poland, not peasant dishes," says Gessler, as I sip a bowl of broth with small Lithuanian dumplings. "Poland actually has a very interesting cuisine which demands very fresh ingredients, often with a lot of labor—something that just couldn't work under communism."

Gessler helped spark a trend of Polish haute cuisine that continues today. Her brother-in-law, Adam, opened his own rival restaurant, Krokodyl, next door to U Fukiera, and then another, U Kucharzy, in the cavernous kitchen of an old downtown hotel, where diners could watch the artistry of a kitchen at work. U Kucharzy became a mandatory stop for businesses and politicians coming through Warsaw, with patrons unaffected by Adam Gessler's increasingly tarnished reputation as one of the country's leading debtors. Adam's business model consisted of renting high-profile locales from the city for many of his restaurants and then not paying rent. He was evicted from Krokodyl, owing the city about ten million dollars in back rent; the restaurant was swiftly taken over by Magda Gessler.[2]

"I pay my rent on time," she notes caustically.

Gessler has taken her brash personality and combined it with the most famous name in Polish cooking to create a personal brand. In addition to a handful of her own restaurants, like U Fukiera, she has struck up a partnership with other restaurant operators in which she lends her signature and offers advice on the menu and décor. She has also become the Polish version of Britain's Gordon Ramsay, appearing in a similar TV show called *Kitchen Revolutions*, where she attempts to overhaul hapless local restaurants. Despite her protests that she is more like Mother Teresa than like Ramsay, she faces a raft of lawsuits from enraged owners put out by her colorful denunciations of their fare—including spitting out a hamburger, saying it stank like a "corpse."

The controversy has simply turned her into one of the most

recognized Polish women. "My name really has become a brand," she boasts.

Gessler's insight that increasingly wealthy Poles would eventually return to their own traditions after dallying with those of other more historically successful countries has been followed by other Polish businesses. Wojciech Modest Amaro won Poland's first Michelin star for his restaurant, which focuses on local ingredients like wild mushrooms, game, pine needles, and single-distilled boutique vodka to create Warsaw's most besieged eatery.

"My dream is for Poland to be like Italy, where people go to their local restaurants all the time," says Adamczewski. "But for that to happen, we need earnings to go up a bit."

That is still some way away.

Michel Moran, whose French-themed Bistro de Paris is one of Warsaw's best restaurants, says there are still relatively few locals with the palates and the wallets to frequent expensive eateries. He jokes that when he goes out to good Warsaw restaurants, he knows half the clients, as only a small group of people in the city make a habit of eating out. "The sector is still pretty small," he says.

A report prepared by Makro, the food wholesaler, estimates that one-third of Poles never eat out. When they do, they often prefer fast food. But once they get wealthier, they become targets for people like Mazgaj. He is tapping into the same nostalgia as Gessler and others for a sepia-toned past of aristocrats and manor houses, opening a line of boutique delicatessens called Krakowski Kredens, evocative of bygone Galicia. Beneath the glass displays, Archduke Ferdinand's hams jostle for place with Prince Sapieha's sausage, and apricot jam once made in Countess Potocka's kitchens.

But as Poland's new elite gains in confidence, nostalgia for a vanished past competes with modern status symbols. Warsaw has Ferrari and Rolls-Royce dealerships. A new shopping mall, VitkAc, looms like a slate-colored ocean liner over one of Warsaw's main downtown streets. Founded by a family of hoteliers and real estate developers, it is aimed at clients who fly to London or Rome to do their shopping.

Inside, spare displays from Gucci and Armani, furniture from makers like Fendi Casa, and wines and olive oils in its delicatessen reflect off concrete floors buffed to a mirrorlike sheen. The tables of the top-floor restaurant are filled with pouty-lipped and botoxed discarded first wives sharing grilled octopus snacks with their gray-templed boyfriends.

The top end of the market that has made Mazgaj rich is still a very narrow one. There are more staff than customers for the high-priced goods carefully displayed on VitkAc's echoing floors. Most Poles can only aspire to such luxury. They may pick up some sausage from Krakowski Kredens, but most still shop at discount stores like the very successful Biedronka chain—marked by a cheerful red ladybug, and built by Portugal's Jeronimo Martins. An annual study by KPMG, the consultancy, finds that Poland only has about forty-five thousand people with assets of more than $1 million: so-called high-net-worth individuals. That's more than Jan Kulczyk and a handful of his peers back in 1989, but still very far from the European average. France, a larger and much richer country little affected by war, has 2.2 million such people. Spain, with a population similar to that of Poland, has more than four hundred thousand.

In its report, KPMG casts the net very wide to scoop in what it calls Poland's wealthy, including everyone making more than 85,000 zlotys (about $25,000) a year, enough to put them in the country's top tax bracket. As of 2013, 786,000 people fit that profile, up from 570,000 in 2008, but that definition of wealth means little to retailers like Ferrari and Gucci. One of the KPMG analysts admits it is a "made in Poland" definition of wealth.

"Out in the countryside, if you ask people what a luxury brand is, they'll say Adidas," Mazgaj says with a grimace. "A lot of people have never heard of Patek Philippe or Armani. We still don't have a luxury market in Poland." He's probably correct. Poland's still hasn't created a global luxury brand. However, Poland does have Irena Eris hotels, Gessler restaurants, and Mazgaj's clothing boutiques. The era of wearing white socks with dark suits has definitely come to an end.

7 The Red Press Baron

A core argument of Poland's right-wing post-2015 government is that the 1989 transition was deeply flawed because it allowed corrupt Communists to seize control of large parts of the new capitalist system with the acquiescence of hapless Solidarity activists. The truth is that very few senior Communist Party members became rich after the collapse of communism, and those who did tended to do so through actually building a business–like Jerzy Urban, spokesman for the military regime in the early 1980s. As Poland normalized, the press changed from being a propaganda arm of the party to a business–enriching both people like Urban, and activists from the Solidarity movement.

Jerzy Urban is a lot of things—an unrepentant advocate of the regime of Gen. Jaruzelski, for which he was a spokesman; a scandalmonger who delights in infuriating Poland's powerful Catholic Church; and a Jew in a country still rife with anti-Semitism—but he is also one of the most economically successful senior members of the long-gone Communist government.

There is a theory, particularly prevalent on the right wing of Polish politics, that the transition to a market economy in 1989 created a massive opportunity to enrich well-placed Communists. They supposedly profited from using their connections and their access to the levers of power to grab juicy bits of privatizing companies, and made themselves rich. The truth is a lot more mundane. It turns out that there was a reason why members of the Party were communists: very few of them were any good at making a go of it in capitalism.

It is certainly the case that former secret police officers, senior military officials, and other well-connected bureaucrats greased their way into positions as board members and senior advisers to many companies, especially in the 1990s. Another few grabbed on to new businesses like Big Bank—the country's first commercial bank largely financed by Communist money. But almost none of them became real entrepreneurs, opening and growing successful businesses. Instead, they coattailed on the success of others.

There was also widespread thievery by former Communist regime officials during the existence of the Fund for Foreign Debt Servicing—known in Polish as FOZZ. This was a plan set up by the Polish parliament in the months before the June 4, 1989, elections to repay some of Poland's outstanding foreign debt. In reality, it was a scheme in which foreign debt was illegally bought up on secondary markets for very low prices. But FOZZ also functioned as a secretive slush fund, doling out huge amounts of cash to well-connected companies. FOZZ had been given $1.7 billion in financing, with which it was supposed to buy up Polish bonds at about a quarter of their face value, often using front companies. However, very little of the money was actually used for that purpose. A later investigation found that about $100 million was transferred abroad. The probe and prosecution lasted more than a decade, ending with a handful of convictions handed down in 2005, but the affair continues to cast a stain on the first years of Poland's transformation, and fuels worries about the nomenklatura of the old regime lining their pockets in the new system.[1]

The most successful of those making a smooth transition from being at the top of the economic pyramid in People's Poland to ascending to the peak of capitalist Poland were the so-called red directors. These were people at senior levels of export-import industries with a good knowledge of how the outside world functioned, who also had access to money and to the resources of the companies they ran. A good example of this type of magnate was Aleksander Gudzowaty, who served as a Moscow representative for a Polish company in the 1970s, later working as the head of a Polish import-export firm before setting up his own company, Bartimpex. Gudzowaty's firm was involved in the crucial and extremely lucrative import of natural gas from Russia—a trade in which his Russian connections played a key role. He died in

2013 as one of Poland's wealthiest men, but Bartimpex's era of greatest profits was in the 1990s.

But the most frequent story of apparatchiks making the jump from communism to capitalism is one of failure. The most resonant example is Marian Zacharski, the former Polish spy convicted of stealing secrets, including technology for missiles and jet fighters, in the United States. He was sentenced to life in prison and traded back to Poland in 1985 as part of a Cold War spy exchange. Useless as a spy because the whole world knew what he looked like, Zacharski was farmed out to take a management job at Pewex, becoming the CEO of the hard currency chain in 1990.

He had ambitious plans of turning Pewex into a modern Polish retailing powerhouse.[2] But a spy whose talents were mainly in the area of looking really good while playing a robust game of tennis turned out not to be a particularly gifted entrepreneur or manager. Although it had one of the most recognizable brands in Poland, with good locations across the country and sound finances, Pewex ran into trouble almost immediately after Balcerowicz's reforms. Shock therapy ended limits on imports and the Polish zloty became convertible, ending Pewex's only-under-communism function as an "internal exporter." Real retailers, both Polish and foreign, made a fortune, while Pewex sank. Its first bankruptcy filing came in 1993, by which time Zacharski had already moved on. It was taken over by French investors in 1997. A year earlier, prosecutors started investigating Pewex's finances. Zacharski left the country for a mysterious existence in Switzerland where he pens spy books, including an autobiography with the Bondian title of *My Name Is Zacharski, Marian Zacharski.*

Just about the only example of a senior Communist Party member becoming rich on his own was Marek Król—and even there, his apparatchik credentials are a little shaky. Król was a journalist who joined the Communist Party just before the formation of Solidarity—although he later admitted that signing up to the party was pure opportunism, simply a way of making a fast career. He had long been associated with *Wprost,* at the time a regional publication published in Poznań. An elegant man with a close-cropped moustache, Król had been a communist ideologue in the early 1980s, joining the party in 1979. But as the decade wore on and his rank at *Wprost* grew, he focused the magazine on the growing free market.[3] He went into politics as a member of parliament from the Communist Party electoral list for the June 4, 1989, elections. In July he was chosen to be the party's Central Committee secretary, a function that would have carried enormous authority in the 1940s and 1950s, but had significantly less meaning when the party lost power a few weeks after the election. Król actually spent much of his short term on the Central Committee bedridden after poisoning himself with steak tartare—a particularly dangerous dish a couple of decades ago, when hygiene and refrigeration practices were significantly sloppier than they are today.

After the Communist Party collapsed following Mazowiecki's ascension as prime minister, Król backed out of politics and returned to journalism. *Wprost,* like many other Polish titles, was owned by the communist-era press monopoly, which in 1990 started shedding its assets. Król ended up becoming the owner, and turned *Wprost* into an unapologetic backer of capitalism. He consciously modeled his magazine on US titles like *Time* and *Newsweek,* breaking with the communist tradition of poorly designed magazines printed on rough quality paper.[4] Aggressive, ambitious, and notoriously hard on his staff, Król turned *Wprost* into the one of the biggest publishing successes of postcommunist Poland. Its color pages and pro-business tilt made it a natural draw for advertisers, who flooded in. By 2006 the magazine included him in its annual list of the one hundred richest Poles, estimating his personal wealth at 211 million zlotys.[5]

But that marked his peak. *Wprost* fell into growing financial difficulties. Król blames the magazine's political opponents, but the broader Polish press market started to run into trouble at that time with dropping circulation, growing competition, and declining ad sales. *Wprost* was not helped by the increasing number of lawsuits it was facing, filed by people charging that they had been libeled or offended by the magazine. Król's taste for provocative covers—like a photoshopped topless German chancellor Angela Merkel suckling the Kaczyński twins, or an image of a celebrity comedian and a politician hanging on crosses, which drove conservative Catholics batty with its irreverence—undercut the magazine's seriousness. Król also committed the fatal error of handing the reins over to a younger generation—in this case his untried son, Amadeusz, who proceeded to run the publication into the ground. By 2009 much of Król's wealth had evaporated, and he was forced to sell *Wprost* for only 8.7 million zlotys.[6] He compared the sale to "placing my only daughter in a whorehouse."[7] By 2010 he had lost his final post, as a columnist for the magazine. But even Król's brief success was significantly more than more orthodox communists ever managed to achieve.

The problem for members of the nomenklatura is that the skills that served them well in communist Poland—a servile attitude towards superiors and a slippery desire to scramble up the bureaucratic food chain—was not of much use in a capitalist country. The trick in building a business is having a good idea and the courage to open a company. Communist skills were closer to what is required in management; but in the case of communists, their strengths tended to be more in dodging responsibility and avoiding decisions—something that may work in an enormous multinational, but which is difficult to pull off in a small and scrappy Polish start-up.

Even if apparatchiks could use their connections after the Wilczek reforms to get easy bank loans, Balcerowicz's later shock therapy and the resulting sky-high interest rates meant that only a gifted real entrepreneur, and not a party hack, would succeed in building a business solid enough to be able to repay the money.

That doesn't mean that the nomenklatura went hungry. The older apparatchiks ended up on pensions, while those with good connections shifted from comfy and relatively well-paid state and party jobs to comfy and better-paid private sector jobs as advisers and board members to the new capitalists. But the big money in postcommunist Poland went to the people with the ideas and the ability to build true businesses.

The reality that most Communist Party members did not become the wealthy elite of postcommunist Poland is a heresy to the political right. The view expounded by Jarosław Kaczyński and Law and Justice is that the 1989 transition was fundamentally flawed. They see the round table discussions as essentially a way for the elite of People's Poland—spies, crooks, and apparatchiks—to grab control of the new capitalist system as it was being born.

"In Poland after 1989 there was a fatal phenomenon—the mechanism of negative selection characteristic of communism was transferred to business," Kaczyński said in a 2013 interview with the newspaper *Rzeczpospolita*, in which he also denounced business for treating workers like "serfs." He further endeared himself to business by calling many entrepreneurs "dimwitted guys" who lavished money on swimming pools and villas and not on innovation.

Kaczyński first held power from 2005 to 2007, winning largely on a campaign against corruption. A key part of his program was to root out and destroy the *układ*, the network of corruption and influence peddling that he claimed actually controlled the country from behind the scenes. The problem was that despite two years of intensive efforts and access to the full power of the justice and interior ministries, no *układ* was found. That is because in large measure it did not exist; failures like Zacharski's were the norm rather than the exception. Even so, Kaczyński's suspicions about business, entrepreneurs, and the 1989 transition form the ideological basis of the post-2015 Law and Justice government.

Even the market value of old communists is much less than that of their old Solidarity rivals. Wałęsa gets a tiny monthly pension of about 4,400 zlotys as a former Polish president, but supplements his income with lucrative speaker fees. He is cagey about how much he makes, but he once admitted to paying about 600,000 zlotys a year in taxes,[8] which would put his post-tax earnings at well over one million zlotys. Aleksander Kwaśniewski, the former Politburo member who succeeded Wałęsa as president, ruling from 1995 to 2005, is much less of a draw on the international speech circuit. Instead of surviving by speaking, Kwaśniewski became a senior adviser to Kulczyk.

Zacharski's bruising experience with capitalism is of little surprise to Urban. "The old nomenklatura didn't understand how to function in the new reality," he says. "Many of them weren't able to turn their contacts into a business. The real nomenklatura didn't get rich—no minister or member of the government became a wealthy person. People like factory directors, trade officials, and bank directors may have been accepted into the Party, but they didn't get rich because they had been in the Party. They became rich because they had economic abilities."

He lights up a cigar, pulls deeply, and launches into an illustration of how little senior communists understood the functioning of a market economy. He tells of how Gen. Jaruzelski tried to help him in 1990, when Urban was scrambling to find a role after the end of Communist rule. and was looking for help in launching his new magazine, *Nie*. "Jaruzelski responded in the only way he knew how. He said, 'I'll call Gorbachev,'" says Urban with a roll of his eyes. And, according to Urban, Jaruzelski did indeed call his comrade in the Kremlin. The order to help Urban wended its way through the channels of Soviet bureaucracy, eventually settling at the Ministry of Foreign Trade, which in turn contacted the trade commissioner at the Soviet embassy in Warsaw. A bemused Urban opened a trading company, getting his secretaries to Telex trade offers to the embassy, and then receiving offers back from Moscow. "I drank a lot of vodka with the ambassador, who would clap me on the back and say, 'We'll do lots of business,'" says Urban. "I quickly saw that this was ridiculous, and closed up shop."

This was at a time when savvier entrepreneurs were making fortunes selling into an exploding consumer market. Still, Urban ended up doing very well for himself in the business he knew best—journalism. That makes him one of the very few financially successful senior officials of the old regime—although, in truth, his official relationship with the Communist Party was even more tangential than Król's.

With a gleaming bald head, round corpulent body, and jug ears, Urban holds court in a sun-dappled villa in an exclusive neighborhood a short walk from central Warsaw. The house and swimming pool and the Jaguar parked outside are tangible proof of Urban's economic success. But he became rich like most other people in Poland: by opening his own business.

Born in 1933, Urban came from an assimilated left-wing Jewish family. He survived the war in Lwów as a teenager by pretending to be a devotedly religious Pole. But his penchant to offend every national symbol was present from almost the very beginning of his life. "In September 1939, I provoked people by laughing at them when they became hysterical in the bomb shelter," he writes in the introduction to his hugely successful book, *Urban's Alphabet*. He goes on to poke fun at the Church and even at the Home Army, the underground force that resisted the German occupation during the war. As a child, he ran into Home Army fighters. "In the evening they cleaned a gun, murmured patriotic melodies, or listened to the BBC," he writes. "I loudly laughed at them but suffered no penalty. They didn't do anything to me because they felt I was an abnormal child, just as I thought they were crazy buffoons."

With his left-wing inheritance—his father was a Communist Party member and a senior journalist in communist Poland—his mordant wit, and his sharp pen, combined with a prickly independence that was very unusual in the darkly oppressive years of early communism, Urban became one of the country's best known journalists. His columns so annoyed Władysław Gomułka, Poland's ruler from 1956 to 1970, that Urban was forbidden from publishing under his own name. But writing in the *Polityka* magazine under a pseudonym (usually Jan Rem), he continued to be so critical of the system that he was banned from journalistic work, returning only when Gomułka was removed from power.

Many of Urban's friends drifted into open opposition to the regime and became leaders of the Solidarity movement after 1980, but Urban steered clear. He denounced the labor union for being unrealistically anti-Soviet and soaked in Polish nationalism and clericalism. His hostility to Solidarity made him a natural candidate as the spokesman for Gen. Jaruzelski's new government, formed in 1981. Urban, a self-declared sybarite, quickly took to the high profile, and to the very well paid but not enormously demanding job. After Jaruzelski sent tanks out onto the streets to crush Solidarity on December 13, 1981, Urban stayed on as the leading apologist for and public face of the martial law junta. He became famous for holding the Polish equivalent of the "Five O'Clock Follies" (the US military's propaganda-filled briefings during the Vietnam War). Urban's versions were weekly televised news conferences attended by the local and foreign media, in which my predecessor as *Financial Times* correspondent, Chris Bobiński, became a star in trying to nail down the slippery spokesman. Because the journalists' questions were uncensored, the conferences became enormously popular, as they gave Poles some inkling of what the rest of the world thought of the government.

Urban became easily the most despised Pole. He reveled in his defense of the unpopular Jaruzelski while attacking the Church and the opposition. In an article published under the pseudonym Jan Rem in the magazine *Tu i Teraz*, he even denounced the popular opposition priest Jerzy Popiełuszko, calling him a "political fanatic and the Savonarola of anticommunism." Weeks later the cleric was murdered by the police.

Urban briefly became a minister in the cabinet of his old editor Mieczysław Rakowski, and ran for parliament in 1989, but failed to win a seat. He also decided to finally join the Communist Party, but his membership application was not processed before the party dissolved itself. "In a sense I was digging my own grave at the round table because I had become a symbol in the battle against Solidarity," he says with a grin. Pushed out of politics, Urban looked at getting back into journalism, but realized he was much too toxic to employ in the new political environment. His ministerial pension was slashed, and by 1990 he was out of work and short of money.

"I thought about opening a restaurant," he says with a half-serious smile. "It seemed to be the easiest business, because 96 percent of the population knew my name, and I figured that I'd pull in a lot of people who would pay simply to see me standing behind the bar. We even started looking for a place to rent." But in 1990 he was saved from pulling beers and wiping tables when a publisher approached him about writing a sort of who's-who book about prominent Poles, complete with biting and sarcastic remarks as to their abilities and achievements. *Urban's Alphabet* took him only two weeks to write and sold 750,000 copies, earning Urban the then enormous sum of $120,000.

Abandoning his plans to open an eatery, Urban decided instead to launch a scandal sheet magazine called *Nie* (Polish for "No"). Although Mikhail Gorbachev didn't end up being particularly helpful, Urban did have a sense of what the market wanted, and he steered his product directly at what he saw was a huge opportunity. This was a time when most of the existing press was scrambling obsequiously to make up for its past sins and ingratiate itself with the new Solidarity government. The *Gazeta Wyborcza,* launched under the leadership of Adam Michnik, soared to become the country's leading newspaper thanks to its dissident heritage and its tight links to Solidarity. But Urban took aim at the people dispossessed by the changes of 1989.

"We were the only opposition paper willing to hit at the government," says Urban, noting that former mainstream publications had a long tradition of editorial servility, and had not yet learned how to criticize the authorities, while the Solidarity newspapers supported Mazowiecki's government. "That left me with a monopoly on criticism of the new government, of privatization, of prosecution of people from People's Poland, on criticizing the Church and the pope. I was supporting the dignity of the people who had lost their jobs and positions with the change of government."

It was a market that no other publication was willing to touch, but it was a category that included an awful lot of people. The Polish United Workers Party had more than two million members when it was dissolved in 1990. Together with family members and other hangers-on, that was a large pool of those displaced and upset about the Mazowiecki government's program. *Nie* started with a print run of 100,000 copies. Urban then raised it to 300,000. At its peak in 2000, the weekly was selling 780,000 copies, and Urban was pulling in three million dollars a year in profit.

As with many good ideas, the market opportunity was obvious when looked at retrospectively. "Despite our sense that we were the nation, a lot of people had been linked to the old system and they looked for an outlet," says Michnik, whose *Gazeta Wyborcza* remains Poland's most influential (albeit much diminished) mainstream daily.

Urban had first tried his idea with the Communist authorities, suggesting that the intensely boring party paper, *Trybuna Ludu* (the Polish equivalent of the USSR's *Pravda*) be converted into a populist British style tabloid with lots of boobs and a left-wing populist approach to politics and economics. The party demurred, preferring to prune the paper's name to *Trybuna* but stick with dense articles about the ideology and internal politics of the postcommunist left. It printed its last edition in 2009.

Nie's popularity was further boosted after only three months of existence by the first of many cases filed against it by the prosecutor's office, this one on accusations of propagating pornography for running a picture of a vagina alongside an article about abortion. *Nie*'s sales jumped to six hundred thousand. Urban's economic success came despite a complete failure to attract any mainstream advertisers to his magazine. The bulk of the ads it runs are for pornography and escort services; most companies are afraid of his controversial reputation. "I even offered prestigious companies free advertising, but no one would take me up on it," he says.

Urban hasn't helped his reputation with his addiction to controversy and offense. He was fined twenty thousand zlotys in 2006 for offending the ailing pope, writing a 2002 column on the eve of John

Paul II's visit to his homeland, in which he described the pontiff as a "senile divinity, a flickering old man . . . the Brezhnev of the Vatican," and a zombie-like "living dead."[9] Urban refused to admit his guilt, and the spokesman of the martial law regime found himself being backed by international journalistic associations, which defended his right to offend. "We know perfectly well that it is still completely taboo to criticize Pope John Paul II in Poland, but that must not prevent the authorities from conforming to the laws regulating press freedom in Europe," wrote Reporters Without Borders.[10]

In 2013, Prime Minister Tusk sued Urban for running a story that purported to be from a recording of a vulgarity-filled conversation between Tusk and one of his lieutenants made at a football match. Urban's later defense, that it was all an April Fool's joke, didn't cut much ice with the courts, which in Poland tend to defer to the dignity of the authorities. "Was it necessary to ascribe such vulgar words to him in order to achieve a satirical effect?" the judge asked in a ruling that forced Urban to apologize for the story.[11] But by then, Urban himself was only a flickering shadow of the force he had once been. Sales of *Nie* have fallen to just over thirty thousand, and the satirical weekly is now a marginal player on the crowded Polish media market.

Still, Urban's publishing adventure has left him a rich man. He edged on to *Wprost*'s richest one hundred list in 2004 at position ninety-eight, with a fortune estimated at 120 million zlotys. He has parked his *Nie* earnings into very conservative investments, mainly bonds issued by blue chips like Ikea and Ford, as well as Polish and Hungarian treasuries. He was also a very early investor in Big Bank. He no longer makes it onto the top one hundred list, but he is still wealthy.

He also feels that despite its satirical and often offensive nature, *Nie* did play an important role in Poland's transformation and the creation of a modern media market. "The orphans of People's Poland have gotten used to the new system," he admits. He plans to guide his fading magazine until he is too old to do so. "As long as I'm alive, even if I have Alzheimer's, I can be the face of *Nie*. We are no longer an opposition paper, but we did teach the market that there was no penalty for criticizing the government—nothing happened to us. We also showed that criticizing institutions like the Church could be profitable, and other papers followed suit."

That was a lesson that *Gazeta Wyborcza*, under the editorship of Urban's old friend Michnik, had to learn painfully, starting in 1990.

Gazeta Wyborcza (Electoral Gazette) was negotiated into existence during the round table talks, when it was supposed to be the mouthpiece of Solidarity and a way of breaking the Communist Party's stranglehold on information. The newspaper was launched as the print embodiment of the opposition; its masthead bore the motto "There is no freedom without Solidarity." With an initial print run of 150,000 copies, thanks to a deal with the Communist authorities that gave it access to very scarce newsprint, the paper was the first national noncommunist daily in Poland since World War II. The paper was first edited in a preschool in downtown Warsaw, with editorial meetings held out by the sandbox on sunny days. When the first eight page issue appeared in kiosks on May 8, 1989, people lined up to grab copies. By June the print run had been boosted to 450,000 a day.

The people in charge of the paper—Michnik, one of Poland's leading dissidents, a stuttering, charismatic chain-smoker who had frequently been imprisoned under communism, and Helena Łuczywo, his workaholic and foul-mouthed deputy—were actually from a background similar to Urban's. Both came from assimilated Jewish families of prewar leftist activists. Like Urban, they grew up within the cocooned world of the Communist elite; Łuczywo even had a nanny looking after her.[12] But, unlike Urban, they broke with the communist system created by their parents, and became dissidents.

Urban's venture with *Nie* was capitalistic from the start; he was simply looking for a way to make money, and chose a likely market. But Michnik and Łuczywo built *Gazeta Wyborcza* out of ideology rather than as a financial venture, although business success did come as the paper grew into one of Poland's leading media empires. The paper's ideology was initially very closely tied to Solidarity, although from the very first there was a bit of friction, largely because from the beginning *Gazeta Wyborcza* was owned by Agora, a specially created holding company, and not by the union itself.

Gazeta's ties to Solidarity and to the new government—Michnik had been personally appointed to his post by Wałęsa—as well as the special deal that gave it access to newsprint, insulated it from the turbulence unleashed both by Balcerowicz's reforms and by the freeing of the media market. By the end of 1989, more than a thousand new publications appeared on the Polish market, many run by journalists who had lost their jobs in the martial law era. Others were pure money-making schemes. I remember speaking in the fall of 1989 to the editors of one of Poland's first girlie magazines, a publication that closely modeled itself on *Playboy*—something completely new in a country that had hewn to socialist prudishness for more than four decades.

Gazeta sailed serenely above the tumult.

Instead of grubbing for money, Michnik was involved in high politics. In a July 3, 1989, article titled "Your President, Our Prime Minister," he proposed allowing the opposition to form a government, but giving the Communists the presidency and thus control of the institutions of power like the military. Michnik was not the first to come up with the idea, but the authority of *Gazeta Wyborcza* made it a national talking point, helping lead to the formation of Mazowiecki's government a month later.

Initially, the dissident journalists who created *Gazeta Wyborcza* had a fairly fuzzy sense of the distance needed between the press and power. That was something they shared with the regime press. RSW Ruch, the national press monopoly in communist times, was 95-percent owned by the Communist Party, and was an important source of the party's finances.[13] That was also Urban's world, from within which he safely needled the Communist authorities in the 1960s and 1970s. The concept of a press distant from the centers of power was a foreign one, both to the regime newspapers and to the vibrant dissident newspapers that existed in the 1980s, when Poland had the communist world's largest illegal book and newspaper publishing industry.

"*Nie* looked at the new government as hostilely as we had looked at the old government," says Michnik, puffing away on a cigarette in his office in the ostentatiously nonsmoking modern steel, glass, and exposed wood office building that now houses the newspaper. "We didn't understand right away that we had to be as scrupulous about our friends now in the government. *Nie* was able to secure its position. It did the same as *Gazeta Wyborcza*, but from the opposite pole."

While Urban was hammering away at the Solidarity government from the pages of his new weekly, *Gazeta* was getting a quick lesson in the dangers of getting too entangled in politics. By mid-1990, Mazowiecki had broken with Wałęsa, as both decided to run for president to replace Jaruzelski. *Gazeta* sympathized with Mazowiecki, causing Wałęsa to demand Michnik's replacement as editor. The Solidarity union also removed the paper's right to use its logo on the masthead, denouncing "the tendentiousness of the articles, which have the goal of discrediting as well as making fun of chairman Wałęsa."[14]

Cut off from its political base, *Gazeta* became more overtly commercial. Its huge sales spurred a rapid increase in advertising; unlike with Urban's weekly, companies clamored to place ads with the country's most popular paper. "In the early days, advertisements were a small part of revenues. But early on, we decided we had to make money from ads," says Michnik.

The trick was to take a paper with its roots in ideology and to turn it into a normal business. While Michnik and Łuczywo provided the intellectual firepower, the new company turned to the investment banker Wanda Rapaczyńska for help on the commercial side. Rapaczyńska, whose family name was Gruber, had left Poland with her family in 1968, part of an exodus of fifteen thousand of Poland's few remaining Jews in the wake of an anti-Semitic campaign by Communist Party hardliners. She made a career with CitiBank in New York before being pulled back to Poland, and *Gazeta Wyborcza*, in 1990. Thin, with short-cropped hair, and fizzing with energy, Rapaczyńska describes how she was brought in to transform the paper into a corporation.

"Nineteen-ninety was the start of a market economy and we needed to function like a normal company in a normal economy," she says. "The people working for *Gazeta* were very experienced reporters, but from the underground. They understood the print side because they had been running illegal printing, but we had to teach people that the only form of an independent press is to be financially independent."

In October 1990, Rapaczyńska brought over a friend from a US advertising agency, and the two sat down with *Gazeta*'s senior staff and gave them a course in "management 101." Traditions learned during years of functioning illegally were difficult to drop; in the paper's early months, one person would bring a big bag of cash to the nursery school to pay salaries.

The first task was to get financing; even with rapidly increasing circulation, the paper actually lost money in 1990. The French paper *Le Monde* was buying new printing presses, and it let *Gazeta* have its old ones. The presses were never actually used by the Polish paper, but they did serve to secure a bank loan. Rapaczyńska then brought in Cox Enterprises, an Atlanta-based media conglomerate, which took a 12.5 percent stake in the business for five million dollars; an investment that repaid itself many times over as Agora quickly grew along with the recovering Polish economy. "Sales were rising like this," says Rapaczyńska, moving her hand up at a steep angle.

By 1998, when Agora went public, the holding's key shareholders had become rich. That does not include Michnik, who refused to accept shares in the company, as he did not want to mix financial incentives with editing the paper. Łuczywo, who did get shares and is now retired, is worth about twenty-five million zlotys, according to a 2014 ranking of the country's wealthiest women by *Wprost*.

Ryszard Bugaj, a former opposition economist now hostile to Michnik and *Gazeta*, estimates that the newspaper's top one hundred people cashed in to the tune of about one billion zlotys in total. "I reject the view of people from *Gazeta* that they were simply being paid a reward for their market success," he wrote in a 2009 article.[15] "I maintain that the people from *Gazeta* paid themselves essentially a bounty for their earlier—undisputed, actually—work in overthrowing communism in Poland. But it was a reward which was many times too high."

Gazeta expanded to include business, tourism, and entertainment sections, as well as regional editions around the country. Agora also grew into areas like radio and outdoor advertising. But there was still one more lesson in store on the dangers of being too close to power for Michnik and his newspaper.

As the company developed, it became interested in acquiring a television channel to expand its market reach. That caused a problem with the ex-Communists, who won the 2001 elections. The government tried to block newspaper groups from also owning television stations, while Agora lobbied to be allowed to do so. On July 22, 2002 (coincidentally the forty-eighth anniversary of the wartime creation of Poland's Communist government), the film producer Lew Rywin dropped by Michnik's paper-strewn office with a very unusual suggestion from what he said was the "group in power." He said he would be able to arrange favorable wording in the legislation to allow Agora to get into broadcasting, in return for a $17.5 million bribe.

Michnik, true to his reporter's nature, recorded the astonishing conversation. But he then sat on his bombshell for about three months—a crucial period during which Poland was finalizing its entry into the European Union. When *Gazeta*, under pressure from leaks appearing in other publications, finally ran the news, a full-fledged scandal, dubbed Rywingate of course, exploded. "We had difficulty explaining why we delayed for three months because Michnik thought it would affect EU negotiations," admits Michnik. "We paid a high price, both justly and unjustly."

Rapaczyńska agrees. "It left a smear on the company. I feel a shadow is still there. It's internal as well; idealists have difficulty with a stain on their honor."

One of the prices was the shredding of *Gazeta*'s reputation, which did not help it in an increasingly difficult business environment. For Polish conservatives, long suspicious of what they saw as *Gazeta's* pro-European and secularist ideology (and of the Jewish background of many senior editors), as well as its reluctance to pursue ex-Communists for their past sins, it led to a final break with the paper. Today, there is a burgeoning market in right-wing weekly magazines, newspapers, and TV channels, all of which have *Gazeta* as a leading foe.

Gazeta made a transition to online publishing, but like most other newspapers it still has not figured out how to monetize its presence there. Agora also flubbed an opportunity to use its early success to grow beyond its national market. Larger and richer German publishers ended up scooping up most interesting media properties in the region. "Whenever you travel in the ex-Soviet bloc, the Germans got everywhere first and bought everything first," says Rapaczyńska, who was hauled out of retirement in 2013 and brought back in to head Agora after several years of turbulence. She finally left Agora in 2014.

Gazeta is now a much-diminished presence on a very fragmented media market; daily circulation is now only about 160,000 copies, just a hair above what it was on its first day of publication. The paper has gone through several rounds of layoffs. However, the advent of the Law and Justice government in 2015 has given the paper a shot in the arm journalistically, if not commercially. Instead of broadly supporting the government as in years past, the paper now leads the opposition, with senior editors taking part in street protests. Kaczyński and Law and Justice have long seen the paper and Michnik as the embodiment of what went wrong after 1989, and as a result state corporations have pulled most of their advertising, and many government departments have halted their subscriptions to *Gazeta Wyborcza* for ideological reasons.

Still, the old moral authority is gone. Michnik is a diminished figure. He has never fully regained the credibility he lost during the Rywin scandal, although he does still pen irregular columns for the paper. His occasional drinking buddy Urban is also smaller. Instead of a controversial hate figure, he has mellowed into an irascible national uncle. Even his vulgar language, which once shocked proper Poles, now makes few waves.

Both *Nie* and *Gazeta Wyborcza* were creatures of the ferment of Poland's transformation, and both have failed to capture a share of Poland's young, who have drifted away from news and newspapers. But whatever their current state, both publications and the people behind them are also examples of capitalist success. "I'm completely incompetent in business," says Urban. "I made money out of my abilities. I didn't have the motives to become enormously rich. I'm not looking for that sort of thing. I wanted to have enough for my needs—which are cultivated but not luxurious."

8 On the Move

Big foreign companies like Volkswagen and Fiat overwhelmingly dominate Poland's car industry, but Polish entrepreneurs have managed to carve out lucrative niches in other areas of transport. This chapter looks at three such cases–ranging from one of the country's (and Europe's) top bicycle producers to successful bus and train makers. As those businesses grew, management faced the challenge of first learning how to run a company, and then how to revamp and retool the business to adapt to shifting markets.

Some of the most visible signs of the changes in Poland are on the roads—and the roads themselves. A quarter-century ago, cars were few and badly built. Poorer people travelled by bicycle for short trips, or crammed aboard wheezing buses and rattling and overcrowded trains for longer ones. But as the country became richer and the roads became better—something apparent over the last decade thanks to an enormous flood of EU structural funds—Poles began to ride, drive, and commute in vehicles more suited to the average European.

Foreign companies like Fiat, Volkswagen, and Opel—all of whom build cars in Poland—as well as train, bus and truck manufacturers, were the obvious beneficiaries of this change. But Polish entrepreneurs were also able to get into the business of moving people, often starting very small. Some of those companies are now the country's largest and most dynamic businesses.

Many entrepreneurs like to think that they are self-created, but Zbigniew Sosnowski acknowledges a debt not just to his father but also to the legacy of centuries of ancestors who farmed the sandy soils of north-central Poland. Sosnowski comes from a long line of petty nobility, proud and hard men who farmed plots of land that were not much larger than those of neighboring peasants and who were, to the casual outsider, almost indistinguishable from them. But in the old Polish Commonwealth the nobility had rights that peasants did not have: the right to vote, the right to carry a sword, and the right to a coat of arms. That world ended ages ago, but long after the collapse of the republic in the late eighteenth century, the noble villagers of central Poland retained their folk memories of being slightly apart from the society surrounding them—something that ended up helping Sosnowski create Kross, now one of Europe's largest bicycle makers.

"My ancestors never worked for anyone else," says Sosnowski, sitting in a boardroom in his factory in Przasnysz, a nondescript town of eighteen thousand, standing on the flat plain about sixty miles north of Warsaw and, not coincidentally, only a few miles from the Sosnowskis' ancestral lands. Coming from the petty nobility who had little land and less wealth, but who retained a stiff-necked pride, seems to have worked better for Sosnowski than for the heirs to Poland's prewar aristocracy. Two generations after their family estates were confiscated, family traditions of education and international contacts have put the heirs of Poland's landed aristocracy firmly in the professional classes. Many have jobs as lawyers, architects, bankers, and teachers—but precious few have the risk-taking genes to start their own businesses.

Sosnowski's father had a seventy-five-acre farm, big for communist times, and Zbigniew, born in 1963, remembers his father fighting to keep the farm going through the bureaucratic hassles and supply difficulties common in People's Poland. But there was never any thought of giving up the land, which is now farmed by Sosnowski's brother. "The land was handed down from generation to generation; that was our culture," says Sosnowski. "That was what a person took out of our house; those values of the past shaped us."

When Sosnowski grew up, he also never thought for a moment of following the route of most other Poles and getting a job in a state company. "I had seen my father's spirit of entrepreneurship as a small boy and I was fascinated by it," he says, noting that the family's effort to improve their farm set them apart from others in their village. His father was one of the first in the region to abandon horses and buy a tractor. "My friends in elementary school talked about going on holiday, but I couldn't even dream about that, because I had to help the family on the farm."

Standing on one's own also carried material benefits. Having a decent-sized farm at a time when there was a shortage of basic foodstuffs made the Sosnowskis wealthier than most other Poles. "We lived on a different level than the family of a factory worker," says Sosnowski. But it didn't spare his mother or, later, his wife from the numbing Polish routine of standing in endless lines. "It was awful, shameful, that people had been reduced to that level."

Sosnowski, who years ago sported a walrus moustache that would have made his sword-wielding ancestors proud, left home in the 1980s and went into business with his father-in-law, who had a car repair shop. The business was a good one, because the cars that Poles were able to buy—mainly the tiny 650cc Fiat 126 and the boxy Fiat 125p—were so badly made that they needed almost constant repairs. In the late 1980s, small service businesses like garages were able to operate legally. But after two years of working with his father-in-law, Sosnowski realized in 1989, at the age of twenty-three, that the earthquake unleashed by the collapse of communist rule was going to permanently change the country. "It was my moment; I knew that I would have to move," he says.

He started looking around for a business. He had neither the experience nor the capital to begin producing anything, so it would have to be sales. He hit on the idea of selling beer or chocolates. However, both Żywiec, a state-owned brewer, and Wedel, the government chocolate maker, were uninterested in supplying an unknown client in Przasnysz. That left his third business idea: selling bicycles.

On earlier trips to Germany to visit relatives, Sosnowski had noticed people riding bicycles for fun. In Poland they were used mostly as a cheap form of transport for people who could not afford a car. That legacy still exists in the Polish countryside today. Driving out to talk with Sosnowski, I passed a couple of wizened men carefully riding their ancient bicycles on the edge of the road as cars and trucks squeezed past them.

But in Germany it was obvious that bikes could be used for more than transporting peasants along rural roads. So Sosnowski contacted Romet, the Polish state-owned bicycle maker, and struck an agreement to sell their bikes in Przasnysz. Relying on advice and capital from his father, Sosnowski rented a shop in the town in 1990 and bought about thirty bicycles. He and his wife, who was in charge of sales, set out their wares and began their business adventure. Their new shop was across the street from a state-owned bicycle shop. The government store had just two or three different bikes in stock, and a sour salesman who reacted rudely whenever any potential customers had the temerity to disturb him. Sosnowski's shop carried all of Romet's products, attractively displayed; and in the form of his wife, it also had a smiling cashier.

"Even though there was another bicycle shop in town, the truth was that we had no competition at all," laughs Sosnowski, who lost the moustache and now sports a fashionable three-day growth to go along with his impeccably cut navy blazer. He sold his first batch of bikes in a few days, and then went back to Romet for twice as many. Within one year he had opened a second shop and hired two drivers who would tour the bazaars and markets that were the main shopping venues in small-town Poland, selling bicycles out of their trucks. A year after that, Sosnowski had another shop and two more drivers. As the business grew, it ended up coming to the attention of Poland's increasingly aggressive tax inspectors. In the very early years of the transformation, tax authorities were unprepared for dealing with thousands of new private business, but they quickly learned.

One day when Sosnowski was sitting in his shop, a man walked in, flashed his ID, and insisted that he close his shop for an inspection. The inspector then demanded all the company's books, and peppered Sosnowski with aggressive questions. "I felt like a beaten dog," says Sosnowski, his blue eyes narrowing in anger at the memory. "It was obvious that he was the master even though he was sitting in my shop." Sosnowski was handed a larger tax bill, but he paid without arguing. "It made no sense to continue the fight; the system was rigged against me, and I would have certainly lost. The tax office generally had a view that I was a thief, that the first million had to be stolen. I was seen as a wrongdoer, not as an honest taxpayer."

Bureaucratic problems didn't stop Sosnowski's growth. By the mid-1990s he was Romet's largest national distributor. He also became a wholesaler to smaller shops, building warehouses, buying up bicycles in the fall, and storing them over the winter. That gave him a leg up, as Romet could not cope with the regular rush of demand every May when Polish parents and grandparents bought their children bicycles as first communion presents.

In order to finance the business, Sosnowski began to take bank loans for operating capital—supplied at rates as high as 50 percent a year, and backed by property owned by him, his father, his wife, and his friends. Sosnowski grew so quickly because, in a country where business ethics was still a pretty new idea, he tried to pay his bills on time, tried to move his product quickly, and spent a lot of time thinking about his clients. "That may not seem very complicated, but it worked for me then and still does now," he says.

In those first years, the Polish customers were simply starved of goods—anyone supplying the market with hard-to-find products did well. But as Poland emerged from the economic crisis of the early 1990s and the economy began to stabilize and then expand, Sosnowski noticed that a growing group of his customers was becoming fussier about the quality of the Romets on offer, and spending much more time looking at British Raleigh and Merida bikes from Taiwan.

There was a reason. "The Romets were really awful bikes," says Sosnowski. "Compared to a Western bike, they looked like a Polish Fiat compared to a Western car. They were heavy, and badly painted. They used Polish and Czech dérailleurs instead of Shimanos; that made them really loud." Romet was still state-owned, and it reacted slowly to the changing market. Like other socialist companies, it worked according to a plan, producing set numbers of bikes aimed at distributors, and never thinking much about what the final customer wanted. Modern manufacturers tend to farm out production of components to other suppliers and concentrated only on a limited part of the assembly process. But Romet made everything in-house—from frames to ball bearings and wheels—almost all of it badly, because it didn't have the volumes to reduce costs and improve quality. It tried to produce its own mountain bike, but again the result was heavy and ugly.

The company's CEO called a meeting of his largest distributors and asked them what should be changed. "Everything," Sosnowski answered.

Worried that Romet was going into a death spiral, Sosnowski decided that it was time to make a leap and become a producer and not just a distributor. He had always wanted to eventually move into production, but first he needed to acquire the know-how. "I had my own distribution network, capital and experience," he says. "If I had had stayed just being a distributor I would have felt that I was working for someone else, and I didn't want that. I'm a free man."

With Western bikes just starting to appear on the Polish market, no company had built up much of a brand, so it was still possible for a Polish business to grab a share of the market. Sosnowski approached five Taiwanese companies about bidding for his business, and ended up choosing one parts supplier. Starting in 1995, the bikes were assembled in Przasnysz and sold very well—to Romet's fury. Sosnkowski had gone from being a leading distributor to being a growing competitor.

It didn't matter much, because by 1998 Romet was out of business. (The brand has since been revived by a private businessman who sells bicycles, motorbikes, and scooters under the Romet name. The renewed Romet is now Sosnowski's leading Polish rival.)

"We moved just in time," says Sosnowski. "If we had waited too long, we could have gone down with Romet."

Sosnowski bought a production line in Italy and shipped it to Poland, allowing him to start building his own bicycles and not just assemble them from parts supplied by others. Sosnowski's company, now dubbed Kross, was soaring, with sales rising by about 50 percent a year as Poland's new middle classes took to cycling for pleasure. By the turn of the millennium, Kross was making more than two hundred thousand bicycles a year, with its own frame and paint shop in Przasnysz. The company became too large for the Polish market, and started to export to the rest of Europe. There the competition was fierce. The high end was dominated by traditional and small-scale manufacturers from countries like Italy, and the low end was dominated by China, which was hampered by tariffs imposed by the European Union. Kross and other Polish bike makers were in the middle: unable to compete with Chinese prices, while not having the brand and reputation to go upmarket.

The middle is a difficult place to be. The answer was to build a brand and escape upward. In Poland, where Kross now controls about 40 percent of the market, the company aimed at customers who wanted a relatively cheap bike, but one that approached the standards of more expensive prestige brands like Giant and Gary Fisher.

As the company grew, Sosnowski saw that his seat-of-the-pants management style, common to most other Polish businesses, was no longer adequate for what was becoming a big company. In the early years he had been a micromanager, hovering over every detail of the company. As he hired more people, that method became impossible, but he saw that his new staff, while capable, lacked management fundamentals. He had been an avid reader of business books, grabbing whatever appeared in translation on the Polish market, as well as taking management courses himself. By the late 1990s he saw that he would have to formalize his company's approach to business. He took all twelve of his leading managers and signed them up for a yearlong Harvard management course in Warsaw, with the team meeting up two or three times a week to learn formal management techniques. "It made an enormous difference," says Sosnowski. "We came out of that speaking the same language; we had the same terminology and used the same techniques. It made management much easier."

In 2002, Kross was approached by Decathlon, the French sporting goods chain, which was looking for partners to assemble the hundreds of thousands of bikes it was selling under its own brand across Europe. While most of the other companies dealing with Decathlon simply put bikes together, Kross insisted on doing more of the work on its own. It built the frames and sourced the parts itself, supplying the French with the finished product. By 2004, when Sosnowski won the Entrepreneur of the Year award from Ernst & Young, part of an annual international competition run by the consultancy, Kross was making about eight hundred thousand bikes a year, more than half of them for Decathlon. The company had a thousand employees, revenues of more than 200 million zlotys, and a generated profit that year of eight million zlotys. Sosnowski had arrived. When he flew off to Monte Carlo for Ernst & Young's Entrepreneur of the Year finals that year, he was rich, and the toast of the Polish press.

Sosnowski's gamble, that Poles would see bikes are more than a cheap form of transportation, was accurate. Cities around the country started to build bicycle paths to cater to the fast-growing middle-class passion for recreational riding. Although Lech Kaczyński, Warsaw's mayor and later the country's president, proclaimed in 2004, "Let's not exaggerate with the construction of bicycle paths," and another city official said that Warsaw was "not a village where one rides a bicycle," the thousands of Poles who now bike to work, and the tens of thousands who clog the paths of larger cities on weekends show that Poland is becoming much more like its neighbor Germany in switching to biking for fun. Spandex-clad road warriors have replaced the peasants who cycled in cloth caps.

But what seemed like the peak of Kross's success was actually a time of great danger for Sosnowski. He was growing increasingly worried about the cost pressure being exerted by Decathlon, which was squeezing its suppliers as hard as it could. He also saw that the Polish market was rapidly changing, with sales of the cheapest bicycles falling while top-end bikes were becoming increasingly popular. It was yet another indication that the country was becoming richer, and that Poland was following in the path of other European countries like Spain, where tastes had shifted upmarket in a similar fashion as it caught up to European standards of living.

Tying the future of his company to the mass production of cheap no-name bikes for Decathlon seemed increasingly risky. It was also becoming obvious that the partnership with Decathlon was becoming incompatible with Kross's own goal of creating an upmarket brand. Initially, teaming up with Decathlon had introduced quality control and modern manufacturing that hugely benefited Kross. "But with time we saw that we were doing the splits, which is an uncomfortable position," says Sosnowski. "Decathlon needed an organization aimed only at effective and cheap production. They didn't need engineers and designers and a research and development team and a sales department, but Kross did. I had the feeling that Kross was becoming product no. 2 in our own company."

In 2007 Sosnowski called representatives from Decathlon up to Przasnysz, and he laid out his terms: either the sports retailer would have to stop cutting its margins, or the agreement with Kross was over. "There was silence," says Sosnowski, sitting at the same conference table where he made the demand. "They were stunned. They kept repeating, 'Are you sure?' But I was. It was a very difficult and risky decision, but I think it was the right one."

It may have been the right decision for Kross's long-term corporate aims, but it was a disaster for the employees who had to be let go once production for Decathlon ended. Sosnowski, who had been Przasnysz's largest employer and a local hero, became a goat. "I was hated in the town," he says.

The company began to slash its workforce. The frame shop, which employed one hundred people to make steel frames for Decathlon, was not needed in a company that used only aluminum frames for its own production. Department after department was in a similar shape. In all, about four hundred of the company's workers had to be laid off. Sosnowski tried to make the process humane, looking at the family situation of each worker and not just their productivity. "If we had a really good worker whose wife had a job in town, he was let go, while another worker who was the only earner in his family was kept on," says Sosnowski, who admits that he became a regular patient at his cardiologist after the layoffs. "These are consequences of running a business. It's not a game; it's a responsibility. You're either strong or you won't be able to handle it and you'll go under."

Kross has survived. It is smaller than when it was cooperating with Decathlon, but Sosnowski says that many of the companies that had relied solely on work as no-name subcontractors for the sports chain went under when the economic crisis hit and the retailer slashed its orders. "Like with Romet, this was another good decision," he says, pointing out that his worries over the future of cheap bike sales proved to be correct. Kross is now putting money into research and development, relying on a core of local talent to push the brand upmarket. "Now we're looking for passionate young engineers," says Sosnowski. "People who sleep with their bicycles, and who are interested in making really cutting-edge products."

Kross's scramble upmarket, where it cannot rely on copying existing technology but instead must develop its own breakthroughs, is an early harbinger of a broader movement within the Polish economy. The cheap but well-qualified labor that fueled much of the growth of the last two decades is no longer enough; only those companies that become truly innovative have much of a chance in surviving over the longer term. "In Europe, cost is less important than brand," says Sosnowski. "What we're doing now isn't a rip-off or copying. This is a group of people with a large budget to design products. Why can't we be as good or better than the US or Western Europe?"

Sosnowski has also dabbled in other businesses, setting up a company making scooters in 2003 and selling it off to an investment fund in 2007. He also has a company that builds apartments in the towns around Przasnysz, and is now involved in a venture that uses space-age construction materials—a break from the traditional Polish methods of steel, brick, and concrete.

Older, rich, and self-assured, Sosnowski has the confidence to hand over most day-to-day management to professionals. "At some point, the owner can be the main brake on a company," he says. "Some of my friends say they have no spare time, but that's ridiculous and that shouldn't be the case—you have to know when to back away. I have several companies, but I go on holidays and I go home every day at 4 p.m. I'm one of the few people in Kross to use up all their annual vacations."

Now Sosnowski's goal is to pass the companies he built on to his two sons—one of whom is interested in real estate, the other in bikes—the first chance to hand on inherited wealth in generations. "I have two sons and they have been working here since they were small," he says. "They started in the warehouse and they have learned and developed. This is the first time in 250 years that we have the chance to build a family company. Of course I could sell, and live off what I've earned by building my businesses, but I was brought up by my father to be patriotic. This is ours, this is Polish, and we are here to make it work."

Sosnowski's success with two wheels has not been mirrored in four. Poland is one of the few Central European countries without its own native car production. Elsewhere in the region, local brands have survived, albeit under new ownership. The Czech Republic had Skoda, now a unit of Germany's Volkswagen, while Romania has Dacia, owned by Renault; but Poland's state-controlled small car factory, located in the northern suburbs of Warsaw, has gone bankrupt.

Instead, many smaller Polish companies supply parts to the big final-assembly car plants, often sending equipment, ranging from car seats to wire assemblies and shock absorbers, across the continent. They are not very visible, and have no recognizable brands—who is aware of which company makes the seals on their car doors?—but they have become important drivers of the Polish economy. However, probably more important for the future of the country are companies creating finished goods under their own name—something that has happened in buses and trains.

Sosnowski used his business to slowly build up his knowledge of the bicycle market and later mastered bicycle manufacturing before he was able to strike out as an independent producer—but there are other ways of gaining needed know-how, as is shown by Krzysztof and Solange Olszewski. They piggybacked on the technical and marketing experience of an established busmaker before starting up their own company, Solaris.

Like Sosnowski, Krzysztof Olszewski was determined never to spend a single day working in a government job. An engineer who studied at the Warsaw Polytechnic University, Olszewski was already showing an independent streak by the late 1970s. Like Sosnowski, Olszewski was the part owner of a small garage in Warsaw, bought thanks to the hard currency he and his young wife had managed to earn in Sweden. He happened to take a business trip to Cologne on December 8, 1981. Taking all of the family's dollars, he went to buy Western car parts for his garage, intending to stay in Cologne only a week before returning to Warsaw. On December 13, however, Gen. Jaruzelski staged his coup and declared martial law to crush Solidarity.

As tanks and armored personnel carriers roared onto the streets of Polish cities, detachments of soldiers and police crushed union protests, and thousands of union activists and members of the political opposition were swept into detainment camps, there wasn't much point in Olszewski crossing back into Poland. "There was nothing to come back to," says Solange Olszewska, a compact and smiling woman who gave up a career in dentistry to take over Solaris after her husband decided to move on from day-to-day management of the company. "We had an agreement that if anything like that happened, he was to stay there and try to bring us to him."

Stranded in Warsaw with two small children and no money, Olszewska tried to get a passport that would allow her to leave the country. Meanwhile, Olszewski's mechanical and engineering experience allowed him to get a job with Neoplan, a German bus maker then opening a Berlin factory.

It took Olszewska a year to get her passport, raising the money to do so by selling their car repair business. She left in September 1982, with the expectation that her two children would quickly get passports and follow. Instead, her three-year-old daughter and two-year-old son were refused travel papers and remained trapped in Warsaw, while their frantic parents tried to get them out of Poland. "It was a nightmare," says Olszewska, who tried to pay for the passports and was even advised to get a letter saying she was terminally ill in the hope that would move the Polish authorities to relent.

In the end, it was a connection made through Neoplan that brought the family back together. The company was selling low-riding buses for disabled people, and one of the officials in charge of the contract was friends with German Foreign Minister Hans-Dietrich Genscher. When the minister heard about the Olszewskis' problem, he appealed directly to the Polish government. A week later, the children were in Berlin; Olszewska still has Genscher's letter as a memento.

The Olszewskis became part of a diaspora of hundreds of thousands of Poles who found themselves out of the country when martial law was declared. Western governments took pity on the refugees, and many countries loosened their visa and work regulations, allowing them to stay legally. Olszewski started as Neoplan's first engineer, hired to work in the company's Berlin factory, and by the end of the decade he was the factory director. The family got German citizenships out of a loyalty to their new country, and they had no plans to ever live in Poland again. But then 1989 happened. Olszewski was enormously excited by the opportunities that he saw in postcommunist Poland, while his wife admits, "I really had no desire to go back at all."

Olszewski sat down for a meeting with the Auwärter family, the owners of Neoplan, and told them he was interested in eventually getting a seat on the board. The dumbfounded owners made it clear that there was a ceiling for nonfamily employees, and that Olszewski had already hit it. "That was as far as he was going to go, because Neoplan was a family company and all the more senior jobs were in family hands," says Olszewska.

Although scrambling up the ladder in Neoplan was blocked, 1989 opened the way for a completely different form of advancement for Olszewski. He quickly saw that there would be enormous possibilities in his homeland, but Neoplan was unimpressed, focusing instead on the more lucrative traditional markets of Western Europe.

On his free time, Olszewski would clamber behind the wheel of a Neoplan bus and drive across the border to show it off in Polish cities. There, transit systems used belching buses made by Ikarus of Hungary and Jelcz from Poland (the company limped on for two decades making underpowered and old-fashioned buses before going out of business in 2010). Low floor designs and luxuries like air conditioning were completely unknown and, to many city officials, a waste.

Olszewski thought Neoplan might do better if it opened a Polish factory, but the company's bosses balked. "The Germans said they had no interest in opening a factory in a country where a former union leader [Wałęsa] was in charge," says Olszewska.

Olszewski persevered, opening a Neoplan sales office in 1994. "Neoplan said they would give us no financial support, but that we would be allowed to sell their buses," says Olszewska.

A year later, the central Polish city of Poznań held a tender for 123 buses and Olszewski unexpectedly won the right to supply 72 of them. There was one problem. The local authorities insisted that the winner had to have a Polish factory. Other busmakers, like Germany's MAN, were already setting up Polish operations; Olszewski faced the potential loss of his first contract. Rather than give up, he began to hunt for a production site, settling on an abandoned ammunition factory in Bolechowo, a town about twenty miles north of Poznań. In communist times the Bolechowo factory had been a key ammunition supplier for Warsaw Pact armies, but the end of the Cold War and the subsequent collapse in Central European defense spending made the factory redundant. By the time the Olszewskis arrived, trees were growing on the roof of the abandoned factory. They didn't have enough money of their own to set up production and, with no financing from Neoplan, had to make the rounds of Polish banks before finally landing a corporate loan.

Tarpan, a nearby factory producing ugly but functional off-road vehicles, was in the process of going bankrupt, so the Olszewskis snapped up thirty-six qualified workers and set up production. (Many of the rest ended up working for Volkswagen, thanks to Kulczyk's deal.) They bought ready-made frames from Neoplan and assembled them on site. This time, when the Olszewskis were desperately hunting for money, Neoplan stepped up and took a 30-percent stake in the new business. It was a cash injection that enabled the company to grow, but which a few years later would almost kill it.

Within two years the Olszewskis had paid off their $3.6 million loan and bought their factory buildings outright. "We started to win one contract after another," says Olszewska. But the boom lasted less than a year. Under the licensing deal with Neoplan, the Olszewskis were supposed to sell their buses in Poland and points further east while Neoplan concentrated on Western Europe. The Eastern markets were growing increasingly competitive. MAN was joined by Volvo, Scania, and other big international producers building local factories.

However, the whole business was upended by the Russian economic crisis of 1998. "Everyone was counting on big sales to Russia, but the economic crisis killed that idea. There were all these new factories in the region, so prices collapsed," says Olszewska.

The frames imported from Neoplan made the Olszewskis' final product too expensive for now cash-strapped governments. Also, buses designed for well-made West European roads were proving too fragile for the brutal conditions in Central Europe, where buses were overloaded with passengers, many of whom were too poor to own cars, and were hammered by potholed roads, and corroded by the salt used keep winter streets clear of ice.

"We thought it was time to create our own brand," says Olszewska. "My husband knew the market well, and we had gathered a lot of customers as well." Olszewski had a lot of technical knowledge, but he had never designed a bus. Instead of wasting time and money trying to do it himself, he turned to a Berlin design bureau that came up with the Solaris Urbino, a low-slung bus made out of stainless steel, which would make it more resilient to the rust that quickly ate through buses made out of conventional steel.

His wife came up with the logo—a green and grinning low-slung dachshund. Green because it was supposed to be environmentally friendly, and a sausage dog to mark the company's main selling point, the low-floor buses. The Solaris brand came from Polish writer Stanisław Lem's science fiction classic, and the name was supposed to be easy to pronounce in many different languages.

The company sold seventy buses in 1999—aiming at the Polish markets and points east, as the old agreement with Neoplan splitting the European market was still in effect. In 2001, Neoplan was taken over by MAN—one of Solaris's fiercest competitors. "MAN was not interested in owning 30 percent of us; they wanted to take us over completely," says Olszewska. "It was clear that they wanted to close us; they didn't need our factory and they didn't need our brand. But we had five hundred workers, and we felt responsible toward those people."

Instead of selling to their much larger rival, the Olszewskis pooled all their money from the company, as well as taking all of their personal assets and loading up with debt, and bought out MAN, taking back full control of their business.

With Neoplan gone, the old agreement was also dead and Solaris could now sell in Western European markets. The problem was that West Europeans weren't particularly keen to buy Polish technology, fearing that anything that came out of Poland would be cheap but badly made. "I didn't think it would be possible to sell to the West," admits Olszewska. "A lot of buyers were scared of taking the risk and buying from us."

Their first breakthrough came in 2000, when a delegation from the Poznań zoo asked to take two Solaris buses to a convention in the German capital. "The Berlin authorities allowed us to use their municipal garages and they got a close look at our buses. The result was that we sold them two," says Olszewska. Other West European markets were also cracked open because the company was desperate and worked harder than its more established rivals. When Olszewski got word that the Swiss city of Winterthur was opening a tender for buses in 2003, he got two buses and drove them to Switzerland. The buses crashed just outside Winterthur, but Olszewski was able to pull mechanics from Poland and repair the buses so quickly that the impressed Swiss bought five. A year later, a crash in a garage in Winterthur destroyed four buses. Again, Olszewski rushed Polish mechanics to the scene and had the buses fixed. This time the story made Swiss papers. "A small company has a much better chance of reacting quickly," says Olszewska. "We can be much faster and more flexible than a big company."

That kind of attention to detail allowed Solaris to overcome the hurdle of being an unknown Polish company. Solaris also takes full advantage of Poland's cheaper labor. The production line in Bolechowo is largely manual, with workers attaching wire harnesses and fitting seats into buses by hand. That gives Solaris the ability to manufacture in small batches—catering to the demands of individual clients. "Western Europe is not impossible for Polish companies, but it is a difficult market and it does take time to do business there," says Olszewska.

Solaris is now the largest foreign bus maker in Germany, with a 13 percent share of the market, and it has made inroads around Western Europe. It also has half of the Polish market, one driven by a flood of funds from the European Union that cities have used to modernize their transport infrastructure. The company is also moving into rail transport, now making trolley cars. The Olszewskis are thought to be worth about eight hundred million zlotys, putting them in the upper ranks of the country's wealthiest people. Like Sosnowski's, their company is in the process of handing control to the next generation. Krzysztof Olszewski has largely retired from running the company, handing control over to his wife. Now their daughter Małgorzata is being groomed to take over the company. "The key is ability," says Olszewska. "We don't want to go the way of Neoplan. If we don't have someone in the family who can manage well, we'll hand it over to a professional."

Poland may not have its own brand of cars, but the thousands of

Solaris buses on the roads from Portugal to Finland do fly the flag for the country's manufacturing abilities.

Not every business success comes from start-ups like those created by Sosnowski and the Olszewskis. Tomasz Zaboklicki pulled off one of Poland's first management buyouts, turning Pesa from a failing rail car repair yard into Poland's largest locomotive makers, one that even won a €1.2 billion contract to supply up to 470 locomotives to Germany's Deutsche Bahn.

The repair yard was one of Poland's oldest, dating back to 1851, when it was set up in the then German town of Bromberg (today's Bydgoszcz). In communist Poland it was one of twenty-seven repair yards serving the sprawling and inefficient state railways—one of the main methods of transportation in a country that was very short of cars.

Even today, Poland's network of railways reflects the legacy of the partitions that ended with World War I. The network in the west, lands that once belonged to Germany, is very dense. The south, which was Austrian, is sparser, while the east, which was Russian, has the fewest rail lines of all. I remember squeezing onto communist-era Polish trains during weekends and summer holidays. The train would roll out of the station filled to the brim with people. Smart travelers shoved their way into toilets to use as handy seats, while slower passengers stood jammed together in corridors that were so tightly packed that conductors could not force their way through to check tickets. Although such sights were still common after 1989, the flow of government money that had kept the whole system creaking along was dramatically cut back. Bydgoszcz lacked the political heft of some of its rivals, and when the railway company decided to slim down, it stopped issuing contracts to almost two dozen repair yards, including the one in Bydgoszcz.

"In one day the company lost more than half of its market," says Zaboklicki, a wiry and compact man with a bristling handlebar moustache who was then the rail yard's business specialist. "The government simply made a decision to kill us off."

Pesa was drowning in debt. It didn't have enough cash to pay employees or to cover its electricity bills, and its management's main goal was to close up the company as smoothly as possible. The rail yard's land in the center of Bydgoszcz, a city of 350,000, was its greatest asset. The idea was to sell off property as a way of managing the decline. One piece of land was supposed to become a new bus station. Another was slated for an open-air bazaar. "Management didn't invest anything and they had no concept of how to save the company," says Zaboklicki, sitting in Pesa's headquarters overlooking the main rail line running through the city.

Zabolicki, an economist and not an engineer by training, was chosen in 1991 to be the union workers' representative on the board despite not belonging to the union. "The reason was that I was telling the truth. We were in a terrible situation. We were a classic case of a bankrupt company. The goal was simply to survive," he says. Zaboklicki and the new management team brought in drastic changes. They began to hunt for new business to replace the state railways. A contract to repair Lithuanian sleeping cars in 1994 helped patch some holes. The company also noticed that there was a market niche in building grain transporters. A lot of grain was being shipped in old coal cars, and that caused high rates of spoilage. The yard came up with the idea of revamping unused military tank transporters—the cars that had been used to ship Soviet tanks around the region for army exercises—and turning them into grain cars which cost a third of new specialized transporters. While the work, which included repairing rail cars in Russia and Ukraine, staved off the immediate threat of collapse, the rail yard still had no clear business model and was in a very tenuous position.

Zaboklicki, who took over as CEO in 1998, pulled together six other managers, and in 2001 they bought the company from the government. But with banks reluctant to lend to buy a failing company, they were forced to clean out their bank accounts and take personal bank loans to scrape together the money needed for the buyout. "I went to the bank and put up everything I had, my apartment and even my wife's salary, to get my share of the money to buy the company," says Zaboklicki, a man who had dreamed of becoming a paratrooper in his youth. "I couldn't sleep; it was really dramatic." The total cost of his quarter share of the company was about one million zlotys ($250,000)—today the price of a small suburban Warsaw house. But with the company deep in the red and revenues of only about $20 million, there were no other takers for the troubled repair yard.

Zaboklicki and his fellow managers knew what they were doing. Pesa had been working for a few years on a project to build a simple rail bus—a diesel-powered train that could be used for short urban commutes. By 2002 it was ready to roll. Zaboklicki also gambled that Poland's looming entry into the European Union in 2004 would open a spigot of cash from Brussels that towns and cities would use to upgrade their ramshackle bus and tramway systems. It was a sensible bet. In Poland's first two years in the EU it got €8.4 billion in structural funds—money that is supposed to be combined with an input from local government to pay for everything from new roads to water treatment plants, garbage incinerators, and, as Zaboklicki expected, buses and trams. In the next EU budget, extending from 2007 to 2013, Poland got €67 billion—the most of any EU country. It gets €73 billion more in structural funds from 2014 to 2020.

But to take advantage of the money that would soon be pouring into Poland, Pesa had to survive. Doing so meant some very unpleasant decisions for a man who had started his corporate career as a workers' representative. The new owners instituted fierce cuts. The workforce was trimmed by more than half, to only 770. Frills like the company brass orchestra and company holiday resorts—standard for state-owned businesses in communist times—were chopped. The union had full access to the company's books, and managers would sit down with union bosses to decide how to spend the trickle of money flowing into the company. "We would have five hundred thousand zlotys in money coming in, and we would have to decide whether that should be used for salaries or for buying equipment. They usually chose the equipment—they were really remarkable," says Zaboklicki, his voice drowned out by the roar of a train racing past his office windows. "Everyone was trying to save us from sinking."

The close cooperation with unions is not the norm in Poland, where labor has more often tried to block privatizations and tends to resist attempts to cut wages and benefits. Companies like KGHM, the state-controlled copper miner, have been dogged with problems from unions, which have forced steep pay increases even in difficult years, and make managing companies a nightmare. "Our story with the unions is actually pretty unusual," admits Zaboklicki.

Pesa's turnaround began with Italy, supplying the southern city of Bari with rail buses. The company also broadened its product range. After repairing one streetcar, Pesa's engineers saw that they were perfectly capable of building such vehicles themselves, and Pesa launched its own line. That approach made Pesa different from most other Polish companies, which largely rely on copying more advanced technology and management techniques from the West instead of figuring it out for themselves. Pesa has a research and development team of more than 150 engineers, and makes an effort to stay in the front rank of international rail companies when it comes to technology and design.

In 2005 the company sold five streetcars to the northern Polish city of Elbląg. "That was a breakthrough," says Zaboklicki. "Cities were afraid of using us because we had no experience." Those first contracts in Italy and Poland settled the nerves of potential buyers, and helped Pesa win a 1.5 billion zloty contract in 2009, supplying Warsaw with 186 streetcars. Pesa beat out much larger and older companies like France's Alstom and Swiss-German Stadler, winning both on price and the flexibility of the contract. Since then, Pesa has gone on to win contracts in the Czech Republic, Italy, Lithuania, Hungary, and a half-dozen other countries.

Zaboklicki also forced Pesa to adopt all the quality and licensing standards used by German rail manufacturers, largely because the disorganized Polish bureaucracy has not bothered to come up with national standards of its own. That was one of the factors that allowed

Pesa to compete for the big Deutsche Bahn contract. Another was Zaboklicki's flexibility. When German unions started to protest about the prospect of such a lucrative contract going to a relatively unknown foreign company during a time of economic crisis, he made sure to include German brakes and engines in his bid. That worked to mollify the opposition. "Deutsche Bahn doesn't buy a cat in a bag," he says. "They buy from all the leading companies. Winning that contract is a signal to the whole railway world that Pesa is a proper international competitor. It's like making it into the Premier League."

Even more satisfying was making that crucial 2012 sale to Germany, which even had a disparaging term, *Polnische Wirtschaft* (Polish economy), as a byword for shoddy, cheap, and "good-enough" manufacturing. That's no longer the case. Pesa is now one of Poland's industrial success stories, competing for contracts with an aggressive Solaris, which is trying to muscle in on local rail and tramway markets. Zaboklicki's gamble in buying his failing employer turned out to be a winning move. He has a 25 percent stake in Pesa, now thought to be worth about 230 million zlotys.

And the twenty-five other railway repair yards? Almost all have gone bust. Some were stolen by rapacious management; in one case a manager bought an airplane while the yard foundered. Others were broken apart and sold for real estate. The only other yard to prosper is now called Newag. Located in Nowy Sącz, in the foothills of the Tatra Mountains, it designs and sells locomotives, much like Pesa, its leading rival. And the ownership? It has been in private hands since 2003.

9 A Question of Scale

In Communist times, the party tolerated only small companies. The 1989 transformation ended that limit of scale, and many new companies grew quickly. But the laws of business as the same in Poland as everywhere else: those companies that adapt and change tend to survive.

Poland's economic transformation has been a huge success, and hundreds of thousands of people have built their own businesses—an explosion of entrepreneurship unprecedented among Europe's transition economies. But only a few of the companies founded in the early 1990s have grown to a sizeable national and international scale. Part of the reason is the normal attrition of capitalism—not every business is destined for success. There is one common denominator among the businesses that did manage the trick: the owners invested in their companies rather than in themselves, and they were never satisfied with their firms' size and market share. They felt they had to grow in order to survive, and growth meant constant adoption of technology and modern management techniques.

Today, the businesses that succeeded are rivals of longer-established West European and international companies, and nothing really differentiates them except for the "Made in Poland" label on their products, as with Pesa locomotives and the buses made by Solaris. There is a recognition that the conditions which existed from 1989 to the late 1990s were unique. It was much easier to open a business in Poland than in many more developed countries. This was a market where customers were starved of something to buy while also having money to spend. Meanwhile, normal retail and production structures—everything from grocery shops to shopping malls, sterile milk production, and factories churning out building materials—didn't exist. What made life less complicated for early entrepreneurs was that the models for such businesses already existed in the West. It was a matter of looking at how things worked in Britain, France, and the United States, seeing that Poland was heading in the same direction, and opening similar businesses in Warsaw, Bydgoszcz, and Rzeszów.

That's what the Krzanowski brothers, Adam and Jerzy, did when they opened their chair-making company in 1992.

The Krzanowskis—Adam, born in 1966, and his younger brother Jerzy, born in 1970—showed a penchant for business as children. Growing up in Krosno, in southeastern Poland (just twenty miles south of Wiśniowa), they had an uncle who was an assessor for PZU, the Polish insurance monopoly. He turned to his nephews, still in elementary school, to take photos of wrecked cars for his insurance cases. "This wasn't just a little bit of money," says Adam Krzanowski. "We were able to buy better cameras, flashes, and other equipment in Pewex shops." That early start in making some private money at a young age, even during communism, is something shared by many other successful Poles. The opportunities that opened up after 1989 were available to most Poles, but those who did best seem to have had a natural drive toward entrepreneurship.

Just down the road from Krosno in the village of Tymbark (now Poland's apple juice capital), and a decade before the Krzanowskis were earning their first money, Ryszard Florek was gathering apples from his aunt's orchard, packing them into suitcases and taking the train to the mountain resort town of Rabka to sell to tourists. "I had to get up at 5 a.m. to pick the apples. They had to be picked and sold on the same day," says Florek, sitting in his office at the headquarters of Fakro, the roof window company he has grown to be the second largest such business in the world. "Other kids in school may have had money from their parents; I had money of my own."

Florek's approach to making money was common among the hardheaded peasants of the hills and mountains of southern Poland, who had successfully resisted communist efforts at collectivizing their small farms and who saw nothing wrong with emigrating to make a few dollars or running sawmills or selling produce in private markets. The collapse of strict rules during the stagnation of the 1980s, followed by the reforms of 1989–90, allowed these would-be businessmen to use their talents on a much larger scale than would have been possible had communism survived.

In the 1980s, Florek had opened a window-making factory with a friend, investing money earned as a construction worker in Germany. But while his business did well, in large part thanks to the inefficiencies of state companies that were unable to satisfy demand, the scale of his operations was very limited. At that time it was possible to run a company with almost no bookkeeping, and paying almost no taxes—as long as the size of the business remained small. Regulations allowed for two owner-workers, four employees, and five students. Any bigger, the business would face a flood of paperwork, and crippling taxes as high as 95 percent.

Leszek Czarnecki, now one of Poland's wealthiest men, got his start in the early 1980s as a twenty-two-year-old scuba diver in his native Wrocław. After trying and failing to get included on lucrative foreign commercial diving trips, he opened his own underwater welding company in 1985. In order to conform to regulations that were suspicious of larger enterprises, he had to qualify as a welder; as a tradesman he was allowed to run a small business.

The Krzanowski brothers also figured out how to make money by taking advantage of tax loopholes and lax enforcement. Jerzy, then just seventeen years old, bought a plane ticket to Istanbul. On board, he struck up a conversation with other Poles flying to Turkey, who explained to him where to go and what to buy to make a profit out of the trip. His brother joined him on four subsequent flights, each of them coming home with two suitcases crammed with jeans and leather jackets. "The customs people at the airport never bothered us," says Adam. "It was obvious what we were up to, but no one caused any problems for us."

After the suitcases were stuffed aboard the rattling train for the long trip home to Krosno, each of them turned a two-hundred-dollar profit per trip. This was ten times more than their parents made in a month of work at the glass factory that was the town's largest employer. The two brothers also took the classic jobs of picking strawberries in Norway and painting houses in Western Europe. They went to university, but were much more interested in starting their own business, despite having no money and no experience. In 1989, Adam managed to get hold of a precious work visa to the United States. Jerzy went to Israel. There, with no contacts, he ended up sleeping first on a beach and then on a balcony in an apartment filled with other Poles looking for work, before finding a job as a cook.

Adam's time in New York was a lot rockier. He tried odd jobs, usually with Polish companies. Many either underpaid or didn't pay him at all before firing him. He prepared to head home with his tail between his legs, and nothing close to the twenty thousand dollars he had hoped to earn to start a business with his brother. But before leaving, he scanned a local Polish newspaper and found a want ad posted for a job as an upholsterer at a chair factory. At five dollars an hour the pay wasn't great, but it convinced Adam that it made sense to stay on in the States—illegally, of course—to earn a little more money. Then he got a spot on the assembly line because one of the workers went to jail for killing someone. He moved on to foreman when that job became vacant, and then to supervisor when that man retired. Within a year he had become a key worker in the twenty-employee business, and a protégé of company owner and founder Henry Stern.

Stern took a shine to the young man in part because of their shared past. Stern had grown up in eastern Poland, in what is today western Ukraine, not far from Krosno. His parents died in German death camps but Stern survived the Holocaust, emigrating to the United States after the war. "He always felt sympathy for the region despite the terrible experiences his family had here," says Adam. "He was an amazing person—like a father to me."

Adam was determined to go home to open a business with his brother, who by that time was back in Krosno running a small poolside snack bar. When Stern saw that there was no way to keep Adam in the United States, he sat down with him to discuss business ideas for Poland. Adam had already thought of making chairs similar to the ones he was making in New Jersey, and had sent sketches and ideas home to Jerzy. "I sat down with my bosses and asked if I could make components for them in Poland," he says.

Instead, Stern suggested that they set up a partnership. He flew to Krosno, met the family, and then kicked in thirty thousand dollars while each of the brothers tossed in twenty thousand. More crucially, Stern went with the boys to visit northern Italy, where dozens of small family-owned factories supplied the wheels, springs, and chromed bits and bobs that are crucial components in chairs. "That was a huge advantage for us, because no Polish company could get payment terms in Italy," admits Adam Krzanowski, an owlish man with close-cropped gray hair (his brother looks like a twin despite the four years of age difference). "When Stern went into the meetings with us, he had very good references in northern Italy. When we'd go to the company after that, they would trust us. No other Polish company would have gotten payment terms; it would have been cash on the barrel. We also got exclusive rights to their products for Poland."

In 1992, the brothers rented a commercial space and started to make their first chairs—models aimed at kitchens and restaurants—with the help of Adam's fiancée, Jerzy's girlfriend, and their mother. They loaded a few models into the back of their Polonez—the heavy and underpowered car that was the Polish car industry's Fiat-assisted attempt at producing a modern model in the late 1970s—and began to look for customers. There were no yellow pages, and even white-page telephone books were a rarity. Instead, Adam and his future wife Agnieszka would drive into the center of a town and look for likely shops to pitch their four models of chairs. They spent their nights in campgrounds, and dried their fluttering towels in the back of the car as they drove on to their next destination.

Their luck changed on the other side of the country, in Poznań. There, they drove up to a furniture shop and began their usual pitch.

"We showed him photos of our chairs, and then brought him out to the car, took the chairs out and showed him," remembers Adam. The owner asked where they had bought the chairs, and was dumbfounded when they told him that the chairs were made in Krosno. The furniture store owner said the chairs were much better suited to offices than to houses, and he ordered 150. He also gave them directions to a friend's shop in Bydgoszcz, in north central Poland. That shop, forewarned of their visit, ordered hundreds more. The orders dwarfed the new company's production abilities.

"We didn't know what to do," says Adam. He raced to a post office and booked a phone call to Krosno. After a suitable wait, he got through on a crackling phone line and was told that Jerzy was next door picking cherries. When Jerzy got the news, he went back and told the neighbor, "I'm not gathering cherries any more. I'm rich and I'm going to be making chairs."

The brothers had managed to hit a sweet spot in the rapidly modernizing Polish economy. Fast-growing local and foreign businesses were opening offices around the country, and needed to furnish them. The chairs that were for sale in the country were imported at a markup of more than 200 percent. The brothers decided that their chairs—less expensive to begin with, thanks to cheaper labor—would have no more than a 50-percent markup. By 1993 the business was growing at about 400 percent a year. "It was an Eldorado," says Adam of those early years.

Despite becoming rich very quickly, the brothers concentrated less on spending their newly earned wealth and much more on continuing to grow their business.

That was the same approach adopted by Florek. He had looked around at post-1989 Poland and saw that his halting steps to move from normal windows to making roof windows would never happen unless he moved very fast. Big international companies like Denmark's Velux, as well as a host of Central European start-ups, were becoming interested in the market. "In 1989 I saw that we'd have to speed up or else we'd never get into the market," he says as we dig into bowls of beetroot soup and pork cutlets at the spartan cafeteria that serves both workers and management at Fakro's headquarters in the Tatry mountain town of Nowy Sącz. Florek put aside a slow-moving partner who was cautious about growing too quickly, and set up a new company with his wife and a friend. As befits a proper start-up, he made his first roof windows in a garage before moving on to rented quarters in a disused bus repair yard. Today the enormous space has been entirely taken over by Fakro and is the company's factory and headquarters.

Florek had visited German factories in the 1970s, taking advantage of an introduction letter issued by one of his engineering professors intended to get his students access to Polish plants. The Germans opened their doors as well, allowing the curious Pole to poke around and see how a modern factory functioned. He also hit the upswing in the Polish economy, as thousands of Poles finally had the money and access to building materials to either modernize their poky apartments or build themselves houses on the outskirts of Polish cities. "In 1990 the conditions were super," says Florek wistfully, referring to the laissez-faire rules brought in by Wilczek a year earlier.

Czarnecki, born in 1962, was also growing fast. He sold his share in the underwater welding company in 1991, again because he wanted to grow but his partner did not. "I was a 50 percent owner of the underwater company, and my partner was sixteen years older than me," says Czarnecki, a tightly coiled man who holds international records for deep cave diving and has a fearsome reputation as a quick-tempered and ferocious negotiator. "I wanted to grow very fast and turn the business into a real estate developer. But my partner had already earned more than he thought he would ever need. He is still my friend, but I asked him to buy me out."

At the age of twenty-eight, despite the fat wallet from selling his company, resting on his early success was the furthest thing from Czarnecki's mind. He had already glimpsed a business that had much more potential. In 1990 his company had to lease equipment, then a form of ownership that was almost unknown in Poland. But with many new companies lacking capital but needing everything from cars and computers to bulldozers, leasing was becoming more common. What leasing did exist was usually run by German financial companies, which charged rates of about 60 percent a year, Czarnecki says; but the business made sense, thanks to favorable loopholes in Polish tax law.

With no experience in the business, Czarnecki's new company, the Europejski Fundusz Leasingowy, focused on items like cars, which were easy to take back in case the client didn't make payments. Local, faster, and cheaper than its foreign rivals, EFL exploded in size. "Twenty-five years ago, it was much easier to succeed. It was much easier to make money," says a grinning Czarnecki, sitting in the headquarters of his bank.

The key to the early success of all three businesses was choosing a fast-growing niche—not all that much of a challenge, as just about every part of the long dormant Polish economy was exploding after the return to growth in 1992. It was also the ability of people with no formal business training to learn to manage rapidly growing companies, and then have the discipline to keep pouring profits back into the company rather than spending on consumption. Many business owners never managed that trick, buying themselves flashy cars and Warsaw villas but then quickly finding that their businesses were losing ground in a rapidly maturing economy.

The Krzanowskis' company, Nowy Styl (New Style), was growing so quickly—making thousands of chairs a month—that it started to run into capacity problems with its Italian suppliers. At first the brothers tried to replicate the Italian model by getting Polish companies to make components. But the Poles, whose sense of corporate ethics was still a little rough around the edges, quickly started to sell the same components to Nowy Styl's competitors (the same problem that many Western companies run into in China). "When we saw that, we decided we didn't want our suppliers to become larger than we were," says Adam Krzanowski.

Nowy Styl started to make its own components, which made the company even more price competitive. Next, it ran into trouble finding enough capacity to chrome parts for office chairs. "There were no chair chroming plants anywhere in Central Europe," says Adam. Instead, they bought a car chrome shop in Krosno, bought modern machinery from Italy, and did the work at home. "The goal is always to earn money and increase the size of the company," he says.

But every growth story has to come to an end. For Nowy Styl, that happened in the crisis of 2008. The company had swelled rapidly for more than a decade, even setting up a subsidiary with partners in Ukraine and expanding into Russia. But the onset of the crisis saw a collapse in real estate development, the lifeblood of the office furniture business. Companies hunkered down, laid off workers, and jettisoned plans to move into larger offices. In 2009, sales in Germany, Nowy Styl's largest market, fell by 35 percent. A year later they dropped by a further 17 percent. For the first time the company was forced to fire workers—a crisis in Krosno, which was already reeling from the bankruptcy of the glassworks in which the brothers parents had worked.

The brothers' seat-of-the-pants management style, which was fine in a period of rapid growth, also faced a crisis. They had fallen into the familiar trap of micromanaging almost every decision at their company. They even decided which cargo was to go in which truck. "For final decisions in just about everything, everyone would come to either me or Jurek," says Adam, using the familiar diminutive for his brother's name. "We'd have thousands of people and directors, but a lot of people would still come to us. The year 2008 marked a definite cutoff in the family style of management. We had become a really large company, and the crisis really hit us hard."

To replace a two-man board of brothers, the Krzanowskis brought in three additional professional managers of an age similar to theirs, but with hands-on experience in production, finances, IT systems, and sales. The brothers had spent so much time building the business that they had not acquired any formal management training at all. They also completely re-engineered the way in which the company was structured. Instead of having country managers in charge of all aspects of operations in their geographical territory, the company broke up its national silos, switching to functions like sales and production that cut across countries. They also found that they needed much faster awareness of what was happening in different parts of the business to get a sense of where changes needed to be made. "We started to bring in very advanced control systems for every aspect of the company," says Adam, waving at his almost paperless desk dominated by a single computer. "I can now sit there and look at everything going on in the company."

Nowy Styl now has budgets for every department, and managers who can see exactly what the production costs are for the furniture they are pitching, allowing them to negotiate rapidly with customers. Productivity is monitored every quarter, forecasts are made three months going forward, and the business calculates six different margins along the production cycle, allowing managers to know exactly how much is being earned. "We stopped being a family business and became a professionally managed company," says Adam.

Similar changes were happening elsewhere in Polish business.

Florek had run into his own troubles in the mid-1990s, but his issue was with Polish bureaucrats, not with the global economy. In 1996, he says he was swamped with overlapping investigations and inspections of his companies by aggressive government agencies. Customers took flight, worried that the company would go out of business, and Florek spent most of his time dealing with official paperwork. "I'd spend half my time fighting off these ridiculous charges," he says. At the same time, the company actually won a national business award, although Polish President Aleksander Kwaśniewski ducked the job of personally handing over the prize to the troubled company. Fakro was eventually cleared of all charges, a process that took a decade to wend its way through the lethargic Polish administration.

Today, Florek bitterly complains that his company could have been significantly larger if he had been able to focus on profits and not prosecutors during the late 1990s. "We were trying to educate bureaucrats about how a market economy functions, but I saw that they were mentally still communists. They were good at destroying, not building." He also blames the delay caused by the investigations for hampering his larger struggle with Velux, the Danish firm that is the world's largest roof window producer. In the mid-1990s, the Danes entered the Polish market more aggressively, cutting their prices. "That was the end of the fun," says Florek. The best escape from battling over the Polish market was to expand abroad. Fakro first grew across Eastern Europe in partnership with a German window maker, and then tried to penetrate Western Europe, Asia, and the Americas. Florek also took his complaints about Velux to the European Commission, which launched an investigation into alleged unfair practices by a dominant market player. To his rage, the European Union found no wrongdoing.[1]

Velux dominates Florek's waking moments. During a long visit to his factory and an interview about his company, he spends most of his time angrily denouncing the Danes, accusing them of foul play aimed at hurting his company, which has about 15 percent of global roof window sales. He waves papers documenting Scandinavian perfidiousness, and launches into angry denunciations of his much larger and better-financed rivals. "Vikings have a genetic predisposition to destroy their enemies," he says. "It's very tough to compete against them because they're very good, but they're also trying to finish us off."

Jørgen Tang-Jensen, Velux's CEO, rejects Florek's accusations. "It seems like he has a personal fight with us," he tells me. "We are trying to concentrate on our business, and we think it is a waste of time and not a benefit to customers to run around and use the courts and taxpayers' money to file these allegations."

Whatever the merits of Florek's complaints against Velux, they have forced Fakro to quickly move up the value chain. Florek has seventy engineers working for him, and the company churns out new models from its factories in Ukraine, China, and Poland. Florek's business is also the first Polish company to become a number-two player in any industry, even a niche one like roof windows.

While the Krzanowskis and Florek have patiently continued to build the businesses they founded, Czarnecki has been a lot more opportunistic. He sold EFL in 2001 to France's Crédit Agricole, earning €412 million in what was at the time one of the largest transactions in Polish history. He went cave diving in South Africa, toyed with the idea of going into space, and became bored managing his former company under French direction, selling his remaining stake in 2003.

Instead of spending on yachts, villas, and swimming pools, Czarnecki was looking to jump back into business within weeks of selling out to CA. That's the first time I crossed paths with him. I had been in Warsaw for only a few months for the *Financial Times* when I was invited to a press conference with Czarnecki and Nathaniel Rothschild. The scion of the famous banking family was much more of a draw than Czarnecki, so I headed off to the sparsely attended meeting. "I believe now is the time for banks," Czarnecki proclaimed during the conference, also announcing that he was taking a small Silesian bank with the corny name of Getin and turning it into a national bank. He added that he had "some experience" with consumer finance. Despite his wealth and obvious head for business, the whole idea seemed a little threadbare.

But Czarnecki had also hit on a segment that was about to explode. Until the early 2000s, Polish consumer banking was stunted in comparison to Western Europe. Car loans and home mortgages were still a rarity. Cash transactions—with the buyer bringing along thousands of dollars in plastic bags, all carefully counted by a notary—were not unusual. But as Poles became richer over the 1990s, and as banks, often with the help of their foreign owners, grew more sophisticated, the demand for lending products was poised to surge.

Getin took aim at that nascent demand. The small bank began to aggressively peddle loans, especially those denominated in Swiss francs. Poles, like those in many other nations before them (there was a time when yen-denominated loans were popular in Italy), took loans in foreign currency because the interest rates were significantly lower than for those denominated in zlotys. Getin started its campaign just as Poland's real estate market began to take off, part of the broader economic impact of joining the European Union in 2004. Both Poles and many foreigners leapt into the market. Even Irish taxi drivers banded together to buy whole floors of planned Warsaw apartment buildings, hoping to replicate their recent success on the Dublin property market.

Getin's growth soared. Starting as a bit player in western Poland, a decade later Getin formed the core of Poland's seventh largest bank. Czarnecki has used Getin, now called Getin Noble Bank (acquiring a patina of grandeur), as the core of a financial group that now includes insurance, mortgage brokers, investment fund management, private banking, car loans in Russia and Ukraine, and a host of other services. The model is to piggyback on either clever ideas or existing start-ups, and to bring them into the Getin family. The founders are brought along as well, and are rewarded with access to the group's financial muscle and lucrative stakes in the subsidiaries they manage. The result has been a fast-growing financial empire that gave Czarnecki stability when Poland was hit by the financial crisis in 2008. The real estate market flattened, and then fell. At the same time, the value of the zloty fell steeply against that of the Swiss franc. The seven hundred thousand people with loans in Swiss currency suddenly saw their monthly payments rise and the overall size of their loans skyrocket, leaving many owing more than the value of their properties. Analysts were convinced that Getin, with 70 percent of its loan book taken up by forex lending, was in terrible danger.

But Czarnecki reacted swiftly. The bank stopped all lending in Swiss francs and clamped down on lending in general, while offering enticements to bring in a flood of deposits, which shored up the bank's finances. He froze a vanity project to build one of Europe's tallest residential towers in Wrocław. The bank continued to make a profit and, despite the crisis, continued to grow. It doubled in size from 2008 to 2012. "The market did not properly estimate our selling power," Czarnecki boasted in an interview after the worst of the crisis (which in Poland was never as bad as in Western Europe) had passed. As his group regained stability, he bought four smaller banks and wrote off billions of zlotys in dodgy loans.

The sector's turmoil also forced Czarnecki to move upmarket and to focus more on service than price. While Getin had the reputation of being a cheap and not particularly cheerful bank, where the institution squeezed every possible zloty out of a client, Getin Noble is at least professing to be more "relational," as Czarnecki puts it. The bank jazzed up its logo and is pushing its Noble Bank private banking branches, where customers are treated to cappuccinos and are met in hushed rooms before being pressed to make investments with the bank. "I've never earned money as easily as I do now," Czarnecki boasts.

Still, the turmoil unleashed by the problems of Swiss franc borrowers eventually hit Czarnecki as well. He's still one of Poland's wealthiest men, but he is no longer a dollar billionaire.

The Krzanowskis were also able to survive the 2008 crisis by scrambling up the value chain. Instead of just making cheap but good office chairs, the company decided to invest in a new factory in Jasło, twenty miles west of Krosno. The factory is completely automated. An architect can now get the company's information on designs for chairs, desks, and other office furniture, incorporate it directly into their blueprints, price it, look at a three-dimensional mockup, and then send the order to the factory, the most modern of its type in Europe. Nowy Styl also has consultants and interior designers who work with architects in planning new offices. This is about much more than putting bums in office chairs.

"We started with economical sales and cheap products," says Adam Krzanowski. "But over twenty years we have raised our quality and our level of service. We spend a lot of time and money on designing and perfecting our product; we want to be innovative and have something new to offer our clients."

The emphasis on quality has also prevented Nowy Styl from shifting production to China. Although cheap Chinese office chairs are now found in hypermarkets across Poland, the company finds that it is better able to keep an eye on quality, and to react more quickly to changing customer demands, by leaving its factories closer to home. Going upmarket has also meant being more focused on costs, and recognizing that Poland is no longer a cheap country in which to do business. "In the past, it didn't matter if we had five people standing on a production line instead of spending a hundred thousand euros on a machine so that only one person would be there. It didn't pay. Now it does," says Adam.

Nowy Styl has also bought two smaller German rivals. One, Rhode & Graal, a German family company, was bought in 2013 because of the brothers' affability and knack for turning rivals into friends. The owner, Peter Rhode, was over seventy-five years old, and his family wasn't interested in taking over the business. He called the brothers and said, "Boys, I'd like to sell and I like you. Do you want to buy the company?"

They did. And after paying forty million euros, they had a German brand in their portfolio. Now Polish engineers are helping the Germans improve their efficiency, a helping hand that many of the Germans still find a little difficult to accept from a neighbor whose economy was once literally a byword for sloppiness and disorganization. Looking back on their breathtaking rise, the brothers, together worth about $180 million, acknowledge that they started at a unique time. "We were in the right place at the right time and met the right people," says Adam. "If it had been a little different it might not have worked. I can't imagine starting a business now. I think young people now have it much more difficult. When we were starting in the 1990s there was nothing here; it was a desert. Now it's not so easy because the market has been occupied. You really have to have a fantastic idea and come up with a truly innovative product or service."

Czarnecki agrees, though not completely. Obviously, conditions in a developed market economy are vastly different from those in a slapdash country racing from communism to capitalism. Until the mid-1990s, success was fairly easy for anyone starting a business, because competition was low and the demand for products was high. The problem was that the size of the economy and its primitive nature meant that truly outstanding entrepreneurs were limited in what they could do. While that may not have mattered to people keen on buying a nice house and a fast car with their company earnings, Czarnecki felt that it placed a ceiling on his ambitions. "Until the mid-1990s, you could not reach a larger scale," he says. "There was no capital, no financing, no qualified workers. But today, if you are truly exceptional, you can build a billion-euro business in just a few years."

The catch, as in other developed economies, is to be truly exceptional.

"Now if you are not exceptional, you have no chance," Czarnecki says, fixing me with his intense stare. "But if you are exceptional, then the sky is the limit. As your business grows, you are in touch with ever more intelligent and demanding people. The abilities needed are harder and harder to attain, and some people can never achieve them."

The first rush of Polish capitalism produced a lot of accidental entrepreneurs. But those who rose to the very top ended up having characteristics similar to those of entrepreneurs who have done well in more advanced countries. Many of the people on the wealthiest list showed a penchant for business even during the unfavorable times of communism. Once they had started a business, they often proved to be more aggressive than their initial partners, eschewing the goal of financing a comfortable life for the greater ambition of building a truly large company.

As Poland changed, becoming more sophisticated and wealthier, businesses had to do the same or else succumb to domestic and foreign competitors. Today, Nowy Styl is the third largest office furniture maker in Europe. Florek has seen off start-up competitors from across Central Europe, and is now doing battle with his sector's leading company. The early 1990s saw a host of often very shaky Polish financial institutions spring up, some of them failing spectacularly and taking investors' money with them. Czarnecki has survived and is now head of one of Poland's leading financial groups.

Although today's business environment is very different, there are still opportunities, but the skills needed to find and take advantage of them are a lot tougher than investing twenty thousand dollars and beginning to build chairs with your mother and girlfriends.

There's also the danger of politics—especially with a ruling party that is deeply suspicious of business and wealth. Jarosław Kaczyński, the Law and Justice Party's leader, told voters in 2015 that he "doesn't believe in" rankings of the richest Poles.[2] "I feel that if someone has money, they got it from somewhere," he said.

Jerzy Krzanowski was one of the first Polish business leaders to feel that suspicion on his own skin. He was arrested in May 2016 in a highly publicized operation by the government's anticorruption agency, on accusations of exerting improper pressure on public officials and money laundering. He insists that he did nothing wrong, and within days it turned out that Nowy Styl had requested the unblocking of a bank guarantee tied to the construction of the Jasło factory—something it had the right to do, as the project had long since been completed.

The issue has since gone quiet, but Nowy Styl isn't the first company to suffer a run-in with Polish authorities.

10 Crushed by Capitalism–

OR BY THE VISIBLE HAND OF THE GOVERNMENT?

There's a bitter Polish joke that Poland's success was built despite rather than because of the government. There's something to that. Although some businesses have been brought low thanks to missteps by their owners and managers–the same kind of thing that leads to bankruptcies everywhere in the world–many have also been undone by the country's bureaucracy, courts, and prosecutors.

Capitalism, to resurrect the hoary quote from Austrian economist Joseph Schumpeter, famously involves "creative destruction." Although the early years of communism were very good at destruction, the creation part was a bit harder for Communist Party cadres. By the mid-1950s, the system lost much of its ability to either destroy or create, and the country sank into a stagnation that left people poor but stable.

Capitalism is different. Communist propaganda had warned about the evils of unemployment, with gripping stories about homeless people roaming the streets of American cities. The experience of unemployment and economic failure were much rarer in the lukewarm bath of Central European communism. All that changed after 1990. Failure became an option, as Balcerowicz's reforms quickly made plain.

In the 1980s, communist Poland was actually an enormously profitable place in which to do business. Of course you needed some level of connections with the apparatchiks who ran the place, but once the paperwork was done, double-digit (and occasionally triple-digit) returns on investment were the norm; failure was a rarity. The reason was that Poles were starved of consumer goods, thanks to the inability of the state to provide exotic items like shoes, jeans, and shaving cream.

Although Polish salaries were derisory when converted into hard currency, hundreds of thousands of Poles regularly worked abroad, picking strawberries in Norway or grapes in France, or painting English houses. That, plus remittances from relatives living permanently abroad, meant that almost every Pole had access to dollars, marks, and pounds, and was keen to spend the money on something better than the tatty goods that could be obtained after standing for hours or days in a grumpy queue.

Jerzy Wiśniewski, who in 1994 founded PBG, an engineering and construction firm, remembers making a return of at least 50 percent a year when he started. "It was a whole lot easier to start a business back then," he says. "There wasn't a lot of paperwork. The whole of Poland was a start-up; regulations still hadn't caught up to the market economy. And our profits were enormous. Whatever you touched at the time turned to gold."

Although the conditions after 1990 may have favored new businesses, that didn't mean there weren't failures. Initially, those hit the hardest were either existing businesses set up as state industries over the decades of communist rule, or the often ramshackle manufacturing companies built up in the 1980s. Many of those private companies existed only because Poland was a largely closed market starved of basic consumer goods. Many substandard local factories churning out "luxury" products like soap and deodorant collapsed when faced with real competition. First there was a wave of imports as Poles took trains to Berlin and Vienna and returned with Western branded products, which were better made and had infinitely more cachet than the stuff made at home. Then foreign producers began to ship products on their own, and many quickly set up production in Poland.

Local businesses faced a double threat: rising competition and the difficulties caused by Balcerowicz's reforms. This was a problem hammered at by Grzegorz Kołodko, who was twice finance minister under the ex-Communists, first from 1994 to 1997 and again from 2002 to 2003. Kołodko, an old classmate and a fierce ideological rival of Balcerowicz, feels a softer approach in the very beginning may have saved more Polish businesses. He has been a vociferous critic of the neoliberal "Washington Consensus," which formed the intellectual basis for Poland's reforms, and of the costs of shock therapy, many of which he feels were unnecessary. He says that Balcerowicz brought about a too-steep devaluation of the zloty, penalized companies too harshly for increasing worker salaries, raised interest rates too high, and opened the country too widely to free trade.[1]

"The fall in production was not accompanied by the elimination of the most ineffective companies . . . in the main it affected companies servicing the domestic consumer market," he writes.[2] "What was eliminated from the market was not the production that was the biggest problem for the budget and for the whole economy, but that which we should have had an interest in retaining."

Added to this were the problems created by Balcerowicz's 1990 reforms, particularly his efforts to stamp out inflation. Soaring inflation had initially been a sweet bonus for nascent private businesses, because Poland's primitive banks had not figured out how to keep real interest rates positive. That meant that inflation quickly eroded the value of loans—only suckers weren't indebted up to their eyeballs. But all that changed under the new government. At the beginning of 1990 the central bank set one of its benchmark rates at 432 percent, and commercial banks went even higher. What had seemed like easy money suddenly turned into a stranglehold on new businesses, which had no way of generating the revenues necessary to repay those loans.

Farmers like Andrzej Lepper, the populist politician who rose to become deputy prime minister, were bankrupted by the steep interest rates, as were thousands of companies. Added to that, hundreds of state-owned companies also failed in the first few years after 1990. Part of that failure was due to managers "tunneling" their company's assets into new private firms, and leaving behind indebted shells. Other state companies tried unsuccessfully to adapt to the new market conditions—but with no experience in marketing, finance, product development, or management, they failed.

Tougher conditions quickly started decimating weaker companies.

In 1990 there were only 168 corporate bankruptcies: 8 state owned companies, 68 cooperatives, and 87 private firms. By 1992 that number had jumped to 940, of which private firms accounted for 552.[3] These companies went bankrupt because of the shock of the reforms. The years since have seen a steady number of corporate failures, many of them going bust for the same prosaic reasons that drive companies into bankruptcy everywhere: mismanagement, incorrect market assumptions, flawed products, and overly aggressive financing. Simply the normal churn of a market economy.

One good example is the failure of William Carey, a stout and sandy-haired American who abandoned the lower levels of the professional golf circuit in the United States to launch a business in Poland in 1990. He was one of the first foreigners to show up in what was still a very unstable economy. He started importing and exporting agricultural products for his father's business, but quickly branched out into importing beer, especially Australia's Foster's (this was the era of *Crocodile Dundee*), to Poles who had had no access to such glamorous brands. By 2005 his Central European Distribution Company was importing and manufacturing vodka, and had taken a quarter of the Polish market.

In 2008, Carey hosted a group of local reporters at a private club for an opulent lunch where he talked about how well his company was doing—it had revenues of $1.5 billion and profits of $250 million—and his ideas for the future. In retrospect, his plan should have set alarm bells ringing, because it was more or less the same vision as those of Napoleon and Hitler: to conquer Russia. This time, though, instead of drowning Russia in blood, Carey wanted to do it in vodka. And he needed an enormous amount of money—almost all of it borrowed—to do so. "Our biggest advantage is that we know what happened in Poland and we can see what is going to happen in Russia," he said at the time. "Russia is almost a mirror of what happened in Poland."

Not quite.

Carey ended up gorging on more than $1 billion in debt in 2008 in order to buy big stakes in three Russian distillers, and for a short time he was the leading vodka producer in the fiery liquor's spiritual home. The problem was that, later the same year, Lehman Brothers collapsed and the global financial crisis started, making life very dangerous for anyone with too much debt. Adding to Carey's troubles, Russia brought in draconian taxes and tough new regulations in one of the government's periodic (and invariably failed) attempts to get Russians to drink less and work more. In addition, Russians, especially richer urban Russians, were following in the footsteps of Poles and shifting away from vodka to more fashionable wine and beer. Hammered on all sides by trends he had failed to foresee, Carey ended up losing control of his largely bankrupt company in 2012 to Roustam Tariko, a Russian oligarch.

Carey's rise and fall was nothing unusual. That kind of thing happens in his native Florida all the time and is increasingly common in Poland, as attested by the turnover in storefronts and restaurants in shopping malls and on Polish streets. However, there was still a subset of Polish business failures that were significantly different from those in many more settled capitalist countries—failures in which the government had a hand. In some cases, the problem was that regulators set rules in a legalistic way without thinking through their full consequences, as happened in the road construction sector.

When enormous sums of money started to flood from Brussels into Poland after 2004, the country finally began to upgrade its terrible roads. In 1990 the country's only highway was a bit of the old Berlin-to-Breslau autobahn, built under Adolf Hitler. The road was in such a terrible state of repair that, although it theoretically was four lanes wide, drivers could really only use two, thanks to the enormous potholes that looked as if they had been laid down by a rolling artillery barrage. Cars had to carefully slalom from one lane to the next to keep the bottoms of their vehicles from being ripped out. There had been ambitious plans to build highways rapidly after 1989, but they came to very little. The problem was a tangled legal system that made it very difficult to expropriate land—a pendulum swing against communist-era nationalizations—and a lack of money. West Germany had almost bankrupted itself in upgrading the tattered infrastructure of East Germany. Poland had no wealthy sugar daddy to foot the bill, so progress was very slow.

That changed after Poland joined the European Union. Money from Brussels revived long-stalled infrastructure projects. This was where Kulczyk showed abilities beyond being a transaction facilitator. Autostrady Wielkopolskie, a construction firm in which he owned a quarter share, first built a section of Poland's main east-west A2 highway near his native Poznań. By 2011 the company had built the final section linking central Poland to the German frontier and the autobahns beyond. Other businesses also expected to make a fortune in construction, and there were good reasons for making that assumption. Building companies looked at the experience of Spain, Portugal, Ireland, and Greece, which had also used the EU's largesse to rapidly build highways and railways. In the process, they had also created huge construction companies that had grown fat from local contracts and then begun to win bids across the continent.

That is what turned Wiśniewski's head as well. Until then he had focused very successfully on the gas market, a sector he understood well. He had been an engineer for Poland's state-owned gas monopoly—supplementing his income with "humiliating" trips to France to pick grapes, where he would earn as much in one day as he would in two weeks back home. In 1994 he opened a business supplying gas pressure systems he had bought in the United States. The company he started with his wife began in a garage; it was another of the many Polish businesses flaunting their garage pedigree. To get his start he pooled all of his money and that of his wife, family, and partners, and scraped together the three hundred thousand dollars he needed to buy equipment from the United States. A decade later, his business, PBG, was listed on the Warsaw Stock Exchange; and by 2007 it had made the index of the country's largest companies.

The business had slowly grown from gas to other utilities. But this was also the time when the Polish government had just won the right to host the 2012 European soccer championships together with Ukraine, and had decided to use the deadline to push through a very rapid road- and stadium-building program. "I thought it was a one-way bet," says Wiśniewski. "There was a danger of losing the market if I didn't jump in."

He leapt in with both feet and he wasn't alone. Lots of other construction companies, many of them with Spanish, Irish, and other European partners, sensed that the government had finally broken open its road construction piggy bank. PBG ended up getting contracts to build three of the four stadiums that would be used to host the soccer matches, including Warsaw's prestigious National Stadium being built atop the old communist stadium that had been turned into one of Europe's largest bazaars. The company also won bids to build sections of highway.

But there was a problem. The Polish government was being extremely careful in how it allocated the contracts. Construction companies raced each other to the bottom, undercutting each other's bids in order to win tenders. In other countries such techniques had paid off, as the contract winner would be able to renegotiate the final price with the government road-building agency when it became apparent that the bid was much too low to actually make economic sense. But the Polish bureaucrats didn't budge. The price bid was the price paid—no wiggle room. Warsaw's worry was that if officials started changing existing contracts, they would get into trouble with other bidders who had lost out on the job. They also feared running afoul of controllers from Brussels, who could demand that crucial EU money be returned. "We could not allow ourselves to lose these funds, not to get reimbursed," said Lech Witecki, head of the road-building agency at the time of the crisis. In addition to those difficulties, fuel, asphalt, steel, and other raw materials saw unanticipated increases in price.

The result was a bloodbath. Many big companies went bankrupt. Poland has not managed to produce a single successful construction firm. And the biggest failure of all was Wiśniewski's PBG. He got into a tremendous fight with the government over payment for his work on soccer stadiums, especially the one in Warsaw. His road-building contracts weren't paying off, and all this was happening while he had over-leveraged himself buying up other infrastructure companies. Banks, worried about the state of PBG's finances, backed away, leaving Wiśniewski hanging. "We were hurt by a domino effect," he says. "As we started to run into financing problems, they would reduce our credit lines."

PBG's shares, which had topped out at four hundred zlotys in 2007, plummeted in value. In the summer of 2012, when the tournament was kicking off in downtown Warsaw, the share price had fallen to less than nine zlotys, a drop of more than 90 percent over its value a year earlier. PBG declared bankruptcy. Two years later it was trading at less than two zlotys a share—a drop of more than 99 percent from its peak, and a painful lesson for punters and for Wiśniewski about the consequences of bad decisions.

Wiśniewski, who had scrambled high in the ranks of Poland's wealthiest people, and who had been seen as an example of an honest and hardworking success story, turned from hero to villain. "All I'm left with from roads and stadiums are disputes and debts," Wiśniewski, a small man with closely cropped gray hair, says sadly. He was also left with a lot of debt, as much as $1 billion, and a lot of very angry bondholders.

He was forced out of the management of PBG, but scrambled back in 2014, determined to revive his company. The plan was to get back to the gas business he actually understood, and to leave behind the nightmare of roads. The problem now is that his reputation is in tatters, banks are still leery of him, and the government has not shown much inclination to step in and rescue PBG. "This is the biggest corporate disaster of Poland's otherwise fantastic economic transformation," Wiśniewski says glumly. "If I hadn't gone into infrastructure, I'd still be beloved by investors." A large part of PBG's collapse stemmed from the problematic interface between Poland's public and private sectors, but the bulk of the blame lies with Wiśniewski and his decision to leap into an area he understood so poorly.

However, there are other corporate failures in which the entrepreneur chose a market well, built up a company, and become a success, only to have the whole effort destroyed by government functionaries who, after many years of desultory investigation, turn out to have been acting entirely incorrectly and sometimes illegally. Those are the cases that give Polish business nightmares and make foreigners wary of investing in a country that otherwise looks very attractive.

Roman Kluska is bald, mousy man with a sandy little moustache, while Tomasz Czechowicz is tall, brash, and a bit of a clotheshorse. But both men were once seen as epitomizing the up-by-their-bootstraps successes of early Polish capitalism, and both crashed thanks to ill-conceived tax investigations that saw one arrested and the other's company driven into bankruptcy.

Kluska hails from Brzesko, a village in the foothills of the Tatra mountains, a place better known for its salty sheep's cheese and for peasants sporting their unique mountain wear of flannel pants and wide-brimmed black hats, than for any business accomplishments. Born in 1954, Kluska began dabbling in computers in the 1980s, when he imported some of the novel machines to the car repair plant where he worked. In 1988 he began importing computer parts and assembling his first computers. The demand for computers sold at accessible prices was so enormous that by 1994 Kluska's company, Optimus, had one of Europe's ten largest computer assembly factories in the mountain town of Nowy Sącz.[4] In that year he sold one hundred thousand computers, half of all the computers sold in Poland. He also launched his company on the Warsaw Stock Exchange. Kluska and Optimus became the symbols of a new and successful Poland—one where a Pole could compete head to head against Western rivals and win. His 1996 meeting with Bill Gates, who advised him to get into the internet, was his crowning glory.[5]

Something similar was happening at the same time on the other side of the country in Legnica, in what had been the largest Soviet garrison in Poland. There, Czechowicz, born in 1970, was building his company, called JTT, also assembling and selling computers into the very hot Polish market. Computers had been a rarity in communist Poland, but Czechowicz saw his first one thanks to his father, who worked at the local technical university. He quickly started to pull them apart, learning how to make and program them. While still in high school, he would assemble Bulgarian floppy disc drives into metal frames, add programs that would allow them to interface with the popular Commodore 64 computer, and then sell them for about $150 at the computer bazaars that had sprung up in most Polish cities. His cost? Ten dollars for each machine. In high school, where his teachers were earning about fifteen dollars a month, Czechowicz drove his own car and spent weekends at Warsaw's fanciest hotel, selling his drives and, later, computer programs.

After 1989 he started traveling to Berlin, trolling the wealthier districts of Germany's former and soon-to-be capital, buying up aging computer hardware. "I was making a thousand marks a weekend. I'd buy three computers there, refurbish them, and then sell them in Poland," says Czechowicz, dressed in a tieless gray suit, explaining his rise and fall and rise again in a loud Starbucks café in central Warsaw. He set up JTT with some friends. First he flooded the Polish market with the popular and cheap Commodore 64, selling more than a million a year and quickly becoming one its largest European buyers. Selling at a margin of only 5 percent, Czechowicz killed off much of the competition by generating enormous volumes. By 1991, at the age of twenty-one, he was a dollar millionaire.

He agrees that it was much easier to start a business in the early 1990s that it is today. "Today, business advances by millimeters; then it was in centimeters or maybe even meters. That means that now you have to be precise, to have a long-term plan, and to be able to manage risk. Then it was mega-chaotic, there was a lot of randomness. But if we could go back, with the knowledge we have now, to those conditions, we'd all be billionaires."

Knowing he had no clue how to run a fast growing business, Czechowicz hired accountants and legal experts from state companies, who had both the knowledge and the connections to protect

JTT. "A lot of companies collapsed because they had problems with receivables," says Czechowicz.

JTT became Optimus's main rival—with the two trading pole position through the 1990s. But by the early 2000s, JTT was out of business, Czechowicz had lost almost all of his money and Kluska had been arrested in a lightening dawn raid by gun toting policemen, handcuffed and forced to spend the night in jail.

The problem was the Byzantine Polish tax code. In December 1989, one of the new government's aims was to quickly improve the quality of Poland's education system and to speed up research and computerization. That's why imports of educational materials and computers were spared a 22 percent VAT payment. But domestic computer makers, somewhat bizarrely, were not. "Looking at the government's priorities, which included the restructuring of the existing economic system, battling the economic crisis as well as reviving the economy, one has to acknowledge that the goal of the regulation was to 'cheapen' so called investment imports," noted a later finance ministry investigation into the affair.[6]

Both JTT and Optimus hit on the same solution: export their computers and then re-import them from subsidiaries in neighboring countries like the Czech Republic, thus avoiding the tax. Even the government seemed to approve of this maneuver, with the education ministry well aware of how Optimus was supplying cheap computers to Polish schools. But the gambit was always a bit perilous. Kluska sold Optimus in April 2000 because, as he later revealed, he foresaw the clouds gathering over his business. Tax inspectors pounced on both companies (JTT in 1999 and Optimus in the new millennium) and demanded enormous sums of back taxes together with steep fines. Kluska was arrested in 2002 and freed on eight million zlotys bail.[7] JTT's management was accused of improprieties, and the company was charged for back taxes. It closed its doors in 2004.

"I was at the very top and I was reset to zero," says Czechowicz.

By 2003, the courts found that tax inspectors had made a mistake in accusing the companies of avoiding the taxes, and that re-exporting was legal. Kluska received five thousand zlotys in compensation for his arrest. He was briefly seen as the symbol of how the state apparatus can easily crush an honest entrepreneur, and was even considered for the post of economy minister in 2005. As for JTT, a court cleared management of charges in 2004, and the government returned twenty million zlotys to the company. In 2006, MCI Management, an investment firm created by Czechowicz that held 40 percent of JTT's shares, filed a case against the finance ministry for losses suffered during the investigation. Since 2011 courts have ruled for and against paying damages—at one point deciding that the company was owed as much as 38.5 million zlotys, while other courts backtracked. The case is still unresolved, but Czechowicz vows to continue fighting for what he says would be the largest ever compensation for bureaucrats improperly killing a company.

The finance ministry report found that, although there had been mistakes in legal interpretation, there had been no wrongdoing on the part of government officials in either case. "The taxes charged have been returned," said the report. "However, there is still the issue of losses, which are difficult to compensate. For that reason, the Finance Minister expresses regrets."

Kluska, a deeply pious man who is a fan of the mystical writings of Polish Saint Mary Faustina Kowalska, has since retreated from the public eye and runs an artisanal sheep's milk cheese business. I once spent several weeks pursuing him to try and do a profile of his experiences; no phone calls were returned. I ran into him in Warsaw and buttonholed him for an interview, but he just smiled wanly and said that he really didn't want any more publicity.

Kluska is still one of Poland's wealthiest people, placing seventy-eighth on the 2014 list prepared by *Forbes*, with assets of 335 million zlotys. Czechowicz, who has since turned MCI into one of Central Europe's leading high-tech venture capital funds, is worth 484 million zlotys, according to the magazine. Both men were rich enough so that their brushes with the Polish authorities, although bruising, were not fatal. The same is not the case for people who lack the financial resources to defend themselves and to mobilize public opinion on their behalf: people like Paweł Rey and Lech Jeziorny.

Today's Poland is in some sense a creation of people like Jeziorny and Rey. They both come from Kraków. A city of universities, cafés, and intellectuals, as well as home to thousands of dispossessed aristocrats (Rey's background), the city was always a center of opposition to the Communists. That was the reason why the party built the hulk of the Nowa Huta steel mill within smoking distance of the city's medieval core, hoping to dissolve Kraków's bourgeois sensibilities in a tide of peasants turned workers. It didn't work. In fact, as the workers' children became educated, they ended up absorbing a lot of the values of the next-door intelligentsia.

Jeziorny and Rey were steeped in that anticommunist culture, and both took an active part in rebelling against the system in the 1970s and 1980s. The authorities interned both men after the 1981 declaration of martial law. Rey spent four months in a communist prison for cementing a memorial plaque commemorating the Solidarity union on Kraków's main square. Once out, Rey, a lanky man with a scraggly beard who is a passionate skydiver, opened a small electronics shop on a dingy Kraków street. After 1990 he set up and sold a couple of computer companies, and then was hired to manage the assets of a government-owned company that had properties across Kraków. Jeziorny, who had spent seven months behind bars after martial law, quickly scrambled up into the higher levels of Poland's new management class, which was being formed after 1990. He was investment director at Magna Polonia, a management firm running one of the investment funds set up to manage the privatization program. He also served on the boards of several large companies.

The two were close friends of the former Solidarity activists who now ruled the country. Intelligent and experienced, they seemed to be destined for the top levels of the postcommunist elite. They both looked at the tangle of properties owned by the new investment funds in Kraków, which included an outdated slaughterhouse not far from downtown. They came up with an audacious plan: to do a management buyout of the meatpacking factory, sell off the factory's potentially lucrative properties in the center of the city, and open a modern meat factory on the outskirts that belonged originally to Magna Polonia.

The two friends, with several other partners, undertook a series of complex transactions. They bought an old milk factory—the site of the future meat packing plant—while securing planning permission to turn the old slaughterhouse, located less than a mile from Kraków's royal castle, into a new shopping mall. By 2003 their plans seemed to be working. They had an agreement with GTC, one of Poland's largest developers, to turn the red brick slaughterhouse into a mall. By April, the new plant had opened. It met all of the EU sanitary rules, and it employed three hundred people. A bishop even showed up in full liturgical regalia to douse the new project in holy water. Next, Jeziorny and his partners decided to find an investor interested in the meat plant and sell either a share of it or the full business. Rey traveled to a trade show in Poznań and made contact with a potential investor; the gamble seemed to be on the verge of paying off.

That's when the tax authorities and the prosecutor's office stepped in. Armed police officers wearing balaclavas swooped in and arrested Jeziorny, Rey, and their partners. They were accused of swindling money from Krakmeat, their meat plant. They also faced accusations of impropriety with regards to Polmozbyt, a car parts company on whose board Rey and Jeziorny sat. Prosecutors triumphantly announced they that had unmasked a powerful group of crooked businesspeople. "We were acting openly and legally," says Rey. "We didn't try to hide anything. We were aware of business risks, but we didn't recognize how things really worked."

Jeziorny was taken off to Kraków's Montelupi prison—an old Austro-Hungarian barracks that had been a prison for the Gestapo during World War II before smoothly shifting to serve as a prison for the Communist secret police. It is now Kraków's municipal jail. Jeziorny remembers sitting in the offices of the Central Bureau of Investigations (Poland's equivalent of the FBI) and seeing Rey's mobile phone, with its ringer turned off, lighting up again and again, the number of the potential investor flashing on the small screen. "We were in the middle of a very complicated transaction and now we were in jail; it was very emotional," says Jeziorny. We are talking in an Italian restaurant at the Galeria Kazimierz shopping mall, the place where Jeziorny and Rey used to sit in their office and listen to the squeals of pigs being herded on the road outside their window to their looming deaths in the nearby slaughterhouse. "Of course, after our arrests, the investor fled," he says.

Rey ended up in an even more primitive prison in Gliwice, in western Poland.

It was nine months before the two were released. Polish prosecutors have a tendency to lock up potential suspects without trial for months or even years at a time while they build cases against them. The practice has been widely condemned by human rights groups and has raised eyebrows in Brussels; various governments have talked of reform, but prosecutors fight hard to keep a method that makes it much easier for them to break suspects.

Speaking at his trial on the Polmozbyt charges, a decade after his initial arrest, Jeziorny said, "In three different jails over nine months I was kept with people who were mentally ill, accused of murder or rape or armed robbery. I was given the status of a dangerous criminal belonging to an organized criminal enterprise and, probably 'just to be safe,' for the first three months I was prevented from seeing my wife and children, and the letters I sent them took a month to reach home."[8]

Once released, Jeziorny and Rey were barred from taking management roles at any company, and their reputation was in tatters. With no investor, the meat plant went bankrupt, costing three hundred jobs. "I came out of jail with 207 zlotys, which was the sum total of all my assets," says Rey.

The case surrounding the Krakmeat slaughterhouse transaction against the two began to fray. Initially, authorities deemed the idea of a management buyout suspicious, apparently not understanding that it was a procedure allowed under Polish law. Although the charges began to disappear one after another, the investigation continued year after year. At the same time, while they were in jail, something strange was happening at Polmozbyt. Sixteen senior managers and board members at the company had been arrested. Jerzy Jakielarz, the head of the local tax inspection office, alerted prosecutors to possible misdeeds. The state treasury, which owned 15 percent of the company, demanded a shareholders' meeting to deal with the situation. When the meeting was called, only 23 percent of the shareholders were represented. The person with power of attorney over the shares of those people being held in jail was prevented from attending the meeting. Jakielarz was made the chairman of the board.

Not long afterward, a savvy investor began to buy up the company's shares far below the market price. A newspaper investigation found that he took control of Polmozbyt for about six hundred thousand zlotys.[9] The company had nine outlets in southern Poland, each with a car dealership and repair facilities. Rey estimates the value of its real estate assets at more than one hundred million zlotys. The whole procedure was investigated, and a court ended up ruling that the takeover was illegal, as the initial shareholders meeting had been improperly called. The court also ruled, however, that the transaction could not be annulled. Jeziorny and Rey had sold their shares in Polmozbyt in 2001 to finance the Krakmeat transaction, but Polmozbyt's shadow continued to follow them.

After six years of investigation, a court in 2009 gave prosecutors until the end of that year to file charges or drop the Krakmeat case. In his ruling, the judge wrote: "The reason for the long investigation is the improper practice of first presenting accusations and then trying to verify them. . . . The procedure should be reversed." The prosecutor's office released a ninety-six-page report finding that Jeziorny and Rey had done nothing wrong in the Krakmeat case. "The evidence does not support the case that the suspects created and led an organized criminal enterprise," it read. It added that the two had been justified in taking an economic risk to save the meat packing plant, because without that the factory was certain to go bankrupt.

"The final report of the prosecutor's office shows that we were the victims of an assault and robbery," says Rey.

"This was something amazing," adds Jeziorny. "These sorts of things happen in Ukraine. They aren't supposed to happen in Poland."

There was one difference. In Poland, unlike in Ukraine, prosecutors were unaffected by politics. Although Jeziorny and Rey were close friends with some of the most powerful people in the country—one of their lawyers went on to become justice minister—the wheels of justice, misguided or not, continued to grind on no matter who was in power in Warsaw.

The two businessmen are still fighting for compensation for the damages they suffered in the case. Rey founded an organization of entrepreneurs who had been harmed by the actions of the state, with dozens of businesspeople sharing stories similar to his own. A film based on their story, *A Closed Conspiracy,* hit the screens in 2013, telling the story of three factory owners destroyed by a conspiracy of tax inspectors and prosecutors. Ryszard Bugajski, the director, was best known for making a powerful film in the 1980s about a brutal interrogation during Stalinist times. The parallels between the two subjects are not completely coincidental.

Jeziorny and Rey are still not in the clear. Prosecutors continued their very slow investigation of the Polmozbyt case, accusing the two businessmen and their partners of illegally draining assets from the company. The two were hauled back into court in 2013. In an emotional speech to the presiding judge, Jeziorny said, "This trial which is coming to a close is a form of judgment on economic freedom and the ability of the prosecuting authorities to interfere with it."[10]

The judge was unmoved, and she convicted them of acting to harm Polmozbyt by extracting money from the company. Jeziorny was handed a two-year suspended sentence and fined 156,000 zlotys. Rey received a suspended sentence of one year and eight months and a

90,000 zloty fine. In her explanation of the verdict, the judge said, "A so-called management buyout is only possible when it is backed by appropriate capital and managers with concrete ideas." She said that was not the case with Polmozbyt.[11] Jeziorny's protests that MBOs were entirely legal in Poland, and that their legality was not dependent on whether they were leveraged, fell on deaf ears.

While cases like Rey and Jeziorny's are rare, they are not completely unknown, and the fear of arousing the ire of the tax authorities or of the prosecutor's office is palpable among Polish businessmen. Part of the problem stems from Polish legal culture and its turbulent historic heritage; Poland's bureaucrats and criminal justice system have an Austro-Hungarian or Russian pettifogging attachment to paperwork and procedures. That is overlaid with a bloody-minded approach dating from communist times. Governments have seen the problem and have tried to tackle it. Some areas have improved. Opening a business is much easier now than it was a decade ago, when reams of paperwork and visits to half a dozen offices for all important stamps and certificates were needed to get the job done. As a result, Poland has seen a steady ascent up the tables in the World Bank's Doing Business rankings, where every country's courts and bureaucratic procedures are compared. The metric has become increasingly important for foreign investors, and Poland has made a particular effort to tackle areas measured by the bank.

But there is a general view among many entrepreneurs that Poland's economic success has been achieved *despite* the government and not because of it. Cases like Jeziorny and Rey's buttress that position. And the new Law and Justice government is likely to be more suspicious of business. Zbigniew Ziobro, the justice minister, has been given control over the prosecutor's office, and there has been a noticeable uptick in high-profile criminal investigations launched against business executives.

11 New Businesses

Most of this book has been about the entrepreneurs who took advantage of the unique circumstances of 1989 to found companies and become rich. That explosion of business creation helped make Poland the most successful of all the postcommunist countries, and powered more than a decade of growth. Although the era immediately after 1989 was singular, younger Poles have continued to open companies–albeit in a much more competitive environment than their predecessors.

In 2012 I got a call from a businessman I had never heard of. Tomasz Kułakowski was calling to see whether he could set up a meeting with a *Financial Times* correspondent to explain how he was building a new business. Not having all that much to do that day, I arranged to meet him at the Blikle café and wandered over. Tomasz, a bald man in his thirties wearing a good suit and a wide grin, sat in a booth along with three of his partners. Their tiny company, CodiLime, had hit on the model of using talented Polish programmers to code for Western businesses, taking advantage of Poland's traditionally strong computer skills and low labor costs. Tomasz ended our conversation by saying, "If you ever come up with an idea for a business, think of us, as we'd be able to help you put it together."

A year later I met him again, this time in the executive breakfast room of Warsaw's Intercontinental hotel, with a window view of the capital's dirty gray apartment blocks interspersed with new glass skyscrapers and the bulk of the Stalinist Palace of Culture. Now, the company was up to twenty-four employees and was breaking even on revenues of just over $1.5 million. The business was having no trouble attracting top talent—people who had the chance to work for big salaries at some of the world's leading IT companies, but who had instead decided to stay in Warsaw. Piotr Niedźwidedź, one of the cofounders, had worked in California for Google and Facebook, and had a résumé mirrored by other top people in the company. "We are showing young programmers that they don't have to leave Poland," said Kułakowski, breaking into his grin. "You can be your own master here and not just a cog in a big machine."

In 2014, Kułakowski met me for a quick breakfast at a fancy café built into the arcade of a communist-era building. Sipping on a green health shake, Kułakowski filled me in on CodiLime's progress over the last year. The company now had eighty employees; had a solid order book from large companies in the United States, Britain, South Africa, and Israel; and was pumping about one-sixth of its earnings into research in artificial intelligence and other areas. "The philosophy is simple," Kułakowski said. "The company earns for itself, which also allows us to invest for the future. We aren't interested in taking all the profits for ourselves. We're more interested in increasing our skills in machine learning. We want to invest for the very long term. That will allow us to finally invent something that doesn't exist yet—to invent the light bulb, if you will."

It's that possibility, of being in at the start of a potentially interesting idea, that is keeping his workers from taking better-paid IT jobs in the United States. "I tell my partners that they are really lucky that they are twenty-five and twenty-six because they have a chance to build a really successful business," he said.

Although CodiLime is still a very small company, what makes it interesting is that it is part of an ongoing wave of business creation that marks Poland as a maturing capitalist economy. Instead of Warsaw, Kułakowski and his partners could as easily be in Berlin, Manchester, or Austin.

The surge of new businesses created in the early 1990s was unique, but Poland is still creating new companies. After the initial frenzy, the rate of new company creation has steadied to almost three hundred thousand a year, according to Eurostat, the European Union's statistical agency. That gives Poland the second highest number of new businesses in the EU after France, a country with 50 percent more people than Poland.[1]

Poles are also more entrepreneurial than are their European brethren. Surveys show that more than 20 percent of Poles are thinking about starting their own business in the next three years, while the EU average is only 13 percent. Half of Poles think it is feasible to become self-employed, while only a third of EU citizens think so.[2] This is partly due to Poland's tax laws, which allow entrepreneurs to skirt many social security taxes. The laws drive companies to push their employees to become outside contractors, and this lowers payroll costs for employers. But it also leaves employees vulnerable as they lose the security and social benefits, like unemployment and maternity leave, that come from having stable contracts. Of the new businesses being created, about 92 percent are one-person operations.[3] This does not mean that all new businesses are being used as tax dodges, but many are. Aside from the tax angle, there is also a deep-seated need to scramble ahead a legacy of the drive that pushed Poles to become black-market traders in the 1980s, and to open formal businesses in the wake of Balcerowicz's 1990 reforms.

Although the most obvious opportunities of the 1990s have gone—Poland is now well stocked with hardware shops, coffee bars, banks. and law firms—the country still does offer interesting, if narrower, niches. For example, CodiLime could only exist thanks to the continuing wage gap between Poland and more advanced countries. Still, the model is changing. Polish salaries are rising sharply and, when cost-of-living differences are taken into account, are starting to earn similar amounts to what they would in Western Europe. "Two people are leaving me and going to work for a Warsaw company that is paying them simply crazy rates," says Kułakowski. He remembers going to the United Kingdom in 2004 to work for Ryanair, the discount airline. His pay there was one thousand pounds a month—a thrilling amount of money for a young Pole at the time. Recently, he hired a twenty-five-year-old mathematician and programmer for three times more money than he was earning in Britain a decade ago.

The maturing economy means that new businesses in Poland now have to find niches similar to what would work in Western Europe and the United States. And people younger than the 1989 generation are doing this.

Piotr Krupa missed the capitalist explosion, because he was still in high school when the old system crumbled. By the time he finished university in 1996 with a law degree, a lot of the easy business heights had already been scaled by the first generation of Polish entrepreneurs. But, instead of looking for a job in one of those newly founded companies, he decided to go into business for himself, setting up a company called Kruk (a play on the last names of the two founders, which also means raven). Krupa hit on a Polish quirk around which he built his first business: The impenetrable, confusing, and fast-changing legal system. He and his partner, Wojciech Kuźnicki, decided in 1998 to write a book explaining the twists and turns of the law dealing with businesses that employ handicapped people. The businesses that did so got a generous tax break, and the idea of employing handicapped people became very popular. But the regulations surrounding such businesses were confusing, and breaking them could have very unpleasant legal consequences.

The initial investment for the book—five thousand zlotys—came from cashing out the presents from Krupa's recent wedding. The partners wanted to move quickly, because a new center-right government, elected in 1997, with Balcerowicz back as finance minister, was promising to reform the mess around tax benefits for companies employing the disabled. "We were terrified that we were about to lose our livelihood," says Krupa, speaking from the nondescript suburban Wrocław office that houses his company headquarters.

The partners managed to get their guide into print and made their first money, quickly moving to publish their next book on Poland's telecommunications law. But while writing their dry legal tomes, they hit on another idea—one that would turn into a significantly more lucrative business. By the late 1990s, almost a decade of fast economic growth had started to create a Polish middle class—something that had not existed since World War II. This nascent bourgeoisie was still earning far less than their counterparts in France and Germany, and had significantly smaller savings and assets. This meant that any consumption had to be fueled by debt. Poles rushed out to buy modern fridges and stoves, signed contracts for mobile phones, and bought themselves cars and computers, all on credit. Both the borrowers and the lenders were inexperienced, and many people quickly got into trouble with repayments.

Krupa started to hear about these problems as he researched his next legal advice book. The partners ended up sending a letter to several companies to see if they would be interested in getting the young lawyers to write legal notes to borrowers in arrears. One mobile phone company bit. Era, now owned by Germany's T-Mobile, sent them a list of 523 problem clients who had fallen behind in paying their phone bills. Kruk, which now had a total of three workers, sent a series of "vaguely threatening" appeals written in formal legal language. Two weeks later, another round of letters went out, and then again and again, over the course of three months.

They went back to Era to see if their method had generated them any success fee. The telecoms company was very pleased, as 40 percent of debtors had paid up—a much higher rate than was usual. They asked Krupa and Kuźnicki if they wanted some more business. Krupa expected to get a few hundred more cases. Instead, the e-mail from the telecoms company had a list with 17,500 names. "We turned the company into a debt-collection agency," says Krupa, who rushed out to hire newly graduated students to begin chasing down debtors. By 2002 the company had more than two hundred employees but was still a fairly ramshackle operation. Krupa had no human resource department, no training programs, and no management experience.

Initially, Kruk was just one small player in a very crowded market. The main technique to extract money from debtors, used by almost all the debt collection agencies, was threats. Debtors were harassed with phone calls and text messages; collection agents would even show up at people's homes to warn them of the consequences of not paying.

Kruk, fined several times by Poland's consumer watchdog agency, wasn't all that different from the others.

But then Krupa had an idea: to treat the people from whom he wanted to extract money like clients, instead of like deadbeats. "Mass marketing was very new in Poland, and ended up scooping up people who couldn't really afford what they were buying," he says. "But these were not people trying to figure out how to game the system. We did large polls and found out that people would pay if they could, but simply weren't able to. They are honest people in a difficult situation. We figured we didn't want to be a debt collection agency any more, but more of a financial planning company for those with debts."

Instead of berating and threatening the clients, Kruk proposed payment plans to get them to start making a dent in their debts—all done in a fairly friendly way. Krupa held companywide meetings, pushing the idea that "the client is king—and in our case, the debtor is king." The new approach was coming online just as the global economy began to lurch into a crisis. Poland did manage to skirt a recession in 2009, but as the economy slowed and unemployment rose, banks and consumer lending companies were keener to sell nonperforming loans for a small percentage of their face value.

Krupa already had experience in this nascent market. In 2003, he roped in Enterprise Investors, the private equity fund, which in total ended up investing $21 million in Kruk, in return for 80 percent of the shares. Kruk used the money to buy loan portfolios. The company also created a credit information agency, and is starting to make small loans to its better customers. It targets those who have paid off past debts but still have tarnished credit ratings that make it impossible for them to get bank credit. The softer approach, combined with the economic malaise, proved to be a winner. The new and friendlier Kruk is now Poland's largest debt collection agency, with more than 1,300 employees. Kruk also controls one-third of Romania's debt collection market, and since 2011 has also been present in the Czech Republic and Slovakia. That was the same year in which Kruk went public on the Warsaw Stock Exchange, netting Enterprise Investors an eight times return on its initial investment. The company's share price tripled over the next three years, making Kruk the fourth largest listed debt collection agency in the world. Krupa is now worth 474 million zlotys—enough to edge him on to the country's hundred wealthiest list—and he wants to make Kruk the leading debt collection agency in Central Europe.

The company's rapid ascent took place in a capitalist economy. Poland in the late 1990s and early 2000s may have been slightly shabbier than the sleek German model across the border, but it was in no sense the postcommunist wasteland of 1990. Krupa's success, and later his international expansion, showed that Polish capitalism was not a one-off phenomenon.

Rafał Brzoska is another example of a later business success. He was only twelve years old when communist rule crumbled in Poland, and he came of age in a proper market economy. The market was actually such a familiar concept to him that he became the family expert on its intricate workings. His parents had been employees of Rafako, a manufacturer of power-generating equipment that was one of the main employers in their hometown of Raciborz. As such, they received a packet of shares when the company was floated on the Warsaw Stock Exchange in 1993. The shares were worth the enormous sum of two hundred thousand zlotys, and the parents made the curious decision of allowing their fifteen-year-old son to speculate with their nest egg.

The result was about the same as handing the keys of a sports car to a teenager. Brzoska hung on to the shares, which soared in value for three weeks. Then the market hit its first downturn since its creation in 1991. Poles had seen the bourse as a one-way bet, but the bear market put a swift end to get-rich-quick dreams. Brzoska's parents' shares lost 90 percent of their value. "I promised them I would get their money back, and I did," says Brzoska. It took him almost seven years of trading on the WSE. He bought business newspapers, studied the market, and made canny trades, slowly clawing back the family money.

His bruising brush with the market so entranced him that he ditched the idea of studying medicine and instead applied to the

Kraków University of Economics. Still, a decade after the end of communism, he and his friends thought that they had missed the boat on becoming entrepreneurs. "There was a general feeling that the people who started a decade earlier selling on the streets and in the stadiums, that that was when the fortunes were made," he says. "There was a feeling that the market was occupied and that all the easy stuff was done. That's the same thing I hear from young people today. But the truth is that the market is changing all the time, so there are always opportunities. If you have an idea, work hard, and have ambitions, you can scale any peak."

That gung-ho appreciation of capitalism wasn't overblown. In 1999, in his third year of college, Brzoska, his girlfriend (now his wife), and some friends saw an opportunity in the rapid expansion of supermarkets and hypermarkets that were opening new locations around the country. The food retailers turned to the same method of advertising that has filled mailboxes with unwanted leaflets across the Western world: junk mail. Brzoska and his partners began to distribute leaflets for the retailers. The field was crowded, but Brzoska hit on two new ideas. One was to offer potential client retailers a low price, and the second was to guarantee that the pamphlets would be delivered in a timely fashion and would actually end up where they were supposed to go. Leaflets dumped in sewers and garbage cans instead of in mailboxes are one of the risks of the trade, so the guarantee raised eyebrows among potential clients. "This was innovative for the time," says Brzoska. His company, Integer, exploded in size and in less than five years had about seven thousand part-time workers. It delivered more than one million pamphlets per year, and had one of the largest market shares in Poland.

But a solid share of such a niche market wasn't enough to keep Brzoska happy. In building the flyer delivery business, he had acquired people, trucks, and a really good sense of logistics. With that experience he decided to aim very high—at the Polish post office, a sluggish and expensive state-owned outfit with a monopoly on all mail weighing less than fifty grams. Taking a close look at the law,

Brzoska had an idea. Why not add something to envelopes so that they weighed more than fifty grams, thus allowing companies like his new outfit, InPost, to deliver them? "The cheapest thing was sand, but that's pretty messy," he says with a laugh. Instead, he decided to glue on metal tabs that pushed each envelope's weight above the post office's threshold.

Brzoska invested six million zlotys and launched his new service in 2006, expecting to start breaking even in only three months. At the same time, the post office went on strike, offering him the gift of two weeks of free publicity as newspapers and television featured the upstart rival to the old monopoly. To the fury of the post office, Polish courts ruled that InPost's gambit was legal.

Despite the boost of publicity, the start was very tough. People who had delivered flyers turned out to have problems with the greater precision needed for delivering mail. Instead of fat profits, InPost struggled through two years of losses. But, fueled by twenty million zlotys in additional investment gained from Integer's IPO, Brzoska soldiered on. "If I had known how strong our opponents were, I probably wouldn't have started this business," says Brzoska, an unshaven and youthful thirty-eight-year-old sporting the close-cropped bristle haircut popular with Polish men. "A lack of knowledge is a common characteristic of many entrepreneurs. But once you start, you can't retreat; then it's like war on the Eastern Front."

By 2008, InPost was making a profit. By 2012, at which time the metal tabs were no longer needed, thanks to EU pressure to liberalize the postal market, the upstart had captured more than 15 percent of Poland's letter deliveries. In 2013, InPost won a contract to deliver official mail from courts and prosecutor's offices.

As InPost grew, Brzoska launched another business, called EasyPack, and took aim at conventional courier companies. "We saw that waiting around for the courier was the 'narrow throat' of the business," he says. He came up with an idea to set up automated package centers. Scattered around Poland, the package centers allowed a customer to drop off a parcel, write in the phone number of the recipient, and pay by credit card. Delivered by the same people who delivered mail using the same vans and trucks, by the next day the parcel would be stashed in one of the compartments at an EasyPack box close to the recipient, ready to be opened with a code sent by SMS. EasyPack now has four thousand stations scattered across nine countries, and plans to have sixteen thousand by 2017. The idea is to capitalize on the growing demand for e-purchases. Brzoska is starting to venture into territory dominated by Jeff Bezos of Amazon.

Brzoska feels that stories like his can still be repeated in Poland today. He does grumble at the bureaucracy that makes life a hassle for business, but he praises the low corporate taxes (a 19-percent flat rate, thanks to a left-wing government a decade ago) and the evident urge to scramble ahead that is still evident among many Poles. "We have a lot of people hungry for success," he says. "We are still a society that wants to achieve and works hard. The energy is still there; the volcano is still bubbling." Brzoska is also an example of the sudden turns of fortune that business can take. His companies sagged after losing several contracts to a revived post office—and in 2017 he handed over a majority stake to Advent International, a US investment fund, and pulled the shares from the stock exchange. He's staying on as a manager to continue developing the mailboxes, but under the eye of the American owners.

The hunt is on to find more businesses like CodiLime and Integer, companies that will drive Poland's continuing effort to catch up with Western Europe. While the first wave of new companies, built up more than two decades ago, started largely by copying existing models from more advanced countries; now the push is to actually innovate and invent new products. But the transition from copying to innovating is very difficult.

One man on the front lines is Zygmunt Grajkowski, a hearty fund manager, with years of experience at Enterprise Investors, who is now managing partner at a Polish-Israeli venture cap fund called Giza Polish Ventures. His goal is to find innovative businesses by roaming around Polish universities to see whether the professors have come up with interesting and marketable things that can be spun off into viable companies. So far, his travels back and forth across the country have been more frustrating than lucrative. "We're not interested in local adaptations of international technology," he says from his office in a luxury business club located in a forested plot of land on the outskirts of the Polish capital. "We don't want copycats."

What he finds as he drops in to universities is that these institutions are often stuffed with the most modern computers and lab equipment available—all thanks to generous financing from the European Union. But a lot of the tech toys aren't being put to good use, and instead stand idle for much of the day. One problem is that they cannot be used commercially, since that would run afoul of EU rules and place the university in danger of being forced to repay the subsidy. "These labs are like museums," Grajkowski grumbles.

Another problem is that the universities are unaccustomed to dealing with the private sector. Technology brokers—basically people like Grajkowski, looking to commercialize academic research—are almost unknown in Poland. The universities themselves are also suspicious of corporate spin-offs. One big danger is those perennial Polish bugbears: badly written legislation and aggressive officials. If Grajkowski finds a great idea, then the university has to place a value on the potential innovation—something very difficult to do in the early stages of a discovery. The danger is that administrators misprice the invention. If they assign too low a value for something that goes on to be a commercial success, they are likely to face a quick visit from the prosecutor's office or from the government's anticorruption agency, and be accused of mismanaging public funds. "Administrators would prefer not to take a decision, because it can only be harmful," says Grajkowski. "In other countries a lot of universities are very interested in commercialization, but in other countries there is also a higher level of trust."

Also, Poland's academic culture does not favor innovation. Universities are governed by powerful administrators, and young professors trying to make a career are under pressure to publish any findings quickly, in order to advance. "The worth of an academic is how much they've published, not how much they've patented," says Grajkowski.

Sluggish universities are coupled with the country's very low levels of spending on research and development. Poland spends about 0.9 percent of its GDP on R&D—one of the lowest levels in Europe. Unlike in more advanced countries, where the spending is three times as high, Poland's R&D spending is dominated by the government, accounting for about half of expenditures. Part of the problem is that many of the country's largest factories, like the Fiat car factory in Tychy in southern Poland, are foreign-owned. For them, Poland is a place to produce, not a place to come up with new products. Polish companies are smaller, and most still tend to be focused on the quite large domestic market. While outfits like Solaris, Pesa, and Nowy Styl are pumping profits back into their businesses to stay competitive, many other companies are content to stick with their proven models, making only marginal investments.

That is not to say that there is no start-up culture in the country. The intoxicating US model of high-tech start-ups has caught on along the Vistula as well. While Kułakowski, with his slightly larger company, makes regular trips to the United Kingdom and the United States to look for contracts and for financing, there is a raft of smaller entrepreneurial companies that are finalizing products and hunting for early investors. This is the model for Krzysztof Kowalczyk, who operates a technology incubator called GammaRebels in a rundown building in central Warsaw. The postindustrial space is right out of start-up central casting: it includes exposed brick walls, a beer-stocked fridge, and a wine bar. People sit in ones and twos in front of their computers. In a backroom, four young men with a company called Intelclinic are working on a sleep monitor—a face mask called NeuroOn, that monitors sleep functions and aims to help users diagnose sleep difficulties. "I'm emotionally involved with Poland," says one of the researchers. "I like the atmosphere here, and that's why I'm starting the company here." A few months after I met them, the team at Intelclinic, led by freshly graduated physician Kamil Adamczyk, raised more than $430,000 through Kickstarter. That was more than four times their initial goal, and Intelclinic then won a competition for best European start-up.

But such truly innovative start-ups are still rarities. Kowalczyk admits that there is a lot of ferment at the very bottom of the start-up ladder, but that very few companies grow to a significant size. His own investment fund, HardGamma, is only interested in businesses that are more than six months old. But the pickings are slim. One issue is that EU funds allow for new companies to tap that money rather than turn to more demanding private investors, who want a share of a company and have very high requirements for their investment to pay off. "We have an aquarium filled with small fish that don't grow into anything larger," Kowalczyk says.

Marcin Hejka, who runs an investment fund for Intel, the global IT company, has noticed that there is a problem of scale in Polish companies. He notes that no innovative Polish company has yet reached a $1 billion size, while two Russian companies—Yandex and Mail.ru—have done so. "A lot of Polish companies aim for the national market, while Czech and Estonian and Israeli companies have small countries, so they immediately focus on international markets," he says. New Polish companies find it hard to clamber across what he calls the "valley of death," the journey from being a start-up to being a company worth about $2 million. At that stage a business is large and solid enough to attract interest from investment funds. Much smaller, and entrepreneurs have to wander through the world of angel financing, Kickstarter campaigns, and other financing methods that are significantly less developed in Poland than they are in Germany, the United Kingdom, and the United States.

Despite issues with regulations, R&D spending, and financing, Poland does have a very good reputation in mathematics, programming, and engineering. Polish mathematicians helped break Germany's Enigma code machine before the war, providing key information for the later Allied intelligence effort that enabled them to read German secrets. That tradition, bolstered by a communist-era emphasis on hard sciences, persists.

Kowalczyk opens a laptop to show rankings from Top Coder, an international computer coding competition. He pushes one key, and three red arrows mark out top Polish universities, right near the head of the list. He flicks another key, and European institutions, largely from Russia and Central and Eastern Europe, are indicated with yellow arrows. Finally, he shows the US institutions: a group of blue arrows pop up near the bottom of the list. "Americans are shocked that Harvard, MIT, Stanford, and Berkeley are not high on the list," he says with a grin. "We could take advantage of the enormous talent pool here and use it to generate faster economic growth in Poland."

While Poles are good programmers, they often lack the soft skills, like financing and management, that would turn them from well-paid employees into successful entrepreneurs. That's the kind of service that Kułakowski provides at CodiLime. "Poland has two models for development in the twenty-first century," says Hejka. "It will either be a cheap labor country or it will be an innovative one. The ability to innovate will decide a country's international status."

12 Halfway There

The past quarter-century has been the most successful in Poland's history. The argument for this conclusion is not all that popular with the current Law and Justice Party government, which came to power in 2015 on a platform arguing that the postcommunist transformation was corrupt and deeply unfair; but the statistics tell a different story. In fact, progress in every area of life, from the quality of the roads to the types of cars people drive and the salaries they earn, has been staggering. But that still leaves Poland as one of the poorest countries in the European Union, one that has seen as many as two million people leave over the last decade to seek their fortunes in the wealthier countries of Western Europe. Frustration at that gap is one of the drivers behind Law and Justice's rise, but the party's populist policies–from lowering the retirement age to trying to impose higher taxes on foreign retailers–could make it more difficult for Poland to continue its exceptional run of economic growth in the future.

On August 24, 1989, John R Davis Jr., the US ambassador to Warsaw, sent a cable to Washington announcing the formation of Poland's first postwar government led by a noncommunist:

> I have the honor to report that Mr. Tadeusz Mazowiecki, a leading member of Solidarity, was today confirmed by a vote of the Polish Sejm in the position of prime minister of Poland and commissioned to form a government. I believe that this development constitutes essential fulfillment of the political tasks assigned to me in my current letter of instructions and await further orders. Davis.

The answer came back from his boss, Lawrence Eagleburger, the secretary of state:

> 1. Department notes with satisfaction the essential fulfillment of the political tasks assigned in your letter of instructions. 2. Your next task is to promote and ensure the realization of economic prosperity in Poland, to include stable growth, full employment, low inflation, high productivity and a Mercedes (or equivalent) in every garage. 3. Best wishes for continued success. Eagleburger.[1]

Eagleburger's note may have been tongue-in-cheek, but the "tasks" he set Davis back in 1989 have mostly been fulfilled over the subsequent quarter century.

First: economic prosperity and stable growth. Since emerging from its economic freefall in 1992, Poland has not seen a recession. That gives it the best track record of any current European country, and one of the best records of any country ever. What Poland has experienced following Balcerowicz's shock-therapy reforms of 1990 is the same thing that many West European countries and Japan underwent during their postwar booms. During the thirty-year span between the end of fighting in 1945 and the oil price shock of the early 1970s—dubbed *les Trente Gloriouses* in France and the *Wirtschaftswunder* in Germany—those countries saw smooth growth and a dramatic increase in wealth. The German economy was more than three times larger in the mid-Seventies than in 1945, while France's was just over six times as large. Japan's economy was eleven times bigger.[2]

Poland, locked into the Soviet camp and with a communist government, lost out on that growth, which had been fueled by postwar recovery and by generous international programs like the Marshall Plan. Poland's economy tripled in size over the thirty years after the war, starting from the low point of utter ruin as the country stumbled into 1945 with millions dead, cities laid waste, borders changed, and huge numbers of refugees and displaced people. But after about 1975, growth stagnated until Mazowiecki took office.

Since 1989, Poland's economy has become almost three times larger.[3] While the rest of Europe fell into recession following the start of the global crisis in 2008, Poland kept growing. That was partly a result of luck; dramatic tax cuts came online in Poland just as the crisis hit, and the currency weakened, which helped exports. But Polish consumers also kept spending, and Polish businesses revamped their models and kept working. The country also benefited from a flood of EU structural funds, in some sense the equivalent of the postwar reconstruction money that Poland had missed out on because of the onset of the Cold War.

The one failing is in the employment rate. Poland has never approached an unemployment level in the low single digits over the whole course of its early postcommunist transition. Unemployment hovered around 15 percent through most of the 1990s, but then soared at the turn of the millennium, when growth slowed, narrowly avoiding a recession. In 2002, 20 percent of Poles were out of work, and youth unemployment was even higher.[4] Unemployment has drifted lower since then; by mid-2016 it was 6.2 percent, according to Eurostat. But one of the reasons for its fall has less to do with local job creation and more with Poland joining the European Union in 2004. Unemployment fell from 19 percent in 2004 to only 7 percent in 2008—a time during which about two million Poles, or about 5 percent of the population, left to find work in Western Europe. Poland's unemployment problem got up and left—and most of those millions of people now working in Manchester, Brussels, and Berlin are unlikely ever to come back. That figure also does not take into account that, while huge numbers of Poles—about 12 percent of the population—are working in agriculture, most are little more than subsistence farmers. The countryside generates only about 4 percent of Poland's GDP,[5] a figure that gives some sense of the enormous waste of potential in having so many people uselessly warehoused in tiny villages tending small patches of land.

Inflation is down from the hyperinflation that Balcerowicz had to battle. By mid-2014, Poland saw its first touch of deflation in decades. Poland's central bank has slowly gained a reputation for sensible policies and inflationary expectations have been drained from society. Polish workers have also become enormously more productive.

In 1993, the average Polish worker generated $10 of GDP per hour worked, about a quarter of the output of his German counterpart. Two decades later, the average Pole was generating $29, not far off the level of some of the poorer West European members of the European Union, like Portugal, and almost half of the output of an average German.[6]

How about the Mercedes Eagleburger called for? He did leave some wiggle room with his allowance of "or equivalent," and if a new Skoda or a well-used Ford or Opel can be considered equivalent to a Mercedes, then that is in fact what is parked in Polish garages. Poland has 554 cars per thousand people, about the same level as France or Germany. In 1989, it had only 128 cars per thousand people, and half of those cars were the ridiculous little Fiat 126p.[7] All in all, Ambassador Davis should be pleased; his second mission has been more or less accomplished.

I saw the results of the rapid change when I returned to Poland with my family in August 2003 as the Warsaw bureau chief of the *Financial Times*. We pulled our bags off the carousel at Warsaw's Chopin airport and walked out through the small terminal building, which looked as if it was made of corrugated iron and painted in a difficult-to-identify blend of burgundy and purple. We piled into a cousin's car, waiting until after our groggy dog had time to pee on the sidewalk outside the terminal, and drove off into Warsaw.

The last time I had been in the Polish capital was in June 1993, on my way to Kraków to attend the funeral of my grandfather, who had died at the age of ninety-five. At that time I had grabbed a bus from the airport straight to the train station, but the one sight that really stood out in the capital was the new Ikea shop in central Warsaw, just a couple of blocks from the station. I pressed my nose against the dirty bus window to take a closer look at this unexpected example of Western business beginning to appear in Warsaw. The Ikea, and huge numbers of billboards, were signs that change was coming to a city that was still obviously Soviet in appearance.

A decade later, a new Warsaw shimmered in the warm summer

sunshine as we headed into the city. In the early 1990s there had been only one modern skyscraper in central Warsaw, the Marriott Hotel. But now other towers poked up around the hulking mass of the Palace of Culture.

My wife Cecelia had been a lot more nervous than me about getting on the plane taking us from the States to my new job in Poland. Her only previous experience with Poland had been a two-week visit in February 1990, while on a break from the University of Toronto. I was then in Warsaw working as a largely unpaid stringer for the largely bankrupt UPI wire service, and living in a cockroach-infested flat I rented from a cousin for one hundred dollars a month. I borrowed a Maluch car from a friend and took Cecelia—at the time my girlfriend—for a quick tour of the country. The roads were narrow and badly lit, and our little yellow car was underpowered and slow. But there was very little traffic on the potholed streets, as the transport trucks and fast cars that now crowd Polish highways were then almost entirely absent. We made good time, driving through the dark and leafless forests south to Kraków, and then again north to Giżycko—a "resort" town in the Masurian lake district in the north of the country.

Cecelia's family was German, and they had lived in Giżycko before the war, when it was called Lötzen. Her grandmother and two sons (one of whom was her father) had fled west in 1944 as the Red Army raped and pillaged its way through East Prussia on its way to Berlin. Taking a nostalgia trip to see if we could find her family's prewar house, we stopped to fill up at a CPN gas station. I walked over to the single window with a low-cut slot, one of the communist world's innovations that forces clients to bend low and assume the posture of a penitent. I dutifully stooped to pre-pay the cashier for my fill-up. Cecelia decided to go to the bathroom.

She came back in shock. The "toilet" was a reeking hole in the ground surrounded by loose billows of soiled paper. We gassed up and continued north, pulling into Giżycko at night to the overwhelming stench of putrid fish from one of the two fish processing plants in the town. The hotel was a cement blockhouse and, to no surprise, the hotel restaurant was closed when we got there. The one open restaurant we could find was in a basement, clogged with clouds of cigarette smoke and surly beer drinkers.

With that as Cecelia's formative experience of Poland, the sight of green parks, asphalt roads, and buildings that were not all various shades of gray came to her as a pleasant surprise in 2003—as did the Polish and foreign gas stations with self-service pumps, snack bars, and clean toilets. A couple of weeks after arriving, we were invited to an annual family reunion on the shores of a lake in the Mazury region, about four hours' drive north of Warsaw. There was no highway. Instead, long lines of transport trucks jostled for place with cars (one result of the rapid increase in car ownership numbers) on the two-lane road. Despite the road's narrow width, slower cars and trucks would drive half on the shoulder, allowing faster and more aggressive drivers—not a rare category among Poles—to pass them. This led to a blood-chilling sight for a Canadian used to more demure driving habits—four cars, two in each direction, racing past each other on a blind curve on a two-lane road. The flower-bedecked crosses planted by the side of the road showed the not infrequent result of that sort of craziness.

We stopped for lunch at a roadside restaurant. Polite service. Decent food. Normal flush toilets with no foul piles of toilet paper.

The camp turned out to be a collection of concrete huts—leftovers from the prefab construction of communist-era apartment blocks—scattered in a forest on the shores of a very pretty lake. The whole property had been part of a Prussian estate. The Junker owners had fled West during the war—probably at the same time as Cecelia's family. The manor house was burned down, and no trace now remains. The Polish settlers who moved into the area after the war had used the Prussian furniture for fuel to stay warm through the damp Masurian winter.

About a hundred relatives of various ages wandered the forest, tanned themselves by the lake, drank and sang at night, and ate fried pork chops and lumpy mashed potatoes in the canteen. The only shopping was in the nearby town of Iława, either at the open air bazaar or at the Biedronka, a chain of discount shops owned by Portugal's Jeronimo Martins.

In the years since, our family has regularly trekked back to Gil Lake for the last two weeks of August. The dank huts are the same, as is the food. But the rest of the country has changed dramatically. Over the decade I worked in Poland for the *Financial Times*, per capita income at purchasing power parity more than doubled—rising from $11,990 to $23,274—and that extra money showed.[8]

Iława, a town of thirty thousand, now has two shopping centers, big box shops, cappuccino bars, and a luxury hotel. The sidewalks have been rebuilt. A modern bypass allows traffic to skirt the town. Yachts bob at anchor in the port. The town hall, dating back to German days, has been repainted and the red brick train station modernized and upgraded. I can't remember the last time I saw a Maluch on the streets (unfortunately, the boys are now too old to play punch Maluch). The locals, dressed about the same as people living in Germany, now drive Skodas, Citroëns, and BMWs—albeit usually used ones imported from Western Europe. Most of the roads leading to Iława have been upgraded and, forty miles to the west, the four-lane A1 highway now runs south from Gdańsk to the center of the country.

Lubawa, fifteen miles away, is home to an enormous Ikea Industry factory—recently expanded by an additional 270,000 square feet. It pumps out shelves and other furniture on production lines where robots are a more common sight than humans. Lubawa itself is a "furniture valley," home to dozens of factories large and small producing for both the Polish and the foreign markets.

These changes over only a decade, in and around Iława, are a microcosm of the continuing rapid pace of Poland's ongoing transformation. The most visible factor has been an enormous increase in the quality and scale of visible infrastructure—roads, highways, local swimming pools and soccer fields, sports stadiums, and new airport terminals. Before 2004, the government was too cash-strapped to finance many of those projects. But after Poland joined the European Union, a flood of cash from Brussels made an enormous difference.

A decade ago, when you drove from Western Europe to Poland, the four-lane autobahn would disappear a couple of hundred yards past the Polish border, replaced by a narrow and traffic-clogged road. The three-hundred-mile trip from the border to Warsaw could take as long as nine nerve-wracking hours. As you passed from the clean and well-lit German road to the bumpy and dark Polish one, which was adorned with billboards, bordellos, and shops selling serried ranks of garden gnomes, it was obvious that you had left Western Europe for a wilder and much poorer place. Today, that line of division between a rich West and a poor and chaotic East has moved to the Polish-Ukrainian border. Except for the language on the signs, there is little to immediately differentiate the Polish highway from the German one.

It's not just roads, shopping centers, and sewage treatment plants that are changing; Poles are changing too. Polish society is being dramatically altered by the combined pressures of the postcommunist economic reforms, which have produced a vastly wealthier society than at any time in Poland's past, and by membership in the European Union, with its resulting wave of migration. In June 2003, Poland held a referendum on joining the EU. The proposition won by 77 percent to 22 percent. The idea was opposed by right-wing nationalists, who feared a dilution of Poland's national character, and by peasants and populists, like Lepper's Self-Defense Party. Even the Catholic hierarchy was lukewarm until John Paul II pressed them to opt for the EU.

The farmers were wrong to worry. They suspected that the promise that the EU would pay Polish farmers generous subsidies was a ruse, and that once exposed to fierce competition, Polish farmers would wilt while the country would be flooded with foreign food. That didn't happen. Brussels was not lying about sending money to Polish farmers—although, as farmers are wont to do, they quickly complained that they wanted more. Almost half of the income of Polish farmers now comes for Common Agricultural Policy subsidies, and the difference in well-being is easily visible. Poland is also now one of Europe's largest food exporters.

A couple of years after arriving in Poland, I had to send a note to the *Financial Times* photo desk. The editors there had fallen into the habit of illustrating every story on Polish agriculture with a photo of a peasant working his field with a horse-drawn plow. I pointed out that there were no peasants in Poland any longer, just farmers, and they were driving tractors and combines. Even farmers with tiny plots of land either have their own mechanized equipment or share. Horses are just a tourist attraction.

But the Church and the conservatives were right to fear that society would change. Poland is still one of the most religious countries in the European Union, but the tectonic plates of Polish society are shifting. Annual surveys by the Church of mass attendance and vocations to the religious life are drifting lower. The number of Poles attending Sunday mass has slipped below 40 percent for the first time, dropping about ten percentage points in the last quarter-century.[9] Poland has so far avoided the dramatic fall seen in other societies undergoing rapid change—like Quebec in the 1960s and 1970s, or Ireland over the last decade, where church attendance collapsed. However, for the official Church the trends are ominous, especially in larger and more anonymous cities.

While gay rights are still a long way off—the constitution says that marriage is reserved to men and women—Poland has had an openly gay member of parliament (now the mayor of Słupsk, a city in the northwest of the country) and Europe's only transgender member of parliament, Anna Grodzka, a former Communist Party apparatchik turned sexual rights campaigner. Abortion is still essentially illegal, but thousands of Polish women travel to Western Europe for abortions.

There has also been a slow change in the character of the people. Poles are still suspicious of authority, something made obvious by their disrespect of traffic laws and of most other forms of government regulation. Part of this is a stubborn peasant orneriness, and part comes from a deep-rooted antipathy toward governments and bureaucrats—one of the legacies of being frequently occupied by other countries. In communist times, suspicion of authority was a given, and most tended to be wary of their neighbors as well. That is changing, but slowly. A survey by the CBOS organization found that in 2002, only 19 percent of Poles felt that most people could be trusted. A decade later, that had edged up to 23 percent.[10]

Making much of an impact on that statistic is a bit of a one-person-at-a-time challenge. In 2005 I took a reporting trip up to the village of Biesowo, a three-and-a-half hour drive north of Warsaw, to interview its mayor, who was doing something very unusual. Janusz Radziszewski, then forty-five years old, had helped unleash a self-help revolution in the village of 350 people. Biesowo was dominated by its post-German red brick church, which had been handed over, like hundreds of Lutheran churches in northern Poland, to a Roman Catholic congregation after the war. It had been a rundown place with potholed roads, shabby houses, and weed-infested vacant lots—indistinguishable from thousands of other Polish villages. But when Radziszewski became mayor, he decided to tackle an abandoned piece of land in the center of the village and turn it into a park. He spent his annual budget of 350 zlotys on loads of sand, then grabbed a shovel and got to work.

"I started alone," he says. "For a day or two, people started coming up and talking and then grabbing a shovel and helping. By the end we had fifty people helping." Volunteering proved infectious. The villagers cleaned up their cemetery, built a soccer field for their children, and set up a crèche for babies. In 2003, Biesowo won the regional contest for most improved village. On the day I was there talking to Radziszewski, a couple of houses had men on their roofs laying new tiles. Most of the buildings in the village were clean and freshly painted. Delegations from surrounding villages trekked over to see what Radziszewski was doing right. "They came to visit us as if were in Germany or something," he said in amazement.

What Radziszewski had helped do in his small village was lay the groundwork for a civil society, something that had been absent in Poland since the war. Little struggles like his are taking place around the country—part of an attempt to turn what was once a badly governed communist basket case into a normal European country. I've seen the same strategy applied to inconsequential but annoying issues, like picking up after dogs. A decade ago, Poland's parks and sidewalks were littered with Parisian-style mounds of dog turds, left by indifferent owners. But years of patient propaganda from city governments are slowly changing minds. Today, the owner of a squatting dog is likely to be upbraided by passersby, something unthinkable a few years ago.

More seriously, Jerzy Owsiak, a charismatic journalist, in 1993 founded the Great Orchestra of Christmas Charity, in which thousands of people collect money to finance the purchase of medical equipment for Polish hospitals. The annual one-day event ends with a televised concert, and just about every person walking the frozen Polish streets of January is decorated with a red heart sticker to show that they've donated. The foundation has raised about $140 million, despite getting flak from the Catholic Church, which is upset at the foundation's secular nature and at the fact that it didn't think of the idea first.

Twenty-five years after the end of communism, Poland is a much better country, as a look at Eagleburger's criteria attests. In fact, Poland hasn't been this wealthy and secure at any point in its history. But in many ways its race is still only half run. The final goal is not to be better off than it was under communism, but to become a normal Western European country. The country has been living off the impact of the explosion unleashed by Mazowiecki and Balcerowicz a quarter-century ago. But a lot of those sources of easy growth are starting to run out. Most of the companies and entrepreneurs described in this book are Poland's elite, the toughest and most innovative of the country's business leaders who built advanced companies, often competing head-to-head against international rivals. But many Polish companies don't fit that model. Many businesses still rely on cheap labor as their main competitive advantage, sticking to the model that they worked out a decade ago or longer. Most are not particularly innovative.

Domestically, the era of easy advances is over. A decade or two ago, there were a lot of easy ideas for business. It didn't take a capitalist genius to figure out that Poland would need grocery shops, shopping malls, pleasant apartment buildings, and clean automobile dealerships. But now that Poles are about two-thirds as rich as West Europeans, the rest of the climb will be tougher. "Poland is like a twenty-year-old," says Jacek Siwicki, the tough-as-nails head of Enterprise Investors, the region's leading private equity fund, whose activities have popped up throughout this book. "It's no longer a teenage emerging market, with all the turmoil and promise that entails. Poland is no longer tormented by hormones, but it's also no longer a super promising emerging market."

Janusz Filipiak, the founder of Comarch, now one of Europe's leading IT companies, says, "I look at my children, who are no stupider than I was; and they have access to capital, but they have a harder time than I did. I couldn't build a company like this today." He started his company in 1991, at the already advanced age of forty. A professor of information technology, he had lectured in Canada and Australia before returning to Poland in 1989, where he saw that, for the first time in decades, there were real opportunities. Back at Kraków's University of Science and Technology, he was trying and failing to bring in Western teaching methods to the Polish school. His salvation came from the government telecoms monopoly, which needed software to figure out how its network was being used. Filipiak was one of the few people in the country with the knowledge to do the work. He signed a contract for about one hundred thousand dollars, left the university, and hired five students to work for him. "Those were the times of very simple decisions," he says from his headquarters at a low-slung corporate campus on the outskirts of Kraków. "Those circumstances can't be repeated."

As Polish companies expanded and their demands for management software become more sophisticated, Comarch grew along with them. But again, Filipiak's initial advantage is one that is difficult to replicate today. "Imagine if now you had access to very well qualified people willing to work for the equivalent of $150 a month. Anybody would have had an enormous success," he admits. "This is a mature market. I was able to start with good people and no knowledge; that doesn't exist anymore. There are no open fields. You now need a lot of capital, and the margins are very thin. I built a company of four thousand people with almost no capital."

New entrepreneurs are entering a market with niches, not gaping opportunities, and with a lot more competition than was the case a couple of decades ago. This means that new businesses have to plan more carefully and be more innovative—something that existing companies will also have to do if they want to at least maintain their current size, or, better yet, grow. A broader range of Polish companies will have to become bigger and more innovative, and start to create their own brands. Despite its large number of successful companies, Poland still has not produced a single globally significant business—something that much smaller Finland was able to do with Nokia, before that company flamed out.

One of the reasons is a matter of scale. State-controlled companies like the copper miner KGHM and the refiner PKN Orlen are relatively large; but private businesses, even successful ones, tend to be smaller and more fragmented. Most companies are still relatively new and are being run by their founders—usually headstrong and ambitious entrepreneurs who do not want to sell their babies to anyone else. But as the founders get older or die, succession issues are starting to arise. Private equity managers like Siwicki are waiting in the wings to buy companies from their founders. "The biological clock is ticking in our favor," he says, sitting in his office suite on the top floor of the Warsaw Financial Center, with enormous windows that provide a bird's-eye view of the capital spread out below. With less emotion invested in their businesses, second-generation owners may allow for consolidations in areas like cosmetics and food processing that will create companies of European scale.

While business is going to have to carry the main burden in continuing to push the country forward (just as it did during Poland's first wave of modernization, two decades ago) part of the response will have to come from the government. Politically, that will be difficult. There was enormous demand for change in 1989, which gave Balcerowicz a window of opportunity to push through reforms of a scale that would have been unimaginable in a more settled and better-functioning country. As an example, the Czechs and Hungarians, whose countries were better managed than Poland when communism ended, had nothing like the Polish stomach for radical change. A second wave of fairly well-planned reforms by the center-right government of Jerzy Buzek in the late 1990s left the country with well-functioning local governments, revamped schools, and a new pension system (albeit one that later was largely gutted, under the pressures resulting from the global economic crisis).

Over the last decade, however, the impetus to continue politically risky changes has largely disappeared. Despite years of promises, government bureaucracy is still fierce. Every year Lewiatan, the Polish employers' confederation, puts out a "Black List" of business barriers, and every year the list gets longer. Pledges to set up a "single window," allowing new businesses to dispense with a lot of the paperwork needed to start a company, are still honored more in the breach than in the observance. There have been some improvements, as seen in Poland's scramble up the World Bank's Doing Business rankings, but on issues like taxes and business registration the country still lags badly.

The government is promising to boost research and development spending, something that is largely being funded by the European Union. But one of Poland's problems is that the state already plays too large a role in R&D, while local companies do not. While some companies, like Nowy Styl, pump huge amounts of cash into modernization, many smaller companies do almost no research at all.

Poland has done a good job of upgrading its schools, which are now among the best in the world, but universities still lag. University education was rationed under communism, and when the system ended, millions of people found they needed a degree for work. As a result, hundreds of new colleges and universities sprang up—many of dubious quality, offering low-tech and largely useless degrees in areas like marketing and journalism. Some of those weaker schools are closing now that just about everyone who needs a diploma has one, but the country has not managed to produce any truly elite universities.

What the country will need is not something on the scale of Balcerowicz's shock therapy. Instead, it will need years of well-thought-out and incremental changes: a tweak to higher education here, a change in tax policies on investment there. That demands an exhausting and never-ending slog of constant improvements, something that needs a competent civil service, well-drafted legislation, and politicians able to take the long view. But the Polish state now functions more like its equivalents in southern Europe, and not like those in the north of the continent, as it aspires to do.

The Polish political system is also deeply flawed. The centrist Civic Platform party of Donald Tusk—who in 2014 was chosen to head the European Council, the most senior job for a Pole since Karol Wojtyla became Pope John Paul II—frustrated business with its caution over further reforms. But their Law and Justice Party replacements are even worse. The right-wing party has a deep populist streak, part of its inheritance when it swallowed Lepper's rabble-rousing Self-Defense Party. A few years ago I was in Krynica, a small spa town in southern Poland that hosts an annual regional economic summit, sort of a threadbare version of Davos. Kaczyński, the Law and Justice leader, was making a rare pilgrimage to a place that his party views, with a shudder of distaste, as exemplifying the unhealthy links between government, business, and well-fed lobbyists. Businesspeople in attendance were eager to hear the party's new softer approach. Instead, Kaczyński gave a fire-breathing interview to the *Rzeczpospolita* daily in which he compared workers to serfs, threatened company owners with punitive taxes if they didn't increase salaries, and worried that Polish capitalism had grown up on twisted roots of corrupt apparatchiks and self-serving businessmen dating all the way back to 1989. "That led to a fatal phenomenon, a mechanism of negative selection characteristic of communism carried over to business."[11] Stunned business leaders watched Kaczyński's speech in amazement and then walked away shaking their heads.

While business was dismayed, Kaczyński's message hit home with voters, especially older people and those from smaller towns and villages who felt left out by the transformation. Those people are scornful of the new middle-class "lemmings," and they hanker for a return to the patriotic traditions and values of an older Poland. The new government caters to them, memorializing the guerillas who fought a no-hope war against the new Communist government after World War II, tightening ties with the powerful Church hierarchy, cooling relations with Germany, and tangling with the European Commission over government efforts to undermine the country's top constitutional court.

These political and institutional worries are layered onto other problems that will make Poland's continued catch-up increasingly difficult. A serious issue is a slowing of growth in Western Europe. The European Union, and particularly Germany, takes most of Poland's exports, and the Eurozone's inability to shake off the consequences of the crisis and return to more robust expansion hampers Poland's growth rate. Another problem that will be more difficult to handle is demographics. Despite its showy Catholicism, Poland has one of the lowest birthrates in the world, with the average woman giving birth to only 1.3 children. That is a rate far below that needed to keep the population stable, and there is no sign of it changing, despite a new government program paying a monthly bonus for larger families. Poland's population, currently about thirty-eight million, will fall to thirty-five million by 2030, and by 2060 there will be only thirty million Poles, and many more of them will be older.[12] That means that public finances will be strained, with fewer workers to pay for their pensions. The obvious answer is to attract more migrants, but that will be difficult in a country that has had no significant minorities since the war. Poland responded to the EU's migration crisis by refusing to take in most asylum seekers; Kaczyński even warned of Muslim migrants carrying "all sorts of diseases and protozoa."[13]

Still, the scale of the challenges facing Poland now is entirely different from that of the ones the country tackled a quarter-century ago. Since 2016, Poland has been considered a high-income country; it is a member of the OECD, the European Union, and NATO. In contrast with next-door Ukraine, which is fighting to keep from being pulled back into Moscow's orbit, Poland seems to have escaped the clutches of its old enemy, taking advantage of Russia's momentary weakness in the 1990s to make good its escape to the West.

Ryszard Petru, a Polish economist turned politician, worked out two predictions of where Poland will be in 2039, fifty years after the elections that brought Mazowiecki to power. Optimistically, both scenarios predict that Poland will be significantly wealthier in 2039 than it was in 2014, in part because of the €105 billion in structural and agricultural funds due to flow into Poland until 2020.

Petru calls his first prediction "inertia," or the "Portuguese variant." Under that scenario, Poland fails to make life easier for business, elects populist politicians, and leaves a large role for the state in the economy, while Polish business remains parochial and tied to the national market (more or less what seems to be happening under Law and Justice). If that happens, Petru guesses that Poland's per capita GDP will not break through much more than about 70 percent of the EU average. "Things would be a bit better, but there would be no breakthrough," he says. "Poland would remain on the periphery." In that scenario, Poland would continue to hemorrhage workers to richer West European countries, and would be too unattractive to lure immigrants to make up for the worsening demographics. Polish industry would continue on its present path of largely supplying

Western Europe, and particularly Germany, with unbranded and semifinished goods.

Petru calls his more optimistic predicition the "active variant." In it, he sees Poland completing its catch-up with the West. There he has company with Balcerowicz, who predicts that within two decades, the Polish per capita GDP could rival that of Germany, if Poland plays its cards right. For that to happen, both government and business need to embark on an exhausting series of "small-step" reforms to make Poland more innovative. This means more money for research and development, better universities, less bureaucracy, sensible government budgetary policy, and a trend toward Polish businesses becoming more like Germany's highly efficient *Mittelstand* companies. If such reforms allow Poland to grow at a rate two or three percentage points faster than Germany over the next quarter-century, then catching up is a realistic goal. "We don't need a great leap forward," says Petru. "We did in the 1990s, when we had to act fast. Now, that's not the case."

One of my first meetings in Warsaw after arriving in 2003 was a dinner at the Canadian embassy, where the ambassador, Ralph Lysyshyn, invited me more for my Canadian passport than for any expertise I might have had on Poland in those early days. After the dinner, various economists held forth on Poland's prospects. Ralph closed with the thought that, while there may be ups and downs and occasional short-term gloom, "no one ever went wrong by being a long-term optimist about Poland. This is a country which will definitely be richer in the future than it is now." He was right in 2003, and odds are that the same sentiment is still correct today, despite the changes undertaken by the new government. A quarter-century after the Mazowiecki government and Balcerowicz's reforms, Poland is returning to the path it would have followed if not for World War II and communism.

• • •

On Sunday, September 10, 1939, my grandfather, Stanisław Cieński, was retreating with his horse-drawn artillery regiment toward Warsaw. From overhead, German fighters and bombers machine-gunned and attacked his column, while in the distance the sound of approaching German armies could be heard. Despite being forty-one, my grandfather had volunteered to serve in the military as war approached. His only preparations for the looming conflagration had been to rush to his tailor in Lwów to have him sew a uniform, and then to badger a reluctant army bureaucracy to take him. He met up with his unit in western Poland as the war started, and had been falling back ever since.

Dirty, exhausted, battling the crowds of terrified refugees clogging the road—which made it impossible to keep the long column of guns and ammunition carts together—and doubled over in pain from a kidney infection, he drove into Jelonki. It was a distant suburb of Warsaw, about five miles from the burning royal castle that marked the center of the city. In Warsaw's ambitious prewar plans, Jielonki was to be one of a ring of "garden cities"—districts of parks, villas, and low apartment buildings that would encircle the Polish capital. But those designs had curled and charred in the flames of war. On this hot September day, German Stuka bombers screamed toward the crowded road, dropping their bombs and then soaring into wide turns as they fired on the panicked people running for cover below. My grandfather, a second lieutenant, sped by a burning house where a man's body hung out of the window, blown there by the explosive force of a bomb. As he and his driver raced along the road to get clear of the bombing, they came up to a thicket of marshes and saw three helmeted soldiers manning a machine gun. It was a German outpost, and the German machine gun raked their car with fire.

My grandfather leaped from the passenger seat and scampered over the edge of the road, diving for cover into a patch of bulrushes. Catching his breath, he saw that he had to move to survive. He pulled out a photo of his wife and children for a last look, broke cover, and ran toward a small house alongside a pond, racing to reach it before the Germans shot him. Once inside the house, he saw three more German soldiers in the courtyard. He pulled out his pistol and fired. One of the Germans fell back; the other two ran toward his hiding place. My grandfather leaned out the window, ready to take another shot as the Germans rounded the house; but they came upon him from behind, and shot him through the shoulder.

Bleeding profusely, he fell back inside the building. A terrified girl inside the house, who had watched the shootout, helped him turn his Sam Browne belt into a tourniquet, but he was very near death. “I was right with God and I knew that dying for Poland, I was fulfilling my duty,” he wrote later in his memoirs. “I knew that my fate was sealed and that nothing could prevent my death.”

But fainting slowed his heartbeat, and the flow of blood from his wound slackened, allowing it to clot enough to save his life. The girl flagged down a police car driving to Warsaw, and bundled him inside. Later that day, despite his wound, my grandfather organized a group of leaderless policemen and soldiers in setting up a strongpoint blocking the road to Warsaw for several hours. There, he was again wounded. And again near death, he was finally taken to a hospital in Warsaw, where he remained for six months. I remember him as an old man years later, showing me the shrapnel scars near his heart.

After the war, Jielonki’s “garden city” plans were scrapped. Instead, part of the district was used to construct barracks for Soviet workers sent to the capital to build the Palace of Culture on the ruins of downtown Warsaw.

Today, the four lanes of Połczyńska Street run through the exact place where my grandfather was shot. On one side of the road where he ran for cover is a large Fiat dealership, while a Lexus dealership and a McDonald’s are on the other side. Low-rise apartment buildings, largely built by private Polish developers, line the road, while modern trucks and cars race toward the city center.

History has come full circle. Bielecki, Poland’s prime minister in 1991, spelled out the scale of the success. “By the end of this decade we’ll be back to where we were before the war, where Romanians called the zloty the Polish dollar, and the Portuguese and Greeks were poorer than us, while the Spanish were only a little richer. History will return to its normal path.”

Notes

CHAPTER 1

1. Angus Maddison, "Historical GDP," http://www.ggdc.net/maddison/maddison-project/home.htm.
2. Stephen Engelberg, "The Spy Who Went into Retailing," *New York Times*, January 22, 1991.
3. "GDP per capita, consumption per capita and price level indices," Eurostat, accessed April 21, 2017, at http://ec.europa.eu/eurostat/statistics-explained/index.php/GDP_per_capita,_consumption_per_capita_and_price_level_indices.

CHAPTER 2

1. World Bank country data, http://data.worldbank.org/country/poland.
2. Alain de Crombrugghe and David Lipton, "The Government Budget and the Economic Transformation of Poland," in Oliver Blanchard, Kenneth Froot, and Jeffrey Sachs, *The Transition in Eastern Europe, Volume 2* (Chicago: University of Chicago Press, 1994), 111.
3. "Polish Hyperinflation and Stabilization 1989–1990," *Economic Journal on Eastern Europe and the Soviet Union* 1 (1991): 9–36.
4. Richard J. Hunter, and Leo V. Ryan. "Poland in 1989: Enter Tadeusz Mazowiecki and the Creation of the Balcerowicz Plan." *Research Journal of International Studies* 11, no. 1 (July 2009): 31–39.
5. Janusz Korwin-Mikke, "Wilczek: Przed Biurem Politycznym Powoływałem Się Na Friedmana a Jaruzelski Dłońmi Zatykał Uszy." *Najwyższy Czas* (Warsaw), March 13, 2012.
6. Ibid.
7. Polish Parliamentary Archives, accessed April 21, 2017, at http://www.scribd.com/doc/444884/Ustawa-Wilczka#force_seo.
8. Jeffrey Sachs, *The End of Poverty: Economic Possibilities for Our Time* (New York: Penguin, 2005).
9. Jeffery Sachs, "What I Did in Russia," March 14, 2012; accessed April 21, 2017, at http://jeffsachs.org/2012/03/what-i-did-in-russia/.
10. Jeffrey Sachs, "Shock Therapy in Poland: Perspectives of Five Years," Tanner Lectures on Human Values, delivered at the University of Utah, April 6 and 7, 1994.
11. Ibid.
12. Mariusz Onufer, Transformacja Systemowa w Polsce: Stracona Szansa czy

otwarcie drzwi do jednoczącej się Europy? *Wydawnictwo Uniwersytetu Wrocławskiego* (2004): 134.

13. Klaudiusz Michalec, "Bogusław Kott Odchodzi Z Banku Millennium: Zaskakujący życiorys Legendy Polskiej Bankowości," *Na Temat*, accessed April 22, 2017, at http://natemat.pl/9761,boguslaw-kott-odchodzi-z-banku-millennium-zaskakujacy-zyciorys-legendy-polskiej-bankowosci.
14. Justyna Sobolak, "Milionerzy Lat 90." *Onet Biznes*, May 28, 2014; accessed April 21, 2017, at http://biznes.pl/magazyny/finanse/milionerzy-lat-90/w3hs9.
15. "Banks Agree to Cut Over 40% of Poland's $12 Billion Debt," *Washington Post*, March 12, 1994.
16. World Bank. http://data.worldbank.org/indicator/NY.GDP.PCAP.CD?locations=PL.
17. Marcin Piątkowski, "Poland's New Golden Age: Shifting from Europe's Periphery to Its Center." Policy research working paper no. WPS 6639, World Bank, October 1, 2013.
18. Leszek Balcerowicz, interview with Radio Zet, May 16, 2016; accessed April 21, 2017, at http://archiwum.radiozet.pl/Wiadomosci/Kraj/Balcerowicz-Ratingi-sa-jak-termometr-nie-atakowac-ich-00022705.

CHAPTER 3

1. Sylwia Czubkowska, "60 Lat Temu Powstały Pierwsze PGR-y." *Dziennik*, November 2, 2009; accessed April 21, 2017, at http://wiadomosci.dziennik.pl/wydarzenia/artykuly/138263,60-lat-temu-powstaly-pierwsze-pgr-y.html.
2. "Państwowe Gospodarstwa Rolne: Sukces Czy Niewypał?" Polskie Radio, February 12, 2014; accessed April 21, 2017, http://www.polskieradio.pl/39/156/Artykul/1045712,Panstwowe-Gospodarstwa-Rolne-%E2%80%93-sukces-czy-niewypal.
3. Jacek Kuroń, "1989: Minister i Zupki. Skąd Wziąłem 50 Milionów." *Gazeta Wyborcza*, June 19, 2004, http://wyborcza.pl/1,136783,2139804.html.
4. GINI Index, World Bank estimate; accessed April 21, 2017, at http://data.worldbank.org/indicator/SI.POV.GINI?locations=PL.
5. Zbigniew Oliwa, "Stół z Kantami: *Przed i w Roku 1989 cz. 4*, March 18, 2009; accessed April 21, 2017, at http://brzeg24.pl/aktualnosci/1826-przed-i-w-roku-1989-cz-4/.
6. Bruce Weber, "Barbara Piasecka Johnson, Maid Who Married Multimillionaire, Dies at 76." *New York Times*, April 3, 2013.
7. Rafał. Kalukin, "O Tym, Jak Barbara Piasecka-Johnson Stoczni Nie Kupiła." *Newsweek Polska*, April 3, 2013.
8. Ibid.
9. Krzysztof Katka, "Solidarni Z Kasą: Na Co Poszły Pieniądze, Które Miały Ratować Stocznię Gdańską?" *Gazeta Wyborcza*, August 5, 2013.

10. "European Commission. State Aid: Commission Approves €251 Million Aid for Gdansk Shipyard in Poland." European Commission press release, July 22, 2009; accessed April 21, 2017, at http://europa.eu/rapid/press-release_IP-09-1178_en.htm?locale=en.
11. John Strongman, Roman Palac, and Adriana Eftimie, "Poland: Reform and Restructuring of the Hard Coal Sector 1998–2006 and Future Prospects." *World Bank Policy Note*, February 7, 2007.
12. Aleksandra Fandrejewska, "Emerytury Górnicze Wciąż Najwyższe." *Rzeczpospolita*, August 28, 2014.
13. Stanisław Tymiński, "'Plan Balcerowicza': Szok Gospodarczy Dla Polski." *Goniec*, December 14, 2012.
14. Wojciech Szacki, "Andrzej Lepper (1954–2011)," *Gazeta Wyborcza*, August 6, 2011.
15. "Stocznia Crist." *Forbes Polska*, December 14, 2014; accessed April 21, 2017, at http://diamenty.forbes.pl/diamenty-forbesa-stocznia-crist,artykuly,169864,1,1.html.

CHAPTER 4

1. "Ustawa O Przejęciu Na Własność Państwa Podstawowych Gałęzi Gospodarki Narodowej," *Government Gazette of the Republic of Poland* (1946), no. 3; accessed April 21, 2017, at http://pl.wikisource.org/wiki/Ustawa_o_nacjonalizacji_podstawowych_ga%C5%82%C4%99zi_gospodarki_narodowej_%281946%29.
2. "60 Lat Temu Komuniści Rozpoczęli bitwę O Handel." Polska Agencja Prasowa, April 12, 2007; accessed April 21, 2017, at http://www.naukawpolsce.pap.pl/aktualnosci/news,28692,60-lat-temu-komunisci-rozpoczeli-bitwe-o-handel.html.
3. Feliks Jabłkowski, *Dom Towarowy Bracia Jabłkowscy. Romans Ekonomicznuy.* (Warsaw, Iskry, 2005), 184.
4. Ibid., 196.
5. Ibid., 198.
6. "Bitwa O Handel W PRL." Polskie Radio, April 13, 2012; accessed April 21, 2017, at http://www.polskieradio.pl/39/156/Artykul/1097907,Bitwa-o-handel-w-PRL.
7. Ibid.
8. Piotr Mieśnik, "Powiesili Go Za Przekręty Z Mięsem!" *Fakt*, May 21, 2013; accessed April 21, 2017, at http://www.fakt.pl/Afera-miesna-Proces-Stanislawa-Wawrzeckiego,artykuly,212137,1.html.

CHAPTER 5

1. Ian Willoughby, "Current Affairs: Why Do Most Czechs Regard Early 90s Voucher Privatisation as Unfair?" Radio Prague, June 1, 2005; accessed

April 21, 2017, at http://radio.cz/en/section/curraffrs/why-do-most-czechs-regard-early-90s-voucher-privatisation-as-unfair?set_default_version=1.

2. "'Pirate of Prague' Kožený Loses Appeal in US Court," *Prague Post*, April 3, 2014.

3. Maciej Bitner, "Narodowe Fundusze Inwestycyjne: Epilog Po 20 Latach." Bankier.pl, February 8, 2012; accessed April 21, 2017, at http://www.bankier.pl/wiadomosc/Narodowe-Fundusze-Inwestycyjne-epilog-po-20-latach-2483607.html.

4. Barbara G. Katz and Joel Owen, "Voucher Privatization: A Detour on the Road to Transition?" Working Papers, Leonard N. Stern School of Business, Department of Economics, New York University, May 14, 2001; accessed at http://EconPapers.repec.org/RePEc:ste:nystbu:01-09.

5. Record of the thirtieth hearing of the so-called Orlen parliamentary commission, December 8, 2004.

6. "Kulczyk Sprzedał Akcje TP." *Polska Agencja Prasowa*, October 14, 2004; accessed April 21, 2017, at http://www.wirtualnemedia.pl/artykul/kulczyk-sprzedal-akcje-tp.

7. Szygulski, Paweł. "Aresztowanie Za Prywatyzację TP SA. Znowu Wielka Afera?" Money.pl, June 14, 2012; accessed April 21, 2017, at http://www.money.pl/gospodarka/raporty/artykul/aresztowanie;za;prywatyzacje;tp;sa;znowu;wielka;afera,105,0,1104489.html.

8. "Miller Oczekiwał Aresztowania Prezesa PKN Orlen," *Polska Agencja Prasowa*, December 4, 2004; accessed April 21, 2017, at http://wiadomosci.wp.pl/kat,1342,title,Miller-oczekiwal-aresztowania-prezesa-PKN-Orlen,wid,6262936,wiadomosc.html?ticaid=1136d4.

9. "Zbigniew Siemiątkowski Notatki Wywiadowcze," *Afery Prawa*, January 5, 2015; accessed April 21, 2017, at http://aferyprawa.eu/content/siemiatkowski.html.

10. Jakub Kopeć, *Utopić Solorza* (Warsaw: Agencja Wydawnicza caRes, 1994).

11. Witold Gadomski, "Solorz gra o wszystko," *Gazeta Wyborcza*, April 26, 2012; accessed April 21, 2017, http://wyborcza.pl/magazyn/1,126177,11624434,Solorz_gra_o_wszystko.html.

12. Aleksandra Stanek, "Od Zera Do Miliardera, Czyli Historia Budowy Imperium Solorza-Żaka." Biztok.pl, April 6, 2014; accessed April 21, 2017, at http://biztok.money.pl/biznes/artykul/od-zera-do-miliardera-czyli-historia-budowy,231,1,2201575.html.

13. Daniel Gąsiorowski, "Zygmunt Solorz-Żak, Jeden Z Najbogatszych Polaków," Money.pl, July 17, 2006; accessed April 21, 2017, at http://manager.money.pl/ludzie/portrety/artykul/zygmunt;solorz-zak;jeden;z;najbogatszych;polakow,31,1,172063.html.

14. Paweł Rożyński, "Komórkowe Disco Polo, Czyli Nowa Jakość W Telekomunikacji." *Dziennik*, June 7, 2011; accessed April 21, 2017, http://

wiadomosci.dziennik.pl/opinie/artykuly/344412,komorkowe-disco-polo-czyli-nowa-jakosc-w-telekomunikacji.html.

15. Daniel Gąsiorowski, "Zygmunt Solorz-Żak, Jeden z Najbogatszych Polaków," *WP Money*, July 17, 2006; accessed April 21, 2017, at http://manager.money.pl/ludzie/portrety/artykul/zygmunt;solorz-zak;jeden;z;najbogatszych;polakow,31,0,172063.html
16. Teresa Kokocińska, "Z Solorzem na cztery ręce," *Sukces* (1993): 13–15.

CHAPTER 6

1. Karolina Szamańska, "Sklepy W Czasach PRL," *Wiedza i Edukacja*, January 18, 2015; accessed April 21, 2017, at http://wiedzaiedukacja.eu/wp-content/uploads/2009/05/karolina-szymanska-sklepy-w-prl.pdf.
2. Marcin Kowalski, "Goniąc Gesslera." *Gazeta Wyborcza*, December 11 2013; accessed April 21, 2017, at http://wyborcza.pl/duzyformat/1,134724,15115854,Goniac_Gesslera.html.

CHAPTER 7

1. Jarosław Jakimczyk, "Mafia FOZZ," *Wprost*, August 16, 2003, 21–23.
2. Stephen Engleberg, "The Spy Who Went into Retailing," *New York Times*, January 22, 1991.
3. Rafał Kalukin, "Gruba Kreska Tow: Marka Króla," *Newsweek Polska*, June 18, 2014.
4. "Imperium Królów Sprzedane Za Bezcen," *Dziennik*, January 9, 2010; accessed April 21, 2017, at http://wiadomosci.dziennik.pl/wydarzenia/artykuly/107482,imperium-krolow-sprzedane-za-bezcen.html.
5. "100 Najbogatszycjh Polaków 2006," *Wprost*, June 12-18, 2006; accessed April 21, 2017, http://rankingi.wprost.pl/100-najbogatszych-polakow/2006.
6. Sebastian Kucharski and Magdalena Lemańska, "'Wprost" Do Nowego Właściciela,'" *Rzeczpospolita* 30 (December 2009); accessed April 21, 2017, at http://www.rp.pl/artykul/412712.html.
7. Marek Pyza, "Żyję w kraju lemingów: Wywiad z Markiem Królem," *Uważam rze*, September 12 18, 2011.
8. Jacek Gądek, "Lech Wałęsa Spiera Się Z Internautami Ws. Pieniędzy," *Onet*, February 9, 2014; accessed April 21, 2017, at http://wiadomosci.onet.pl/tylko-w-onecie/lech-walesa-spiera-sie-z-internautami-ws-pieniedzy/29x5p.
9. Urban Zapłaci Za, "Breżniewa Watykanu?" *Wprost*, March 7, 2006; accessed April 21, 2017, at http://www.wprost.pl/ar/87632/Urban-zaplaci-za-Brezniewa-Watykanu/.
10. "The Editor of a Satirical Paper Sentenced for Making "Insulting" Comments about the Pope," *Reporters Without Borders*, January 25, 2005; accessed April 21, 2017, at https://rsf.org/en/news/editor-satirical-paper-sentenced-making-insulting-comments-about-pope.

11. "Urban Kpi Z Sądu Po Wyroku Za żart Primaaprilisowy. Ubrał Się W Togę I . . ." *Gazeta Wyborcza*, October 18, 2013; accessed April 21, 2017, at http://wyborcza.pl/1,76842,14800891,Urban_kpi_z_sadu_po_wyroku_za_zart_primaaprilisowy_.html.
12. Luiza Zalewska and Piotr Zaremba, "Pani Na Agorze," *Dziennik*, February 14, 2009; accessed April 21, 2017, http://wiadomosci.dziennik.pl/opinie/artykuly/87053,pani-na-agorze.html.
13. Tomasz Leszkowicz, "Prasa Na Gruzach Partyjnego Koncernu: Likwidacja RSW 'Prasa-Książka-Ruch,'" Histmag.org, June 29, 2013; accessed April 21, 2017, at http://histmag.org/Prasa-na-gruzy-partyjnego-koncernu.-Likwidacja-RSW-Prasa-Ksiazka-Ruch-8099.
14. "Kartka Z Kalendarza III RP." *Gazeta Wyborcza*, September 3, 2013; accessed April 21, 2017, at http://wyborcza.pl/politykaekstra/1,133669,14543421,Kartka_z_kalendarza_III_RP.html.
15. Ryszard Bugaj, "Jak Uwłaszczali Się Ludzie 'Wyborczej,'" *Dziennik*, February 18, 2009, accessed April 21, 2017, http://wiadomosci.dziennik.pl/opinie/artykuly/87132,jak-uwlaszczali-sie-ludzie-wyborczej.html.

CHAPTER 9

1. Svend Albaek and Adina Claici, "The Velux Case: An In-Depth Look at Rebates and More," *Competition Policy Newsletter* 2 (2009): 44–47; ec.europa.eu/competition/publications/cpn/2009_2_10.pdf.
2. Molga Tomasz, "PiS rozpoczął wojnę z bogaczami," *Na Temat*, May 16, 2016, http://natemat.pl/179751; accessed April 21, 2017, at pis-rozpoczal-wojne-z-bogaczami-pierwszy-niewypal-jerzy-krzanowski-juz-na-wolnosci-za-to-z-dosc-naciaganym-zarzutem.

CHAPTER 10

1. Grzegorz Kołodko, "Od Szoku Do Terapii," *Rzeczpospolita*, December 27, 2009; accessed April 22, 2017, at http://www.rp.pl/artykul/411644.html.
2. Grzegorz Kołodko, *Transformacja Polskiej Gospodarki: Sukces Czy Porażka?* (Warsaw: Polska Oficyna Wydawnicza BGW, 1992), 104.
3. Herbert L. Baer and Cheryl Williamson Gray, "Debt as a Control Device in Transitional Economies: The Experiences of Hungary and Poland." *World Bank Policy Paper* 1480 (June 1995): 30.
4. Michał Matys, "Roman Kluska: Legenda O Dobrym Pasterzu," *Gazeta Wyborcza*, June 19, 2013; accessed April 22, 2017, at http://m.wyborcza.pl/wyborcza/1,132748,14128202,Roman_Kluska__Legenda_o_dobrym_pasterzu.html.
5. Jakub Noch, "Onet Nie Po Raz Pierwszy Trafia Z Rąk Do Rąk: Od Romana Kluski Przez TVN Do Ringier Axel Springer," *Natemat*, January 25, 2015; accessed April 22, 2017, at http://natemat.pl/17363,onet-nie-po-raz

-pierwszy-trafia-z-rak-do-rak-od-romana-kluski-przez-tvn-do-ringier-axel -springer.

6. Poland Finance Ministry, *Biała Księga JTT Computer Sa I Optimus SA*, /bip/_files_/podatki/biala_ksiega/biala_ksiega.pdf.
7. Małgorzata Werner, "Optimus: Ofiara Chorego Systemu, Który Od Lat Niszczy Polską Przedsiębiorczość," Forsal.pl, Februrary 27, 2014; accessed April 22, 2017, at http://forsal.pl/artykuly/780660,optimus-ofiara-chorego -systemu-ktory-od-lat-niszczy-polska-przedsiebiorczosc.html.
8. Robert Gwiazdowski, "Układ Zamknięty," Warsaw Enterprise Institute, May 6, 2014; accessed April 22, 2017, http://wei.org.pl/blogi-wpis/run,uklad -zamkniety,article,734,language_code,en.html%20pp4.
9. Jarosław Królak, "Urzędnik I Prokurator Dopadli Polmozbyt," *Puls Biznesu*, October 28, 2011, accessed April 22, 2017, at http://pwp.pb.pl/2507621,7063 ,urzednik-i-prokurator-dopadli-polmozbyt.
10. Gwiazdowski, "Układ Zamknięty."
11. Maciej Pietrzyk, "Skazani, Ale Będą Walczyć," *Dziennik Polski*, November 23, 2013; accessed April 22, 2017, http://www.dziennikpolski24.pl/artykul /3289108,skazani-ale-beda-walczyc,2,id,t,sa.html?cookie=1.

CHAPTER 11

1. Anna Tarnawa and Paulina Zadura-Lichota, "Report on the Condition of Small and Medium-Sized Enterprise Sector in Poland in 2011–2012," Polska Agencja Rozwoju Przesiębiorczości, 10, accessed April 22, 2017, at https:// badania.parp.gov.pl/images/ReportonSMESectorinPoland_2014.pdf.
2. Ibid., 11–12.
3. Ibid., 18.

CHAPTER 12

1. Roy Rosenzweig Center for History and New Media at George Mason University, "U.S. Reaction to a New Prime Minister in Poland: Making the History of 1989," accessed April 30, 2017, at http://chnm.gmu.edu/1989 /items/show/409.
2. World Economics Global GDP Database, *World Economics Journal*.
3. World Bank data Poland, http://data.worldbank.org/country/poland.
4. Ibid.
5. World Bank, http://data.worldbank.org/indicator/NV.AGR.TOTL.ZS.
6. OECD labor productivity statistics; accessed July 25, 2017, at https://data .oecd.org/lprdty/gdp-per-hour-worked.htm.
7. Maciej Górecki, "Rynek Motoryzacyjny w Polsce 1980–1989 (cz. 1): Co Jeździło Po Polskich Drogach?" Histmag.org, May 24, 2013; accessed April 30, 2017, at http://histmag.org/Rynek-motoryzacyjny-w-Polsce-1980–1989-cz.-1.-Co-jezdzilo-po-polskich-drogach-7965.

8. World Bank.
9. "Analiza Wyników Badania Dominicantes i Communicantes W 2013 R," Episkopat.pl, January 24, 2015; accessed April 30, 2017, at http://old.episkopat.pl/kosciol/kosciol_w_polsce/statystyki/6014.1,Analiza_wynikow_badania_dominicantes_i_communicantes_w_2013_r.html.
10. "Zaufanie Społeczne: Centrum Badania Opinii Społecznej," Cbos.pl, March 2012; accessed April 30, 2017, at http://www.cbos.pl/SPISKOM.POL/2012/K_033_12.pdf.
11. Andrzej Stankiewicz, Michał Szułdzryński, and Paweł Jabłoński, "Kaczyński: Biznes Często to Przystań Ludzi PRL," *Rzeczpospolita*, September 4, 2013; accessed April 30, 2017, at http://www.rp.pl/artykul/1044683-Kaczynski—Biznes-czesto-to-przystan-ludzi-PRL.html.
12. Poland ZUS Social Security Agency, "Prognoza Wpływów i Wydatków Funduszu Emerytalnego Do 2060," July 8, 2013; accessed April 30, 2017, at http://www.mpips.gov.pl/bip/projekty-aktow-prawnych/projekty-programow-i-inne/prognoza-wplywow-i-wydatkow-funduszu-emerytalnego-do-2060-r-/.
13. "Cholera na wyspach greckich, dezynteria w Wiedniu," *Kaczyński pyta o uchodźców*, October 13, 2015; accessed April 30, 2017, at http://www.tvn24.pl/wiadomosci-z-kraju,3/kaczynski-zastanawia-sie-czy-imigranci-sprowadza-do-europy-zarazy,585502.html.

Other Sources

Balcerowicz, Leszek. 2014. "Poland: Stabilization and Reforms Under Extraordinary and Normal Politics." In *The Great Rebirth: Lessons from the Victory of Capitalism over Communism*, ed. Anders Åslund and Simeon Djankov. Washington: Peterson Institute for International Economics.

Belka, Marek. "How Poland's EU Membership Helped Transform Its Economy." Occasional Paper no. 88, Group of Thirty, Washington, DC. October 2013.

Gomułka, Stanisław. "Transformacja gospodarczo-społeczna Polski 1989–2014 i współczesne wyzwania." *Nauka* 3 (2014): 7-16.

Kawalec, Michael. "20 Years of Economic Transformation: Did Poland Apply a Successful Big Bang?" Master's thesis, Faculty of Economics and Business, University of Amsterdam. August 12, 2010.

Kowalski, Tadeusz, et al. *Institutional Change in the European Transition Economies: The Case of Poland*. Poznań: Wydawnicwo Uniwersytetu Ekonomicznego w Poznaniu, 2010.

Koźmiński, Andrzej. *How It All Happened: Essay in Political Economy of Transition*. Warsaw, Diffin, 2008.

Index